Uncommon
CARRIERS

60

FARRAR
STRAUS
GIROUX

BY JOHN McPHEE

Uncommon *CARRIERS*

John McPhee

FARRAR, STRAUS AND GIROUX

NEW YORK

Farrar, Straus and Giroux
18 West 18th Street, New York 10011

Copyright © 2006 by John McPhee

Printed in the United States of America
Published in 2006 by Farrar, Straus and Giroux
First paperback edition, 2007

Large parts of the text of this book appeared originally in
The New Yorker. "The Ships of Port Revel" appeared in
The Atlantic Monthly.

The Library of Congress has cataloged the hardcover edition as follows:
McPhee, John (John A.)
    Uncommon carriers / by John McPhee.
      p. cm.
    ISBN-13: 978-0-374-28039-0 (hardcover : alk. paper)
    ISBN-10: 0-374-28039-8 (hardcover : alk. paper)
    1. Freight and freightage.   2. Transportation.   I. Title.

  HE199.A2M39 2006
  388'.044—dc22

                                2006007953

Paperback ISBN-13: 978-0-86547-739-1
Paperback ISBN-10: 0-86547-739-6

Designed by Cassandra J. Pappas

www.fsgbooks.com

20 19 18 17 16 15

To Sam Candler, *of the Boarskin Shirt,*
of Cemocheckobee Creek,
of the Shad Alley and the Coal Train,
all aboard

Contents

Uncommon
CARRIERS

A Fleet of One

The little four-wheelers live on risk. They endanger themselves. They endangered us. If you're in a big truck, they're around you like gnats. They're at their worst in the on-ramps of limited-access highways, not to mention what they do on horse-and-buggy highways. They do the kissing tailgate. They do passing moves over double yellow lines. They make last-second break-ins from stop signs on feeder roads. The way they are operated suggests insufficiency in, among other things, coördination, depth perception, and rhythm. When I went to bad-driver school, the opening lecturer did not imply any such flaws in his students. He was a real bear. He wore blue-and-yellow trousers and a badge. In a voice he fired like a .45, he began by asking us, "How many of you people think you're good drivers?"

We had all been singled out in four-wheelers. My own car had a tendency to ignore stop signs without previously sensing the presence of bears. It lapsed in other ways as well. After I reached twelve points, I was offered admission to the New Jersey

Driver Improvement Program, on the following voluntary basis: enroll or lose your license. Among the twenty-five people in the class, two smart-asses stuck up their hands in positive response to the instructor's question. He looked them over, then swept the room. "Well, you must all be good drivers," he said. "If you weren't, you'd be dead."

Then he darkened the room and rolled a film showing cars hitting cars in on-ramps. A, looking left, accelerates. B, looking left, accelerates. B rear-ends A, because A hesitated, and B was still looking to the left. This primal accident, the figure eight of bad driving, was the base of a graphic montage that ended in high-speed collision and hideous death on the road.

These memories of bad-driver school ran through me in eastern Oregon after Don Ainsworth, at the wheel of his sixty-five-foot chemical tanker, gave some air horn to a step van that was coming fast up an on-ramp on a vector primed for a crash. A step van is a walk-in vehicle of the UPS variety, and, like all other four-wheelers, from Jettas to Jaguars, in Ainsworth's perspective is not a truck. FedEx, Wonder Bread, Soprano Sand-and-Gravel—they're not trucks, they're four-wheelers, even if they have six wheels. A true truck has eighteen wheels, or more. From Atlanta and Charlotte to North Powder, Oregon, this was the first time that Ainsworth had so much as tapped his air horn. In the three thousand one hundred and ninety miles I rode with him he used it four times. He gave it a light, muted blast to thank a woman in a four-wheeler who helped us make a turn in urban traffic close to our destination, and he used it twice in the Yakima Valley, flirting with a woman who was wearing a bikini. She passed us on I-82, and must have pulled over somewhere, because she passed us again on I-90. She waved both times the horn erupted. She was riding in a convertible and her top was down.

If the step van had hit us it would only have been inconvenient, the fact notwithstanding that we were hauling hazmats. The step van weighed about ten thousand pounds and we weighed eighty thousand pounds, minus a few ounces. Ainsworth said he could teach a course called On-Ramp 101. "We get many near-misses from folks who can't time their entry. They give you the finger. Women even give you the finger. Can you believe it?"

I could believe it.

"Four-wheelers will pass us and then pull in real fast and put on their brakes for no apparent reason," he said. "Four-wheelers are not aware of the danger of big trucks. They're not aware of the weight, of how long it takes to bring one to a halt, how quickly their life can be snuffed. If you pull any stunts around the big trucks, you're likely to die. I'm not going to die. You are."

We happened to be approaching Deadman Pass. We were crossing the Blue Mountains—on I-84, the Oregon Trail. He said, "Before you know it, we'll be sitting on top of Cabbage. Then we're going to fall down." He had mentioned Cabbage Hill when we were still in the Great Divide Basin. He mentioned it again in Pocatello. After crossing into Oregon and drawing closer, he brought it up twice an hour. "It's the terrific hill we fall down before we come to Pendleton. Pretty treacherous. Switchbacks. Speed restricted by weight. You'll see guys all the time with smoke flying out the brakes or even a flameout at the bottom."

From the Carolina piedmont to Hot Lake, Oregon—across the Appalachians, across the Rockies—he had not put his foot on the brake pedal on any descending grade. In harmony with shrewd gear selection, this feat was made possible by Jake

Brakes—a product of Jacobs Vehicle Systems, of Bloomfield, Connecticut. Ainsworth called the device "a retarder, generically—you're turning a diesel engine into an air compressor." On a grade we descended in Tennessee, he said, "If you choose your gear right, and your jake's on maxi, you can go down a hill with no brakes. It saves money. It also lengthens my life." Crossing the summit of the Laramie Range and addressing the western side, he geared down from twelfth to eighth and said, "I won't use one ounce of brake pressure. The jake is on maxi." As big trucks flew past us—dry boxes, reefers—he said, "These guys using brakes with improper gear selection don't own the tractor or the trailer. Using brakes costs money, but why would they care?" Ainsworth owns the tractor and the trailer. As he glided onto the Laramie Plains, he went back up to eighteenth gear: "the going-home gear, the smoke hole; when you got into this gear in the old days, your stacks would blow smoke." On a grade at Hot Lake, however, he tried fifteenth gear, and his foot had to graze the pedal. He seemed annoyed with himself, like a professional golfer who had chosen the wrong club.

And now we were about to "fall down Cabbage." In ten miles, we would drop two thousand feet, six of those miles on a six-per-cent grade. Through basaltic throughcuts we approached the brink. A sign listed speed limits by weight. If you weighed sixty thousand to sixty-five thousand pounds, your limit was thirty-seven miles an hour. In five-thousand-pound increments, speed limits went down to twenty-six and twenty-two. Any vehicle weighing seventy-five thousand pounds or more—e.g., this chemical tanker—was to go eighteen or under. A huge high view with Pendleton in it suddenly opened up. I had asked Ainsworth what makes a tractor-trailer jackknife. He had said, "You're going downhill. The trailer is going faster than the tractor. The trailer takes over. It's almost impossible to bring yourself out of it. Brakes won't do anything for you. It's a product of going too fast for the situation. It can happen on a flat highway, but nine times out of ten it's downhill." The escarpment was so steep that the median widened from a few feet to one and a half miles as the northbound and southbound lanes negotiated independent passage. Ainsworth had chosen eighth gear. He said, "Most truckers would consider this way too conservative. That doesn't mean they're bright." Oregon is the only American state in which trucks are speed-restricted by weight. Feet off both pedals, he started the fall down Cabbage praising the truck for "good jake" and himself for "nice gear selection." My ears thickened and popped.

"Six per cent is serious," he said. "I've seen some sevens or eights. British Columbia drivers talk about tens and twelves."

In two strategic places among the broad looping switchbacks were escape ramps, also known as arrester beds, where a brakeless runaway truck—its driver "mashing the brake pedal and it feels like a marshmallow"—could leave the road and plow up a very steep incline on soft sandy gravel. In winter, the gravel may not be soft. Ainsworth recalled a trucker in Idaho who hit a frozen ramp. His load, bursting through from behind, removed his head. On Cabbage Hill, deep fresh tracks went up an arrester bed several hundred feet. After trucks use a bed, it has to be regroomed. The state charges grooming fees. Some drivers, brakeless and out of control, stay on the highway and keep on plunging because they don't want to pay the grooming fees. Ainsworth said, "Would you worry about your life or the Goddamned grooming fee?"

He was asking the wrong person.

A little later, he said, "Bears will roost at the bottom here."

Fulfilling the prediction, two cars were in ambush in the median where the grade met the plain. Wheat fields filled the plain—endless leagues of wheat, big combines moving through the wheat, houses far out in the wheat concealed within capsules of trees. We passed a couple of dry boxes, both of them Freightliners. Among truckers, they are also known as Freightshakers. "What's the difference between a Jehovah's Witness and the door on a Freightliner?" Ainsworth said.

I said I didn't happen to know.

He said, "You can close a door on a Jehovah's Witness."

We crossed the Columbia River and went over the Horse Heaven Hills into the Yakima Valley, apples and grapes in the Horse Heaven Hills, gators in the valley. To avoid a gator he swung far right, over rumble bars along the shoulder. A gator is a strip of tire, dead on the road, nearly always a piece of a recap. "A gator can rip off your fuel-crossover line, punch in your bumper, bomb out a fender."

The Yakima River was deeply incised and ran in white water past vineyards and fruit trees, among windbreaks of Lombardy poplars. Hops were growing on tall poles and dangling like leis. There was so much beauty in the wide valley it could have been in Italy. Now, through high haze, we first saw the Cascades. On our route so far, no mountain range had been nearly as impressive. We had slithered over the Rockies for the most part through broad spaces. Now we were looking at a big distant barrier, white over charcoal green, its highest visible point the stratovolcano Mt. Adams. We met three new Kenworths coming east—three connected tractors without trailers. One was hauling the other two, both of which had their front wheels up on the back of the tractor ahead of them. They looked like three dogs humping. It was here that we were first passed by the scant bikini in an open Porsche, here that Ainsworth touched his horn for the second time on the journey. I was marginally jealous that he could look down into that bikini while I, on the passenger side, was served rumble bars in the pavement. I had long since asked him what sorts of things he sees in his aerial view of four-wheelers. "People reading books," he answered. "Women putting on makeup. People committing illicit acts. Exhibitionist women like to show you their treasures. A boyfriend is driving. She drops her top."

We skirted Yakima city. " 'Yakima, the Palm Springs of Washington,' " Ainsworth said. "That was written by a guy on laughing gas." He reached for his CB microphone. "Eastbounders, there's a pair of bears waiting for you. They're down there right before the flats." Now ahead of us was a long pull up North Umptanum Ridge. "We're going to give 'em hell," he said. In the left lane, he took the big tanker up to eighty-three, pressing for advantage on the climb. He was in the fast lane to overtake a flatbed hauling fifty thousand pounds of logs. The distance had almost closed; we were practically counting tree rings when the logging truck began to sway. It weaved right and then left and two feet into our lane. Ainsworth said, "Oh, my goodness!"

Ordinarily, I tend to be nervous if I am riding in a car driven by someone else. Like as not, the someone else is Yolanda Whitman, to whom I am married. On trips, we divide the driving time. I make her nervous and she makes me nervous. She was a student in bad-driver school in the same year that I was. While she is at the wheel, I sometimes write letters. I ask the recipients to "excuse my shaky penmanship," and explain that I am "riding in a badly driven car." Coast to coast with Don Ainsworth was as calm an experience as sitting in an armchair watching satellite pictures of the earth. In only three moments did anxiety in any form make a bid for the surface. None had to do with his driving. The first was over the Mississippi River on the bridge to St. Louis—the big arch in the foreground, the water far below— where we seemed to be driving on a high wire with no protection visible beside us, just a void of air and a deep fall to the river. The second was in St. Joseph, where we swung through town on I-229 for a look at the Missouri River, and the narrow roadway, on high stilts, was giddy, a flying causeway convex to the waterfront. Falling down Cabbage Hill, concern for safety hadn't crossed my mind. And now this big logger was bringing up a third and final shot of adrenaline. We got by tightly. The driver was smoking something.

The ridges were dry in that part of Washington—rainfall less than eight inches a year. At elevations under three thousand feet, the ridges were not notably high—certainly not with the Pacific Crest becoming ever more imminent at twelve, thirteen, fourteen thousand feet. We made another long pull, over Manastash Ridge, and drifted down from the brown country into another paradise of irrigation—instant Umbria, just add water. It was a dazzling scene, the green valley of hay, wheat, and poplars; and here the string bikini passed us again, goosed by the air horn and waving. By Cle Elum, we were pulling at the mountains themselves—less than a hundred miles from Seattle and approaching Snoqualmie Pass. Listening to his engine climb, Ainsworth called it "operatic."

Ainsworth thinks his chemical tanker is at least as attractive as anything that could pass it in a car. He is flattered by the admiring glances it draws. He is vain about his truck. That day in particular had started in a preening mode—at a nylon-covered building called Bay Wash of Idaho, next to a beet field west of Boise, where we drew up soon after six and went off to have breakfast before the big doors opened at eight. Ainsworth will not go just anywhere to have his truck's exterior washed. All over the United States and Canada, for example, are washes called Blue Beacon, and they are known among truck drivers as Streakin' Beacon. Ainsworth passes them by. He insists on places that have either reverse-osmosis or deionized rinse water. He knows of three—one in Salt Lake City, one in the Los Angeles Basin, and Bay Wash of Caldwell, Idaho. To the two guys who washed the truck he promised "a significant tip" for a picture-perfect outcome, and he crawled in granny gear through the presoak acids, the presoak alkalis, the high-concentration soap, and warm water under such high pressure that it came through the seams of the windows. "They're hand-brushing the whole critter," he said admiringly a little later. And soon he was getting "the r.o. rinse" he had come for. Ordinary water dries quickly and spottily. This water had been heated and softened, sent through a carbon bed and a sand filter, and then introduced to a membranous machine whose function was distantly analogous to the gaseous diffusion process by which isotopes of uranium are separated. In this case, dissolved minerals and heavy metals failed to get through the semipermeable membranes of the reverse-osmosis generator. Water molecules made it through the membranes and on to rinse the truck, drying spotless. The Army and the Marine Corps use reverse-osmosis generators to go into swamps and make drinkable water. (Deionization is a different process but does the same thing.) Ainsworth paid sixty dollars and tipped fifteen. We were there two hours. "If you go into a Streakin' Beacon, you're going to be out in twenty minutes," he said. "You see the amount of time we fuck around just manicuring the ship? If I were in a big hurry, I wouldn't be doing it. Lord help us." We were scarcely on the interstate rolling when he said, "This is as close as a man will ever know what it feels like to be a really gorgeous woman. People giving us looks, going thumbs up, et cetera."

This is what raised the thumbs et cetera: a tractor of such dark sapphire that only bright sunlight could bring forth its color, a stainless-steel double-conical trailer perfectly mirroring the world around it. You could part your hair in the side of this truck. The trailer seemed to be an uncomplicated tube until you noticed the fused horizontal cones, each inserted in the other to the hilt in subtle and bilateral symmetry. Ainsworth liked to call it "truly the Rolls-Royce of tanks," and then he would deliver "Ainsworth's Third Axiom: if your stainless-steel thermos seems expensive, wait till you break three glass ones." The tank looked new. He had hauled it three hundred and eighty-seven thousand miles. It was so cosmetically groomed that its dolly-crank handle was stainless steel, its fire extinguisher chrome-plated—costly touches of an optional nature, not in the Third Axiom. Ainsworth uses tire blackener in the way that some people use lipstick. The dark tractor, still in its first ten thousand miles, had several horizontal bands, red and powder blue. On its roof, its two principal antennas were segmented red, white, and blue. Its bug screen—forward, protecting the nose—was a magnified detail of a flying American flag. His earlier tractors all had similar bug-screen bunting, long before 9/11.

When Ainsworth slides into a truck stop, if there are, say, two hundred and ten trucks on the premises, he is wary of two hundred and nine, not to mention others that follow him in. At a Flying J in Oak Grove, Kentucky, he went completely around the big parking lot looking for the space where he was least likely to get clipped. "You're inside the truck stop and you hear your name on the P.A.," he said. " 'Meet So-and-So at the fuel desk.' At the fuel desk is a guy with a sheepish look. Nowadays, they usually don't show up." In Little America, Wyoming, he circled a couple of hundred trucks before parking beside a light pole so only one truck could get near him. He said, "We're fifty per cent protected and that's better than one hundred per cent vulnerable." He has never been dinged and nothing has ever been stolen from his truck. " 'Constant vigilance is the price of freedom,' " he remarked. "Patrick Henry."

Ainsworth wore T-shirts with the truck's picture on them. Tall and slim—wearing tinted glasses, whitish hair coming out from under the band at the back of his cap—he had pushed sixty about as far as it would go. Only in one respect was he as well dressed as the truck. His boots, fourteen inches high, had been custom-made from the tanned hide of a water buffalo by the bootmaker J. B. Hill, of El Paso. Hanging in the sleeper behind him as he drove were boot-shaped leather bags containing other boots, like fly rods in burnished tubes. His caiman boots, he wished to point out, were made from the skins of farm-raised caimans. "Most people think they're either gator or croc. They're not custom-made. They're off the shelf."

"Whose shelf?"

"Cavender's, in Amarillo."

In his boot library, as he calls it, are mule boots, eel boots, anteater boots, gator boots, crocodile boots. All these boots are in the Third Axiom, he says. Why? "Because they last forever." His elk and bison low walkers are made by H. S. Trask, of Bozeman. Most truck drivers are content with running shoes. Ainsworth is content never to wear them.

I rode with him as "part-owner" of the truck. I didn't own even one hub nut, but was primed to tell officials in weigh stations that that's what I was. I never had to. My identity in truck stops was at first another matter. Hatless, in short-sleeved shirts, black pants, and plain leather shoes, I had imagined I would be as nondescript as I always am. But I was met everywhere with puzzled glances. Who is that guy? What's he selling? What's he doing here? It was bad enough out by the fuel pumps, but indoors, in the cafés and restaurants, I felt particularly self-conscious sitting under block-lettered signs that said "TRUCK DRIVERS ONLY."

So, a little desperate and surprisingly inspired, I bought a cap. Not just any cap. I picked one with a bright-gold visor, a gold button at the top, a crown of navy blue, an American flag on the left temple, and—on the forehead emblem—a spread-winged eagle over a rising sun and a red-and-green tractor-trailer and the white letters "AMERICA—SPIRIT OF FREEDOM." On the back, over my cerebellum, was a starred banner in blue, white, red, green, and gold that said "CARNESVILLE, GA PETRO." I put on that hat and disappeared. The glances died like flies. I could sit anywhere, from Carnesville to Tacoma. In Candler, North Carolina, while Ainsworth was outside fuelling the truck, I sat inside in my freedom hat saying "Biscuits and gravy" to a waitress. She went "Oooooo wheeeee" and I thought my cover wasn't working, but a trucker passing her had slipped his hand between the cheeks of her buttocks, and she did not stop writing.

I would pay for my freedom at the Seattle-Tacoma airport, when—with a one-way ticket bought the previous day—I would arrive to check in for home. Sir, your baggage has been randomly selected for radiation therapy. Please carry it to that far corner of the terminal. My boarding pass was covered with large black letters: "S S S S S S." At the gate, I was once again "randomly selected" for a shoes-off, belt-rolled, head-to-toe frisk. I had become a Class 1 hazmat. At home was a letter from Visa dated two days before my return. "Please call 1-800-SUSPECT immediately." Yes? "Please explain the unusual activity: Georgia? Oregon? Petro? Flying J? Kirk's Nebraskaland? Little America? What is your mother's maiden name?"

"Was."

Self-employed, Ainsworth has an agent in North Salt Lake. Ainsworth rarely knows where he will be going, or with what, until a day or two in advance. "I am in a very specialized portion of trucking," he had once told me. "I have chemicals in a tanker. The whole game hinges on tank washings. Without tank washings, tankers would roll loaded one-way, then go back to origin to load again. In the old days, it was all dedicated runs. Now, due to the widespread existence of interior tank washes, we can move around, taking different things."

For example, when I joined the truck, in Bankhead, Georgia, he was hauling a load of concentrated WD-40 east from San Diego. He had called the day before, from Birmingham, to say that he had just learned that after delivering the WD-40 in Gainesville, Georgia, he would be going to the Spartanburg Tank Wash, in South Carolina, then deadheading to Harrisburg, North Carolina, where he would pick up the hazmats for the haul west. We had been corresponding for four years but had never met. I was at Newark airport two hours after his call.

Before San Diego, he had hauled a surfactant from Salt Lake to New Mexico. He had washed in Phoenix and deadheaded west: To Hill Air Force Base, in Ogden, Utah, he once hauled parts degreaser for F-16s. From Philadelphia to Superior, Wisconsin, he hauled "a secret ingredient" to the company that manufactures Spy Grease. After bouncing to Neenah to wash, he loaded at Appleton a soap used in the making and curing of bricks. It was bound for Dixon, California. He has hauled weed killers, paint thinners, defoaming agents that form a broth in the making of explosives, latex for sandwiching plywood, and dust suppressants that are "kind to horses' hooves." To Fresno he took latex for a dye that turns brown cardboard white. Wood squeezings, or lignin liquor, is used in curing cement. He has carried it from Bellingham to Rancho Cucamonga—northern Washington to southern California. He turns down a job maybe once a year. "I don't want to haul any more cashew-nutshell oil—I believe it harms my barrel," he said. Cashew-nutshell oil arrives in ships from Brazil. "You can't make any friction device—clutches, brake shoes, brake pads—without it. It looks like creosote or asphalt. It's a hard wash. It calls for a stripper."

South of Pocatello, in a brightly greened irrigation valley, we met a Ranger reefer coming the other way. "They're out of Buhl, Idaho," he said. "They raise trout. I took some liquid fish guts up there last year—out of a tuna place in L.A. Harbor." Before the liquid fish guts, his load had been soap. Generally, the separation is distinct between food-grade and chemical tankers. You haul chemicals or you haul food. The vessels are different, the specs are different—mainly in protective devices against the aftermath of rollovers. Ainsworth used to haul wine, orange juice, and chocolate. He mentioned a load of concentrated cranberry juice worth five hundred thousand dollars, a load of chocolate worth seven hundred thousand. He said orange-juice haulers sometimes carry sizing agents on the return trip (sizing agents control shrinkage in textiles). Very few companies carry both foods and chemicals even in completely separate tankers. Ainsworth remembers a California carrier with a fleet of about twenty trucks who carried paint thinner, washed, and then picked up wine. He said, "Your brother better be F. Lee Bailey if you're going to engage in practices like that."

In Gainesville, north Georgia, less than fifty miles from Atlanta, we arrived at Piedmont Laboratories, Inc., on Old Candler Road, at 7:59 A.M. Piedmont is an independent packer of everything from hair spray and shaving cream to WD-40. "If it's rainy and your car won't start, rip off the distributor cap and spray it in there," Ainsworth said. "The WD means water displacement." A man named Bomba Satterfield came out—brown shirt, brown trousers—and took a sample of our brown liquid. Ainsworth hooked up a Piedmont hose to force out the cargo with compressed air. By nine we were discharging. Ainsworth said, "We're flowin' and a-goin' right now, Bomba. It'll be about an hour." Satterfield disappeared. Ainsworth said, "Got to take a whiz." As he started off in search of a men's room, he said to me, "If the cargo starts to spill or all hell breaks loose, turn that stopcock and pull down the lever of the internal valve." All hell stayed put, to the relief of the part-owner.

When the load was gone, air was hissing from a valve at the top of the tanker. "If we let air go into the company's tank it would roil the waters," Ainsworth said, adding helpfully, "That's r-o-i-l." He climbed up the steel ladder on the side of the vessel and began, gingerly, to undog the dome. The dome cover was nearly two feet in diameter and was secured by six dogs. "Bleed before you break," he said. "Air is bleeding. Pressure can kill you if you break early." He said he had "heard of guys being blown off the tops of their trucks and into walls and killed." He had "heard of guys having their heads blown off." Other discharging methods could result in negative pressures no less serious. You could implode the tank. If you worked on railroad tank cars, which are made of carbon steel, you could crush them with implosion and twist them like beer cans. Your head would not come off but you would surely be fired. From the dome, we looked down inside the vessel. It looked almost clean. The heel, or residue, was—as we would learn at the interior wash—scarcely more than one ten-thousandth of the six thousand gallons that had been there.

The Spartanburg Tank Wash charged him less than two hundred dollars. It consisted of four parallel bays in what had recently been country. After three pints of heel went into a bucket, a Texas spinner was lowered through the dome. "They're using ultrahot water—just below steam—and detergent," Ainsworth said. "It's an easy wash." A Texas spinner is a Gamma Jet, directing blasts of water at a hundred pounds of pressure per square inch. The procedure took two hours. "They use steam for caustic, and strippers for supercorrosive solutions," Ainsworth remarked while we waited. "You clean out cement mixers with sugar and water." He had a chemical dictionary in his truck to help tank washers break down any unusual product he might be carrying. "But wash guys usually know. Are you aware that a lot of wash guys get killed every year by nitrogen blankets? Customers sometimes use nitrogen to force a load out of a truck. Then the driver goes to a wash. A wash man goes into the tank. He dies. The driver should have alerted him." Some tank washes that service food vessels are kosher. A rabbi is there, supervising.

Directions supplied by Chemical Specialties, Inc., to 5910 Pharr Mill Road, Harrisburg, North Carolina, were written for vehicles approaching the region from the direction opposite ours. When Ainsworth is given imperfect directions, he sometimes asks, on arrival at the company office, "How did you get to work?" Often the answer is "I take the bus." Ainsworth: "That's apparent." At Chemical Specialties, he nosed onto a scale that was under a loading rack lined with bulbous vats. Releasing air, locking the brakes, he said, "O.K., we're in the tall cotton." Variously, the tall cotton was zinc nitrate, manganese nitrate, D-Blaze fire-retardant solution, monoethanolamine. Before filling our vessel, a company handler of hazmats rattled off questions while Ainsworth nodded affirmatively: "You got a wash-out slip? Is your outlet closed? Can you take forty-five thousand pounds?" Ainsworth, for his part, had a question he was required to ask the shipper: "Do we have to display placards?" But he knew the answer and he had the four placards— diamond-shaped, bearing the number 8 and the number 1760 and an inky sketch of test tubes spilling. If you dipped your fish in this hazmat, you would lift out its skeleton, but the hazmat at least was not combustible, not flammable, not explosive. The "8" meant "Corrosive." The "1760" stood for monoethanolamine.

We took it in by hose through the dome. As we filled, Ainsworth sat in the cab plotting his way west. Hazmats had to stay off restricted routes and avoid all tunnels except exempted tunnels. With your tire thumper, you did a tire check once every two hours or hundred miles, whichever came sooner. "Any fines that have to do with hazmats you take a large number and multiply it by a grandiose number," he said. "There's a twenty-seven-thousand-five-hundred-dollar maximum fine." A Class 6 hazmat is poison. A Class 9 hazmat with zebra stripes is "as close to harmless as you're going to get." Explosives are Class 1. Even Ainsworth develops wariness in the presence of a Class 1 placard. Seeing one at a truck stop in Cheyenne, he said, "You might not want to park next to him at night." If a placard with a 3 on it is white at the bottom, the load in the truck is combustible. If a placard with a 3 on it is red at the bottom, the load in the truck is flammable. Odd as it may seem, Gilbert and Sullivan did not write the hazmat codes. A flammable substance has a lower flash point than a combustible substance, according to the codes. "Hazmats" may soon be a word of the past. In Canada they are called "Dangerous Goods" and the term may become international. Hard liquor is a Class 3 hazmat. Depending on its proof, it is either combustible or flammable. The Glenlivet is combustible. Beefeater is flammable.

I got out of the truck to look at the hose in the dome. Ainsworth said, "Get back in. We're almost loaded and your weight has to be part of the total." He should not exceed eighty thousand pounds, and the part-owner's hundred and fifty would matter. We were, after all, parked on a scale. Drawing on his knowledge of nineteenth-century rifle-sighting, he said, "Kentucky windage and Tennessee elevation is what you are doing if you're not right on a scale."

And moments later Ainsworth said, "He's hammering on my dogs. We're getting ready to get out of here." He backed away from the loading rack, stopped the truck, and went off to sign papers and receive from a laboratory his Certificate of Analysis. As if in a minor earthquake, the truck trembled for minutes after he was gone, its corrosive fluid seiching back and forth. As we began to roll for the Pacific Northwest, he said, "We're weighing seventy-nine thousand seven hundred and twenty, so we'll have to plug our brains in to see where we're going to fuel."

In this trade, if you were "grossed out" you were flirting with the weight limit. In weigh stations, they could "make you get legal"—keep you right there until you discharged enough cargo not to be overweight. "Grain haulers, they may know a farmer who will take it, but this corrosive stuff is something else," Ainsworth said. His twin saddle tanks, one on either side of the tractor, could hold three hundred gallons, and "a full belly of fuel," at seven pounds a gallon, would weigh twenty-one hundred pounds. We never had anything like a full belly. Constantly he had to calculate, and cut it fine. With no disrespect for the Chemical Specialties scale, he sought a second opinion, pulling into a Wilco Travel Plaza forty miles up the road, where he came to a stop on a commercial CAT Scale (Certified Automated Truck Scale). While Ainsworth waited, while a truck behind us waited, and while the cashier in the CAT booth waited, the load in the big steel vessel took five minutes to calm down. Ainsworth paid $7.50, got a reading of 79,660, and renewed his fuel calculations. In Candler, North Carolina, at TravelCenters of America, he took on fifty-five gallons of fuel—"just a dab." Always near the intersections of interstates, truck stops have also tended to sprout on the leeward side of weigh stations. Approaching a Flying J just west of Knoxville, he said, "We're going to take on some Mormon motion lotion." Flying J is based in Utah. Waiting behind trucks at fuel bays, Ainsworth sought to avoid being trapped, because some drivers park at the pumps, go inside, eat, and shower. Farther west, where space expanded, he could show more generosity to the saddle tanks. At the Nebraskaland Truck Stop, in Lexington, he bought a hundred gallons. In the bays, there was always a pump on either side of the truck, one for each fuel tank. Truckers call the two pumps the master and the slave. One pump has the rolling numbers, the other is blank. As a general rule, if you take on fifty gallons or more at a truck stop, you get to shower and overnight free.

Many weigh stations have sensors that provide, as you enter, a ballpark assessment of your respect for the law. If a green arrow lights up after you go over the sensor, you bypass all other apparatus and move on. The stations have dynamic scales that you slowly roll across and static scales on which you stop. The weight on each axle is critical as well as the gross. You obey brightly lettered, progressively stern, electrically lighted signs: "AHEAD," "STOP," "PARK BRING PAPERS." Sometimes in weigh stations the I.R.S. is present—there to check the color of fuel. Clear fuel is the only fuel you can legally burn on the highway. Red-dye fuel is maritime fuel, farm fuel, or for use in stationary engines. If you are caught with dyed fuel, the fine starts at a thousand dollars. Ainsworth recalled disdainfully a trucker-negative television piece in which "they only interviewed people in the failure line at scales—outlawish people, running around with no sleep, pinching asses, and going a hundred miles an hour." Park bring papers. In a weigh station east of Boise, we passed a painted wooden sign that said "LEAKING HAZARDOUS MATERIALS NEXT RIGHT." We weren't leaking. We proceeded on.

While the common weight limit for five-axle eighteen-wheelers is eighty thousand pounds, in some states you can carry a greater load if, on more axles, you spread the load out. Near Lincoln, for example, when we met a seven-axled ag hopper, Ainsworth said, "He can gross maybe a hundred thousand pounds. He takes grain from Nebraska to Salt Lake and brings salt back." The more axles you add, the more you can legally carry. In 1979, westbound at Rawlins, Wyoming, Ainsworth, in a reefer hauling pork, came up behind a "LONG LOAD OVERSIZE LOAD" surrounded by pilot cars, a press car, a spare tractor, a tire truck, mechanics, and bears. A lowboy, it had eighteen axles and a hundred and twenty-eight tires. From Argonne National Laboratory, southwest of Chicago, to the Stanford Linear Accelerator Center, in Palo Alto, California, it was carrying a super-conducting magnet that weighed a hundred and seven tons. At close to half a million pounds gross, this was the largest legal load ever to move in the United States, a record that has since been eclipsed. To Don Ainsworth, the magnet was just a magnet. But the truck—the tractor! "It was a Kenworth—olive and glossy—with an olive trailer, a sharp-looking rig."

The most beautiful truck on earth—Don Ainsworth's present sapphire-drawn convexing elongate stainless mirror—gets a smidgen over six miles to the gallon. As its sole owner, he not only counts its calories with respect to its gross weight but with regard to the differing fuel structures of the states it traverses. In western Idaho, we took on fuel, and an hour later, in Oregon, passed pumps that were selling it for eight per cent less. He said, "It's much better for us to take Idaho fuel than that phony-assed Oregon fuel. It's expensive fuel that looks cheap." The Idaho fuel included all Idaho taxes. The Oregon fuel did not include Oregon's ton-mileage tax, which Oregon collects through driver logs reported to each truck's base-plate state (in Ainsworth's case, Utah). Oregon feints with an attractive price at the pump, but then shoots an uppercut into the ton-mileage.

In general, he remarked, fuel is cheaper on or below I-40, and north of I-40 it's costly. He particularly likes the "fuel structures" of Georgia, South Carolina, Tennessee, Missouri, and Oklahoma. To save a couple of thousand pounds and commensurate money, some hazmat-carrying chemical tankers are made of a fibreglass-reinforced quarter-inch plywood with balsa core. Ainsworth's aesthetics do not include balsa cores. He would rather be caught dead in running shoes. In Idaho, in a heavy quartering wind on the huge plateau beyond Mountain Home, he could barely get into eighteenth gear and could feel the wind getting into his wallet, running up the cost of fuel. In the Laramie Basin, where we passed a collection of wrecked trucks, he said, "This place is Hatteras for box trailers. Those six wrecks, probably, were blown over in the wind. In terms of hurting your fuel economy, a side wind is every bit as bad as a headwind. The smaller the gap between the back of the cab and the nose of the trailer the better off you are in terms of fuel economy." In his mind as on his calculator, he paid constant attention to cost efficiencies. The Wyoming speed limit was seventy-five. Driving into a setting sun near Rock Springs, he said, "All day long I've been going seventy in an effort to save fuel." He asked if I knew what heaven is. Heaven is "this month's Playmate in the passenger seat, last month's in the sleeper, and diesel fuel at ten cents a gallon tax paid." Time and again, as we crossed the continent, he said, "I am a businessman whose office is on eighteen wheels. I have a fleet of one."

Most owner-operators own just their tractors. They haul company trailers. In the hazmat-tanker business, Ainsworth knows of only one other driver who owns his whole truck. Insurance is near prohibitive. Per vehicle per accident, the limit of liability for a dry box or a flatbed is seven hundred and fifty thousand dollars. For a chemical tanker, the limit of liability is five million. So why did Ainsworth want to own the whole truck? "First," he answered, "my piece of the pie increases. Second, I maintain her. I know what kind of shape she is in." The "wages" he paid himself were $1.08 times the odometer. But that pie he referred to was filled with more than hours driven. What did he and the truck earn in a typical year? A good year? His responses were strictly elliptical. He would sooner tell you what he paid for his water-buffalo boots, and he was not about to reveal that, either. Instead, he said, "Would we be waltzing around in a brand-new Pete and a virtually new tanker if there was no money in this business? And would my banker back me up? It's good money. It really is." He said truck drivers make about seventy thousand a year if they are Teamsters, but few are. "Teamsters don't even organize trucking companies anymore. There's no point. Trucking is overpowered by non-union drivers." And companies pay them thirty-five thousand a year. Specialists like auto-haulers can make a hundred thousand a year. An owner-operator may gross a hundred thousand, but roughly half is overhead: payments on the tractor, road taxes, insurance, maintenance, and about twenty thousand dollars' worth of fuel. There are some three hundred and fifty thousand independents on the road, hauling "mostly reefers and flats." And what about the people in local six-wheelers—dump trucks, delivery trucks? "Those guys who drive these little shit boxes around make thirty to forty grand a year. But, as I've said, they're not truck drivers. A truck driver drives an eighteen-wheeler. The skill level to drive those little step vans is like a kid riding a trike."

Don's father, Arthur Ainsworth, was born in Lancashire, and came to Canada, and then to western New York, near Rochester, after the Second World War. He became the editor-in-chief of *Screw Machine Engineering*, a magazine whose name a hyphen would have improved. In 1952, he gave up journalism and began rebuilding machine tools, specifically the Davenport Automatic Screw Machine. He also bought fifteen acres south of Rochester—a truck farm. "I'm a farm boy," Don says often, and that is where he grew up, one of seven kids, in the "muck empire" around Honeoye Falls, growing celery, sweet corn, onions, and cucumbers, and hauling them to the farmers' market in the city.

He went to Honeoye Falls High School, class of 1960. After four years as a billing clerk for the Mushroom Express trucking company, he joined the Army, and served in the Azores and at the Defense Language Institute in Monterey ("a lot of those people were spooks"). He was a reporter on the base newspaper. Out of the Army, he found a billing-clerk job in California, and in 1971 was married. He has two children. Jeff, who lives in Sioux City, hauls livestock in his own truck. Alisa lives in Newport Beach, California, and is a programmer/analyst.

Divorced in 1975, he has not remarried. In 1976, thirty-four years old, he began to hang around truck stops in the Los Angeles Basin, seeking informal training on the road. At a Union 76 in Ontario, near Riverside, he saw a guy changing a headlamp, chatted him up, and learned that he was independent. His name was Tim, and sure, he said, why not? Don could come along. They took a load of lettuce to Iowa, and returned with pork, team driving. Four months later, Don bought Tim's truck—"a 1973 Peterbilt cab-over with a skillet face." With it, he did "endless pork-and-produce loops," and in 1977 bought his own refrigerated trailer. When "the produce market went to hell," he sold his reefer and found a tanker outfit—Silver Springs Transport, Howey-in-the-Hills, Florida—that would teach him the ways of tankers and take him on as an independent contractor. In addition to the orange juice and the chocolate, he hauled liquid chicken feed, lard, and tallow. It was a living, but after a while he was running empty too much of the time, getting too much deadhead. So he switched to chemical transport.

He watches his diet. Ordering dinner from a Waffle House

menu in Smyrna, Georgia, he asked for a salad with his T-bone instead of the eggs. In the Kingdom City Petro, Kingdom City, Missouri, he had a big sirloin for breakfast with eggs over easy and toast. We went past Kansas City, up through western Iowa, and had lunch in Nebraska that day. Typically, we had lunch eight hours after breakfast. He described himself as a teetotaller and a non-smoker all his life. He said "nor'west" for "northwest" and "mile" for "miles" ("It's twenty or thirty mile down the road"). He spoke trucker. A dump truck was a bucket. A moving van was a bedbugger. A motorcycle was a murdercycle, or crotch rocket, driven by a person wearing a skid lid. A speedo was a speeding violation. A civilian was someone not a truck driver. A lollipop was a mile marker. A "surface street" was anything off the interstate. On a horse-and-buggy highway, look for William Least Heat-Moon. He also used words like "paucity" and spoke of his "circadian rhythms." He frequently exclaimed, "Lord help us!" He said "shit" and "fuck" probably no more than you do. He seemed to have been to every jazz festival from Mt. Hood to Monterey. He had an innate pedagogical spirit, not always flattering but always warm. Twenty-two miles into Oregon, he explained the time zones of the United States. "There's four time zones with an hour's difference between them," he said. "Spread your four fingers. There's three zones between them." Or, as a Montrealer is said to have said to a Newfoundlander laying sod, "Green side up!"

Each morning, everywhere, he hunted for "the Walleye," often in frustration, because the Walleye tended not to be where his truck could go: "You just don't roll around with hazmat placards looking for *The Wall Street Journal*." He referred to the *Journal* conservatively as "the best-written paper in the world." In the course of a day that began in central Tennessee and went on through Kentucky and southern Illinois, he found no Walleye until we pulled into a QT in St. Peters, Missouri—"a convenience store on steroids that has grown into an El Cheapo truck stop"—where we parked between the pumps in a fuelling bay, left the truck, went inside, bought *The Wall Street Journal*, Xeroxed fifteen pages from "Hazardous Materials Transportation: The Tank Truck Driver's Guide," bought sandwiches to go, took a whiz, went back to the truck, pumped no fuel, and departed.

"Do you know of a writer named Joan Didion?" he had asked me in North Carolina.

I was too shy to say, "Take the 'of' out."

"She is a powerful writer," he went on. "She was raised in the San Joaquin Valley and now lives in New York City. Do you remember an author—he's dead now, twenty or thirty years; they celebrate him up there in the valley . . . ?" Silent for a mile or two, working on it, he eventually said, "Saroyan. William Saroyan." He had Cormac McCarthy's "Border Trilogy" in the truck. "It's the third time I've read it," he said, "but it's like 'Moby-Dick,' you learn something new every time." Out of the blue, in widely scattered moments, he mentioned other writers, editors. They seemed to come up out of the landscape like cellphone towers. On I-85, George Plimpton: "Is he head of *The Paris Review* today?" On I-40, William Styron: "He really knows his cured ham." *Esquire* materialized on I-640 in Knoxville: "I don't know how you can run a man's magazine if you're a lady." As we crossed the Missouri River for the first time, Heat-Moon rose for the first time, too. Seeing two combines and a related house trailer in Little America, Wyoming, Ainsworth said he had read "a great book, a terrific book" called "Dream Reaper" that described a new machine for harvesting wheat, but he couldn't remember the name of the author.

"Craig Canine."

The ten-acre parking lot behind the Kingdom City Petro, in Missouri, was covered with steel biscuits, by now familiar to me—yellow humps, about a foot in diameter, protruding from the asphalt. "When the Martians land and try to figure things out, the toughest thing is going to be the yellow hump at the truck stop," Ainsworth said, but actually any self-respecting extraterrestrial would go straight to a yellow hump and start plugging into jacks for cable TV, the Internet, and the land-line telephone system. After dark, the big parking lots appear to be full of blue fireflies, as drivers lying in their sleepers watch TV. For team drivers, many trucks have in-motion satellite TV. Tractors come with built-in television trays. They're not an option. A truck with no television is about as common as a house without TV in Van Nuys. Ainsworth's TV shelf had boots on it.

Explosives are carried in liquid form in tankers. The more prudent truck stops have designated "safe havens"—Class 1 parking spaces situated, if not in the next county, at least, as Ainsworth put it, "a little away from the rest of the folks who may not want to be there when the thing lights off." Meanwhile, the main parking areas are always decibelled with the idling sounds of diesel engines and refrigeration units. At night in Bankhead, under the full moon, six hundred trucks were idling. It was hot in Georgia but the drivers were cool. Iowa, Oregon, everywhere, the trucks in the truck stops are idling, summer and winter, adjusting personal levels of coolness and warmth. When you are walking in a lot through the throaty sound of hundreds of idling trucks, it is as if you were on the roof of a co-op beside the air-conditioner. From the sidewalks at impressive distances, some drivers can hear their own trucks within the chorus, their own cicada reefers.

The concatenation of so many trucks can be intimidating to new, young drivers. Parking spaces are often designed so that trucks can enter them and exit them moving in the same direction. But not always. Sooner or later, you have to back up, or make some other maneuver that raises the requirements of skill. "In truck stops, you see guys with stagefright," Ainsworth said, as we entered the Flying J in Oak Grove, Kentucky. They take their stagefright with them when they leave. Some years ago, a young tractor-trailer driver, new in his job, picked up a load in Minnesota bound for New York City. He got as far as the apron of the George Washington Bridge, where he became so nervous and scared that he stopped the truck, left it there, and headed for a bus station.

Ainsworth's favorite line in truck-stop restaurants is "I see a lot of civilians in here, a very good sign. You see a civilian and the food is good." My own first choice comes off the public-address system like this: "Shower No. 275 is now ready." While guys in truck stops are waiting for showers—or just killing time—they sit in the TV rooms and stare. One hour a week they are asked to clear the TV rooms for Sunday religious services. They gripe and yell obscenities. Ministers are provided by Truckstop Ministries Incorporated, of Atlanta; Transport for Christ International, of Ephrata, Pennsylvania; Truckers' Christian Chapel Ministries, of Enon, Ohio. Some truck stops have mobile-unit chapels permanently parked in mid-lot. "Sometimes they take you to a real church, and return you," Ainsworth said. He seldom misses a Sunday service.

He locked the cab wherever he parked. "Dopers are every-where," he explained. "And they know the value of everything. In truck stops it's not truckers who bother me, it's pimps and whores, people who want to steal, and people who want to sell you Rolex watches with Timex guts." He said of a truck stop in the backcountry of eastern Oregon, "At one time it was a whorehouse with fuel pumps." Generally speaking, though, the seaminess of truck stops is in inverse proportion to their distance from major cities. In fact, you could generally call them whole-some if they're out in the tall corn. He described certain truck stops in the eastern Los Angeles Basin as "dangerous" and said they were full of burglars who would "hit you over the head," pushers, fencers of stolen goods, and hookers known as "sleeper leapers," who go from truck to truck. "The stops have security, but once the sleeper leapers get in there's no getting rid of them. You don't say 'Get lost.' They might hurt your truck. You say, 'I just left mama. I'm O.K.' "

In a bitter ice-cold winter wind at a truck stop on I-80 in South Holland, Illinois, he had seen a hooker going around the lot dressed in only a blouse and a miniskirt. Outside New York City, in his experience, no regional truck stop was less safe than the service area on the New Jersey Turnpike named for Vince Lombardi. His description of it was all but identical to his de-scription of the truck stops of Los Angeles: "The Vince Lom-bardi plaza is a real dangerous place. Whores. Dope. Guys who'll hit you over the head and rob you. A lot of unsavory people wandering around, and not your brethren·in transport." About his brethren in transport, the most unsavory item that Ainsworth pointed out to me was lying beside a curb at the edge of a truck-stop parking lot in Kentucky. It was a plastic quart-size fruit-juice bottle with—apparently—apple juice in it. He said, "That isn't apple juice. It's urine. They generally leave the bottles by the trucks. Other trucks run over them. When you see wet pavement, that isn't rainwater."

You see children playing in the truck-stop parking lots, especially in summer—eight-year-olds in baggy short pants like their parents'. A woman in Little America was walking her dog beside a closed auto-hauler with a custom sleeper. A closed auto-hauler hauls concealed expensive cars. A custom sleeper is a family home, stretched onto a bobtail. Indiana Custom Trucks, of LaGrange, Indiana, makes kitchen-bedroom-parlors that cost more than the tractors themselves and, of course, have in-motion satellite TV. "People think truck drivers are all evil and mean," Ainsworth said when we were still in North Carolina, and even earlier in our acquaintance he said, "Please do not entertain any stereotypical notions about truck drivers—i.e., that they are tobacco-chewing, ill-educated, waitress-pinching folk raised on red beans and rice and addicted to country music." He is dour about the brethren's obscenities and profanities while talking with one another on CB radio. "A lot of four-wheelers have CBs," he said. "The truckers' language reinforces the stereotype that truck drivers are fourth-grade-educated grease-under-the-fingernails skirt-chasing butt-pinching dumdums. Dodos." Sometimes you look into trucks and see big stuffed animals on the passenger seat. "Lots of real dogs, too. The dog of choice is poodle."

I think it can be said, generally, that truckers are big, amiable, soft-spoken, obese guys. The bellies they carry are in the conversation with hot-air balloons. There are drivers who keep bicycles on their trucks, but they are about as common as owner-operators of stainless-steel chemical tankers. At the Peterbilt shop in O'Fallon, Missouri, we saw a trucker whose neck was completely blue with tattoos. Like many other drivers in the summer heat, he was wearing shorts, running shoes, and white socks. Some still wear bib overalls—the Idaho tuxedo, according to Ainsworth. Sometimes it's the Louisiana tuxedo. Bull racks are trucks that carry cattle. If a bull rack has a possum belly, slung down inches from the pavement, it can variously carry "hogs, sheep, goats, cattle, vicuñas—whatever." Bull-rack drivers, according to Ainsworth, are "all macho guys." In Wyoming, we passed a Freightliner driven by a slight Asian woman in a baseball cap. She wore glasses and her hair was gray. In Oregon, an England company dry box out of Salt Lake overtook and passed us. Ainsworth described the driver as "a lady who looks like a grandmother." Women are now about five per cent of all truck drivers. "You have to have half-ass mechanical skills," he said modestly. "Women don't have such skills." Quite rare are "single lady drivers" and two-female teams. Man plus woman, however, seems to work out as a team. "For a husband and wife it can be a very simple chore. They have drop trailers at both ends. Dropping and hooking, they can easily do a thousand miles a day." The sun never sets on the languages spoken by American truck drivers.

Drug use is "not rampant" among truckers, he said. "Random drug screening is fairly effective. Preëmployment screening, too. If they see you staggering around and your eyes are red, you're going for a for-cause screening—urine test, blood test, et cetera. They test for five things: cocaine, marijuana, angel dust, amphetamines, and heroin. Many times, they'll give you a saliva test, just like a horse, right on the spot." Alcohol? "I don't smell it on guys." As a teetotaller, he is a particularly qualified smeller. Truck stops sell beer, and Ainsworth approves. "Better to have it right there than to be rolling around in your bobtail looking for a liquor store."

Just as the body of a fish tells you how that fish makes a living, the body of a tanker can tell you what it contains. In Ainsworth's words, "The architecture of the tank says what is in it." If a tank has gasoline inside, it has a full-length permanent manway on top, and, seen from the rear, is a recumbent oval. If a truck is a water wagon, the tank—rear view—is rectangular. A perfect circle ambiguously suggests asphalt, milk, or other food. If the vessel is all aluminum and shaped in tiers like nesting cups, it is a food-grade pneumatic hopper full of flour, granulated sugar, and things like that. If stiffeners are exposed—a series of structural rings circling and reinforcing the tank—the vessel is uninsulated, generally operates in a warm climate, and often hauls flammables and combustibles. Ainsworth said, "That is what mine looks like without the designer dress" (the stainless mirror sheath). The double conical side view speaks of chemical hazmats. Since September 11, 2001, all these shapes have scattered more than fish.

"Since 9/11, people see a tanker and they think you've got nitroglycerin in it," Ainsworth said.

Responding to a suggestion that we use a Wal-Mart parking lot while making a visit in Laramie, he said, "There's no way I'm putting these hazmats in a Wal-Mart. People in places like that think the truck is going to explode." In the fall of 2001, near St. Louis, a cop in a weigh station asked what he was carrying. "Latex," said Ainsworth. "Latex is a hazardous commodity," said the cop, but let him go. In a weigh station near Boise with a tankful of phosphoric acid, he got the "PARK BRING PAPERS" sign, as did all trucks with hazmat placards after 9/11. Everywhere, though, drivers were being scrutinized even more closely than the contents of their tanks. Drivers quit "because they looked Middle Eastern and were stopped left and right." If not native born, drivers with hazmat endorsements on their licenses became subject to police checks. "At truck stops, you used to be able to drop your trailer and bobtail into town. Now they don't want that. Something may be ticking." Signs have appeared: "NO DROPPING TRAILERS." The asphalt pavement at many truck stops used to be laced with dolly slabs. If you wanted to drop your trailer and go off bobtailing, you used a dolly slab or you might regret it. The retractable landing gear that supports the front end of a detached trailer could sink deep into asphalt and screw you into the truck stop for an extended stay. Rectangles just large enough for the landing gear, dolly slabs were made of reinforced concrete.

September 11th did not create in Ainsworth a sensitivity to law-enforcement officers which was not already in place. He describes the introduction of photo radar as "another encroachment of our rights." On I-10 once in Florida, a cop pulled him over and tried to put a drug-sniffing dog in his cab. He said, "I'm allergic to dogs." The officer said, "It's O.K. We can spray the cab." Slowly, Ainsworth said, "I'm constitutionally allergic to dogs." The bear got the message. The bear, of course, had "run a make" on him—"a cop phrase for plugging me into the N.C.I.C." The National Crime Information Center is a system within the F.B.I. "A cop stops you, runs an N.C.I.C. on your license, your whole history—your hit-and-runs, your D.U.I.s, your drug arrests. He's ready to give you a field sobriety test— walk a straight line, et cetera. Around San Francisco, that's called the Bay Shore Ballet."

"What did the cop find in your record?"

"Zero. There's nothing that exists on me. We don't really believe in interviews with police. It just gums us up. I run a legal ship, and the equipment is well maintained." Ainsworth added that he can afford water-buffalo boots because he obeys the law, keeping the buzzards out of his wallet. Buzzards, a word of broad application, extends from police to the Department of Transportation and the Internal Revenue Service and beyond. In the argot of the road, D.O.T. stands for Death on Truckers.

A female police officer is a sugar bear. A honey bear. A diesel bear is a cop who deals with truckers only. On a surface street in Puyallup, Washington, we happened by a municipal cop parked in his police car. Ainsworth said, "That's a local. That's not a real bear. Truck drivers would say, 'That's not a full-grown bear.' "

It had been well over a decade since he had acquired his last speedo. At one time, he thought "speedos were merely a form of doing business," but he had completely changed his mind. Individual bears have idiosyncratic speed thresholds that range from zero to ten miles above the limit. So Ainsworth sets his cruise control exactly on the speed limit. "Cops are suspicious of everybody," he said as we were starting to roll from Charlotte. "You have to think like a cop." His thinking is assisted by his radio scanner, which homes in on the highway bands for state police. In Malheur County, Oregon, he heard a bear on the scanner say that he had a dump truck in Vale and was going to weigh it on a portable scale. "Vital information," Ainsworth said. "It's vital for you to know where the predators are." He bought the scanner mainly to detect "bears in the air." How does he know they're in the air? "You learn cop talk: 'That blue truck in lane No. 3—we've got him at 82.5.' " On the Pennsylvania Turnpike he once heard an air bear say to five chase cars on the ground: "We're going home early. We've got our work done for today." In other words, a quota had been met. The quota mattered more than a full shift of the cops' contribution to safety. Speedos, evidently, were for them a form of strip-mining more profitable than bituminous coal. On I-15 in Idaho, after we met a four-wheeler getting a speedo on the shoulder from a bear with flashing lights, Ainsworth turned on the scanner. "We want to know everything about cops," he said. "We want to know if that cop is going to turn and come along behind us after signing the ticket." He did.

"On I-90 in Montana it was legal to go any speed until about two years ago," Ainsworth said. "Guys went a hundred miles an hour. There were too many wrecks. You'd need a big parachute to stop this thing at a hundred miles an hour. I wouldn't think of doing a hundred miles an hour. You're going to Beulah Land."

Backing blindsided at the Peterbilt dealer's in Missouri, he said, "Sometimes you do this by Zen." He had never been to driver school. "I'm a farm boy," he explained. "I know how to shift. There are two things you need to know: how to shift, and how to align yourself and maintain lane control—exactly how much space is on each side. In city traffic it's critical." In the open country of western Kentucky, he said, "Out here, you look way ahead. It's the same as steering a ship. There's a silver car about a mile ahead that I'm looking at now. When you steer a ship, you don't look at the bow, you look at the horizon. When I'm in a four-wheeler, I stay away from trucks, because if a tire blows or an entire wheel set comes off I'm going to Beulah Land."

Gratuitously, he added, "Atlanta has a lot of wrecks due to aggressive drivers who lack skill. In Los Angeles, there's a comparable percentage of aggressive drivers, but they have skill. The worst drivers anywhere are in New Jersey. Their life cannot mean a great deal to them. They take a lot of chances I wouldn't take—just to get to work on time."

From Harrisburg, North Carolina, to Sumner, Washington, the load in the tank behind us kicked us like a mule whenever it had a chance. The jolt—which Ainsworth called slosh, or slop— came mainly on surface streets and on-ramps when gears were shifting at low speeds. On the open road, it happened occasion- ally when we were gearing down, mashing on the accelerator, stepping on the brakes, going downhill, or going uphill. Ains- worth minimized the slosh with skills analogous to fly casting. "You coördinate shifting with the shifting of the load," he said. "You wait for the slop or you can pretzel your drive line." The more ullage the more slop. The density of the mono- ethanolamine had allowed us to take only six thousand gallons in the seven-thousand-gallon tank. The ullage was the difference was the mule.

We would deliver it to Sumner after a day's layover in the Cascades. We were running twenty-four hours early. For the spectacular plunge in christiania turns down through the moun- tains from Snoqualmie Pass, Ainsworth's gear selection was No. 14 and his foot never touched the brake. The speed limit for trucks was, of course, restricted, but not by weight, causing Ainsworth to say, "They're not as bright as Oregon." The State of Washington was bright enough, however, to require that a truck stop in that beautiful forest of Engelmann spruce and Douglas fir be invisible from the interstate, right down to the last billboard. About thirty miles uphill from Puget Sound, we turned off I-90 at a nondescript exit, went through a corridor of screening trees, and into the Seattle East Auto Truck Plaza, where a freestanding coffee hut named Cloud Espresso dispensed americano one-shots and mondo latte—truck-driver drinks, strong enough to float a horseshoe. In the lot, at least a hundred trucks were parked and humming. On one flatbed, a guy had a yacht he had hauled from Fort Lauderdale for a Seattle couple who had sailed around the Horn. He was getting ten thousand dollars to take the boat home.

As we began to roll on the second morning, I asked Ainsworth what time it was. He said, "0600 local." Sumner is down near Enumclaw and Spanaway, southeast of Tacoma. On Eighth Street East at 6:50 A.M., we turned into a large, elongate, and already busy lumbermill, where lanes were narrow among high piles of raw logs and stacks of lumber in numerous dimensions, from rough-cut ten-by-tens down. We saw a machine called a C-claw, or grappler (basically a crab's claw with a six-foot spread), go up to an eighteen-wheeler that had just arrived with fifty thousand pounds of fresh wood—forty-foot logs of Emperor fir. As if the huge logs were bundled asparagus, the big claw reached in, grabbed them all, and in one gesture picked up the entire fifty thousand pounds, swung it away from the truck, and set it on the ground.

A man appeared from behind some stacked lumber and shouted, "You guys got chemical?"

"We're not here with his morning orange juice," Ainsworth muttered.

"Did you know you've got a hole in your tank?"

A living riot, this guy. He directed us to "the second dry

shed" in the vast labyrinthine yard. It was a cloudless day. From the roof of that dry shed, you could have seen the white imminence of Mt. Rainier, twenty-five miles southeast. But we were soon parked under the roof and looking instead at a bomb-shaped horizontal cylinder rouged with rust. This was the destination to which Ainsworth had hauled the monoethanolamine 2,884 miles. "What is the capacity of the tank?" he asked. Answer: "It's big." Eventually, he determined that the receiving tank's capacity was nine thousand gallons. He got out his tire thumper and thumped the tank. "Sounds pretty empty to me," he concluded, and from tubes on his tanker he removed two twenty-foot hoses two inches thick and a ten-foot jumper with double female ends. He hooked them together and forced out the hazmat with compressed air. As the fixing preservative in pressure-treated wood, chromated copper arsenate and ammoniacal copper arsenate were being phased out by the pressure-treated-wood industry. Some people had built their houses entirely of pressure-treated wood, and from the arsenic in the preserving compounds the people were going the way of old lace. Adults had been hospitalized. Children were at particular risk. So arsenic compounds were out now, and we had brought the base of the broth meant to replace them. In an hour, the six thousand gallons were discharged. We climbed to the dome, Ainsworth eased it open, and we looked down into the vessel. There remained what turned out to be a pint and a half of heel. It was a very dark and glistening, evil-looking blue. If blood were blue, it would be like that monoethanolamine.

At 0900 local we were back on the road. Ainsworth was headed for a wash in Portland, and then would bounce to Kalama, near Kelso, and take a load of K-Flex 500 to Kansas City, and then bounce to Gastonia, North Carolina, for latex bound for White City, Oregon. From the lumbermill, he took me fourteen miles to the Flying J Travel Plaza, Port of Tacoma Truck Stop, Interstate 5. As he departed, the long steel vessel caroming sunlight was almost too brilliant to look at. I stood on the pavement and watched while the truck swung through the lot and turned, and turned again, and went out of sight. As it did, the Flying J's outdoor public-address system said, "Shower No. 636 is now ready."

The Ships of Port Revel

The captain says, "Midships." I say, "Midships." He says, "Starboard twenty." I say, "Starboard twenty." He says, "Dead slow ahead." I say, "Dead slow ahead." He is a licensed master of ships of any gross tons upon oceans. I am his helmsman, third mate, engineer. My talent consists of following orders. "Hard to starboard." "Hard to starboard." We leave the Suez Canal.

The Suez Canal runs along the east sides of Manhattan Island and Staten Island from Cape Horn to Cape Fear. On Range 195 you head from the Bay of Biscay to the steel island of Ras Tanura. This is Port Revel, in Dauphiné, near Grenoble, where ship captains and ship pilots from all over the world take a five-and-a-half-day course in ship handling for a room-board-tuition fee of fifteen thousand dollars. Since the nineteen-sixties more than six thousand skippers and pilots have come here for advanced training, in classes as small as four and no larger than eight. Port Revel is a pond in the foothills of the Alps. It was dug for potter's clay by Trappist monks in the sixteenth century, and was later used to raise fish. "Ease to ten." "Ease to ten." "Midships." It would dumbfound those monks to see what is happening on their pond today.

The ship Normandie is traveling west. The Brittany is docking in a forty-knot wind. The Europe is doing a Williamson turn. The Normandie is new, and was built to carry containers on a fast-ship hull. The skippers agreed after their first two hours on the pond that these model ships behave very much in the way that big ones do. They are not canoes. They feel like ships. They are replicas of real and specific ships, to scale, with bulbous bows and working anchors. The model tanker Europe is forty feet long. It is a mini-clone of the Esso Europa, one thousand feet long. My canoe at home weighs fifty pounds and turns on a centime in ponds. The model Europe weighs 41,013 avoirdupois pounds. You don't turn it with a paddle. When it moves, and develops what the instructor Philippe Delesalle refers to as "the inertia," it does not want to stop. He says it is "like a large lorry with a moped engine and no brakes." He has warned us: "If you try to treat them as toys, they don't like that and they won't forgive you. Don't use your hands to avoid collisions. You can break your wrists. Remember, this is a finger, not a fender." In an earlier class one ship hit another so hard that its bow broke off under the other ship's hull. The pond, with its kilometre of shoreline, represents three miles by two and a half miles of confined navigable water. When we go half ahead for a bit, and get up to the scale equivalent of six or seven knots, the skippers had better be thinking at least five ship lengths ahead—figuring in ship lengths their stopping distance. Five ship lengths at full scale is almost a mile. To do a Jordan stop you turn hard left or hard right—increasing greatly your underwater resistance—and then go full astern. You stop like a skier.

My captain at the moment is Björn Grandin, of Wallenius Lines, Stockholm. He is behind me on the "bridge"—a cockpit designed so that his eyes look out upon the surrounding buoys, channels, and shoreline from a level analogous to the bridge level of the real ship. I sit in a lower cockpit, my eyes about even with this tanker's long and unencumbered steel deck. One of my hands is on the ship's wheel, the other on the engine-order telegraph. Before me is a rudder-angle indicator, a relative-wind-direction indicator, a relative-windspeed indicator, a speed log, and an r.p.m. indicator. Björn has all that duplicated in front of him, along with a port-anchor-chain indicator, a starboard-anchor-chain indicator, a bow-and-stern-thruster panel, and a compass. I have already responded to one of his commands by repeating it verbatim while turning the wheel hard over in the direction opposite to the one he spoke of. The ship does not just swing over and hit something. It takes some time to respond. Realizing my mistake, I shift the rudder at once, but the precision of Björn's maneuver is blunted. Which he never mentions. In real life he is the skipper of Traviata. Wallenius ships are named for operas. Faust and Fidelio fly the American flag, because they carry American military cargoes, which by law must travel in "American" ships. On Traviata, Björn carries cars around the world. To Yokohama he carries Japanese cars made in the United States. To the United States he carries Ford tractors made in Japan. From Sweden to the world he carries Saabs and Volvos, keys in the dash. He has also delivered for Mercedes-Benz—keys in the ship's safe. ("It's the radios.") Björn lives in Malmö and drives a Ford. He is wearing a gray sweatshirt that says "YANKEE BYLINE U.S. SPORTS."

We're in the Brittany. The model weighs sixteen tons. We go northbound in the deepwater channel, turn right on

Range 97, soon pick up Range 15 by the stern, keep four red buoys on our port side, and turn thirty degrees left onto Range 162. "Every half mile you have a ninety-degree turn, so don't go too fast," Philippe has instructed. "Have power on reserve. Keep something in the pocket." Turning works better with powered kicks ahead. The telegraph speaks in parables. Dead slow ahead, you cannot turn easily and may drift or skid off course. Full ahead, you make a snappy turn, but try keeping it up and disaster will present itself.

You begin your big turns well in advance or you finish up aground. This condensed roadstead of channels, shoals, and islands is intolerant of inaccuracy. As the ship begins to swing one way, it drifts the other—skids. You feel the force of the inertia—massive, inexorable, immense—moving at an angle (the "drift angle") to the axis of the ship. Sedately the vessel skids, like a cornering car. This is the Indianapolis 500 in geologic time. "You skid onto the range," Philippe says. "If it skids too much, it's on the buoys." "Overturning"—an odd word in this context—means turning too far in order to kick ahead on the engine and correct a skid. "You turn too far to the right, then kick ahead to the left. The engine is part of the steering equipment. You cancel the skid."

At times in these tight waters the ships in their glide seem unstoppable by anything but docks, wharves, rocks, and trees. It would flatter the students to call such moments rare. Continuous shifting of the rudder from hard left to hard right, hard right to hard left, has considerable slowing effect, but not always enough. The ship might as well be sliding on ice. The Sperry Hydrobrake is essentially a pair of rudders that stick out like wings in opposite directions; these ships are not equipped with Sperry Hydrobrakes. Devices like parachutes have been proposed, and bulbous bows that open like flowers; but neither exist, here or on the oceans. The situation calls for the crash stop maneuver—emergency full astern. First the shaft has to stop spinning, and with it the propeller, and then it has to pick up revolutions in the opposite direction until it has reached full astern. By now, if several million barrels of oil are not already calming the seas around you, the propeller may cavitate. Every ship has its window of cavitation. As it slows down, with its propeller reversed, and reaches a zone of, say, twelve to eight knots, a dramatic change in pressure occurs around the screw. The water is suddenly flashing, making bubbles; the propeller is churning a high percentage of air. Philippe says, "When you have cavitation, the propeller is not working. The propeller is just making mayonnaise, you know. The crash stop maneuver is not a helpful piece of knowledge. When they use it, they just go and crash somewhere."

A very good way to stop, if there's water enough around you, is to do a Williamson turn. A ship that will stop in thirteen ship lengths after going full astern at a speed of sixteen knots will stop in ten ship lengths at full astern with the rudder cycling, and in three ship lengths with a Williamson turn. Generally known as a device for picking up a person overboard, the Williamson turn is impressively precise. You turn the wheel hard right or hard left until the ship is sixty degrees off the course it was on. Then you shift the wheel to the other extreme. The ship circles and returns to the place where it left the original track. On the training ship of Maine Maritime Academy the cadets do Williamson turns all day long around a floating life jacket, and at the end of the day they pick it up.

The Williamson turn was invented by Butakov, Philippe informs us. Williamson did it during the Second World War as a lifesaving device. Butakov did it in 1903, on the eve of the Russo-Japanese War. "The maneuver was known as the Butakov pipe. It was not to recover a man fallen overboard, because at that time, you know . . ." The Russians fired guns and then did the turn they called the Butakov pipe in order to keep the guns at the same distance from the enemy.

Philippe is on the dock like a swimming instructor—in white shorts and a striped shirt across a wide space that has processed a lion's share of exceptional food. He calls it his bulbous bow. It is supported by athletic legs. In his long career he has been a pilot in Algiers, the Persian Gulf, the Wouri River of Cameroon. On the dock he has placed a small block of wood marked "BRIDGE," meaning that Björn should finish exactly there, but Björn says "Hard to port" when he means "Hard to starboard," and his careful approach splays. "In such a ship you never use the wharf as a brake," Philippe says. "Your stern is falling down the wind."

With a hook on the end of a pole he pulls a mooring line off the ship and secures it to a bollard, where it acts as a lever to assist the docking. The mooring lines are just nylon rope, but—because they, like everything else, are meant to function to scale—they each include a breakable section of fishing line of a pound-test appropriate to the tonnage of the ship. Everything about these models has been worked out according to a principle of similitude developed in the nineteenth century by the English hydraulic engineers William Froude and Osborne Reynolds. According to the math, the length scale (1:25) is squared to find the area scale (1:625) and cubed to find the scales of volume, weight, and force (1:15,625). Time is the square root of the length factor—1:5. Time is five times quicker than in real life. What takes one hour on a real ship takes twelve minutes here, with commands falling like rain. "Port twenty. Slow ahead. Midships. Full astern." Forty hours on the pond equals two hundred hours of real ship handling. Astonishingly, the model ship Europe develops less than half of one horsepower in order to replicate the real ship's thirty-two thousand. No tugs. A tug at scale would be too small. The models' bow and stern thrusters—pumping water in either direction—can be used to simulate tugs. "We are here to make ship handling, not tug handling," Philippe has said dourly, condemning the thrusters.

Mallards by the dozen cruise among the ships. At scale the mallards are thirty feet long. All the life rings mounted on trees around the pond are fifty feet across, and the trees—spruce, fir, oak, beech, chestnut—are fifteen hundred feet tall. The old hunting lodge set back from the water approaches the size of Versailles. The instructors have a collection of little toy sailors not quite three inches high. They place them for perspective on the long plain decks of the tankers. The toy sailors are almost unnoticeable, and at scale they are six feet tall. Real sailors use motorbikes on the decks of such tankers. Despite a sign by the pond—"PÊCHE ET BAIGNADE INTERDITES"—a pike was caught here that weighed eleven pounds. At scale (1:15,625) the fish weighed eighty-six tons. With respect to center of gravity and gross tonnage, the weight of a two-man crew is obviously important. Skipper and helmsman combined weigh twenty-five hundred tons.

The models, nine in number, are worth about two million dollars. Their hulls—variously fabricated in foam, steel, and glass-reinforced plastic—are made in boatyards elsewhere but are fitted out at Port Revel. They are powered with electricity and laden with electronics. When a light glows at the top of their masts, they have the undivided attention of a tracking infrared theodolite, which sits at the top of a twenty-metre tower with its head cocked. Captain Chase and I call it the Owl.

Andy Chase was a card-carrying second mate some years ago, when I followed him into union halls looking for a ship. We went to Colombia, Ecuador, Peru, and Chile on the SS Stella Lykes, with a captain so gifted that he frequently and lengthily spoke with the ship. In Buenaventura, parallel docking between two other ships without the assistance of tugs or a pilot, he worked the seven-hundred-foot Stella Lykes into a seven-hundred-and-fifty-foot space as if he were inserting a coin in a meter. Andy later became a first mate and then a licensed master of ships of any gross tons upon oceans. It is in part a reflection of the rapid disappearance of American-flag ships that Andy is less often a master now than he is a schoolmaster. As a professor at Maine Maritime Academy, he teaches courses in celestial navigation, meteorology, seamanship, nautical science, watchkeeping, rules of the road, and ship handling, his reason for being here. Skippers do not come here at a given point in a career. Their companies seem to send them randomly. In the real world masters seldom handle ships. Harbor pilots and docking pilots and river pilots and bar pilots and canal pilots do. When a severe situation arises in which a captain must handle his ship, he might wish he had been to Port Revel. Meanwhile, the pilots who enroll here are testing the limits of the considerable ship handling they know, searching what is possible. The author of "Auxiliary Sail Vessel Operations" (Cornell Maritime Press), Andy Chase is in his forties now, his beard still blond, tattoo still blue, his temples turning gray. He does a complete circle at full ahead in deep water with the Owl watching. The Owl confides in a computer, and so does a ship-to-shore radio that transmits every engine change, every turn of the wheel, the heading, the degrees of rudder, the turn rate, the wind knots, and the ship's velocity backward, forward, and sideways. Andy is in command of the Europe, with me as crew, and his deepwater turning circle is three and a half times the length of the ship. When shipyards test ships in deep water, they go to a place where the depth is greater than six times the draft of the ship—a definition of "deep water." At six plus, the bottom has no effect on the hull. Andy now turns a complete circle in shallow water, where the distance between the hull and the bottom is less than half of the draft. The ship is sluggish, difficult to steer. Water can't pass underneath. The ship can't skid. The turning circle is twice as large.

A ship in shallow water loses maneuverability and can be difficult to control. Backing in shallow water becomes quixotic. On its own the backing ship will turn left or right or not at all. A ship is heavier in shallow water and particularly difficult to stop. The virtual mass of the ship increases, because you have to stop not only the ship but also the shallow water you take with you. Captains lose time who go into shallow water in order to cut corners and save time.

As a ship moves in deep water, it creates a wave at the bow, a wave at the stern, and a trough between. This is the wave profile, or the wave form, of a ship. The ship descends in the trough—a phenomenon known as squat, which increases as the square of the ship's speed. A two-hundred-thousand-deadweight-ton tanker goes down more than seven feet at sea speed. In shallow water squat increases. Go too fast and you may go too low. To reduce sinkage, reduce your speed. When the Queen Elizabeth 2 went aground in the Elizabeth Islands of Massachusetts, she may have been deep in her own trough, going too fast.

A British captain who came to Port Revel some years ago and went too fast in shallow water continued to give crisp, authoritative maneuvering orders—"Port ten," "Midships," "Port ten," "Midships," "Starboard twenty," and so forth—although his ship was stuck firm. You can navigate in the cream of mud, as the uppermost bottom is sometimes called, but you can't maneuver in potter's clay.

Europeans say "port" and "starboard." By law Americans must say "left" and "right."

If we could rise from the pond and above the screening trees, we could see Alps. On certain days we would even see Mont Blanc, about a hundred miles northeast. Through the clearest air Mont Blanc is visible from the Peugeot van that daily brings the skippers from the Hôtel Bonnoit, in the small village of Viriville, to this isolated pond on the Plateau de Chambaran. Better that we not see the great mountain, we are told, for if we do see it, rain will come within two days. In the Bonnoit's felicitous dining room, over duck pâtés, frogs' legs, *écrevisses* on lettuce like trout just caught and lying in green grass, *pommes de terre dauphinoises*, mussel soup, Guinea fowl, *girolles avec sauce à la crème*, *quenelles de brochet*, poached-egg salad, or *lapin braisée*, the skippers exchange superstitions of their own.

Lapin braisée. The word *"lapin"* is not to be uttered on a French ship, remarks Yvon Satre, of Compagnie Générale Maritime, who is captain of the Pascal, which, like the full-size Normandie, shuffles containers between southern Europe and the Far East. Rabbits were carried as food on old French wooden ships, and—sometimes with disastrous results—they chewed not only the rigging but also the ships' wooden structures. You do not say *"lapin"* for fear of very bad luck, Yvon tells us. You might mention a small, flexible-bodied lagomorph with very long ears, but you never say "*lapin.*" Yvon once carried twenty tons of coneys from Japan to Barcelona. He might have been at greater risk, he says, if the rabbits had not come aboard at a uniform temperature of minus twenty degrees.

Scott Parker, of Interlake Steamship, in Cleveland, says that a profound superstition in Great Lakes shipping is that you never leave a repair yard on a Friday. After Scott left a repair yard one Friday, a boiler blew up. Philippe, over lunch at Port Revel, remarks that roughly five times a year a bulk freighter leaves a port somewhere in the world and is never heard from again. This evolves into an exchange of French and American expressions for dying. With uninventive phrases like "kicked the bucket," "bought the farm," and so forth, the Americans quickly run up something of a trade deficit, for the French—over the Camembert—mention the gentle announcement "He has stopped eating," and add to that what appears to be the ultimate word on this topic: "He has swallowed his birth certificate."

Back on the pond the reversible-current generators, which can stir the whole of Port Revel in varied swirls and convolutions, are sending a two-knot flow along Pier G at Cape Fear and across the entrance to the Antwerp Locks, simulating, as well, the entrance to the Oakland Terminal, in San Francisco Bay. Cape Fear in the real world is the place in North Carolina where Bermuda came out from under the North American continent, but here it is only the south end of Staten Island. The skippers are to dock, port side to, against the current. "Docking is difficult if current is coming toward you parallel to the dock," says the instructor Joseph Le Sciellour. "Remember, if you double the current speed, you square the force on the ship. The current is setting you off the pier." Yvon will attempt to dock the container ship Normandie.

Yvon Satre, in comparison with the other skippers, is stately. It is a special pleasure to be his third mate and helmsman. There is less to do. Where others might give thirty or forty commands (playing checkers with the engine, fine-tuning the prow), Yvon may give six. "Starboard ten," he says. An eternity goes by, and then he says, "Midship the wheel." His voice is solemn and musical. "Wheel" as he pronounces it is a drawn-out linkage of *"oui"* and "eel." Whereas the other skippers turned up for the course in sneakers, blue jeans, and polo shirts, Yvon appeared at dockside on the first day in buckled shoes, slacks, a striped shirt, and a blazer. Not tall but solidly constructed and with a neatly trimmed black beard, he seemed like an opera singer preparing to ship out on a swan. He is Armorican, a Breton from birth, son of a jeweller, graduate of the Ecole Nationale de la Marine Marchande. On one of his three annual trips to the Far East he can take his wife but no children. Since he has no children, that's not much of an inconvenience. (Björn Grandin has a boy and a girl, and his family can travel on the Traviata whenever he likes.) Yvon is fifty-three. His metal-rimmed spectacles dangle from a cord around his neck. His manner is not only quietly and commandingly assured but scholarly and philosophical as well. When someone remarked on this, Philippe Delesalle muttered, *"Ce n'est pas Sartre."*

Now in the Normandie, Yvon negotiates the Manhattan channel on his way to the dock on Staten Island. Like everyone else in the class, he is not immune to disaster. The captains are here to learn difficult maneuvers. On his first trip past the current generator, Yvon hit it six times. He was sucked into it. As his helmsman, I was in a position to hear him softly comment, *"C'est difficile!"* The Normandie, its bulbous bow glowing red in the ceramic-green water, approaches a critical bend in the Manhattan channel, where the current is not so much a problem as a trap. "Hard to starboard. Full astern. Midship the wheel." He goes aground so hard that the draft of the ship decreases by ten scale feet. He smiles and says, even more softly, "We have spoken about the rabbit yesterday."

A four-hundred-thousand-dollar wave maker is emitting, to scale, a ten-foot wave every eight seconds. Parallel to the crests, the ships roll, dead in the water. Going half astern and achieving sternway, they are drawn—without any additional commands or maneuvers—toward the waves and away from shore, automatically turning ninety degrees as they back up, and moving in the direction of safety. It's a good way to stay off the rocks.

While waves and currents matter plenty, nothing affects these big heavy ships so much as wind. When engineers at SOGREAH (the Société Grenobloise d'Etudes et d'Applications Hydrauliques) were first designing this evident combination of a miniature golf course and Caltech, their most sensitive consideration was wind. In any marine setting—any Atlantic or Mediterranean port—there was much too much of it, because wind, like all else, had to be figured to scale. The math said that a ten-knot wind against the models would equal a fifty-knot wind on the actual sea. There was too much wind in the three deep valleys of Grenoble. So the company went to the foothills and found what Philippe Delesalle describes as "a small lake in the middle of nowhere sheltered by forest." When a breeze ruffles the surface, our wind-speed indicators will read thirty or forty knots, and although the model ships may weigh twenty actual tons, they can be blown off course.

A weathervane, turning into a shifting wind, revolves about

its pivot point, which—needless to say—stays where it is and does not change. In the behavior and handling of ships nothing is more significant than the captains' and pilots' sense of the point on a ship that is analogous to the place where a weather-vane swings, with the difference that on a ship—in varying situations having to do with, among other things, center of gravity, speed, torque, and direction—the swinging place moves. It is known in ship handling as the peripatetic pivot point. On a ship moving forward the pivot point is about a third of the way back from the bow, and the ship turns around that point. If the ship stops and moves backward, the pivot point travels aft and settles even closer to the stern than it was to the bow. If two tugs push the ship on the same side at opposite ends, the tug that is farthest from the pivot point will turn the ship. A bow thruster will have scant effect on a ship that is moving forward, but will easily turn a ship that is moving aft. If you can sense the peripatetic pivot point—in your mind following it around the ship as if it were a spotlight—you can back around a corner and into a pier using engine and rudder alone. "With the real ship you can do that, of course," says Joe Le Sciellour, showing limitless confidence in his students. They attempt the maneuver with the models. This academic drill illustrates the role of the pivot point in ship handling, and the skippers learn by failing at it, one by one. To back into the pier, put the pivot point off the corner of the dock and "saw wood," they are told. *"Scier du bois."* You kick with the engine, short pulses—full astern, full ahead, full astern, full ahead. "It's a matter of transferring the pivot point from stern to bow and bow to stern," Joe says. The kicks, proportionally, are more astern. Philippe is so intent on this that he has wired himself to a bullhorn. "As long as your pivot point is ahead of the corner, you'll turn," he broadcasts. Joe adds, "You transfer the pivot point and finish parallel." Joe Le Sciellour, who lives in Dunkirk, is an animated teacher—short, trim, and intense—and formerly a North Sea pilot and skipper of a Channel ferry. Like Philippe, he once worked as a pilot in Algiers, where depths were routinely given in feet and lengths in metres.

Gradually a sort of catechism of ship handling is rising in everyone's mind. Steer with your engine. Understand the limits of what you can do with your ship. You do it more by feel than by math. You have to bear in mind the varying effects of wind, current, swell, and momentum. You have to bear in mind the ratio of your wet longitudinal area to your rudder surface. You have to bear in mind that a ship having headway fetches to windward. The farther aft the bridge, the more she wants to come into the wind. You have to bear in mind the bank effects in narrow channels, the bottom effects in shallow water. You deal with current in a narrow channel not by speed but by setting a good drift angle. At the right angle to an oncoming current you can cross it without slipping backward. (In a canoe you would call that ferrying.) You have to bear in mind not only your speed through the water but also your speed over the ground. Know your knots of wind drift. What is your draft? You won't know exactly. What is the depth of the water due to tide? It is hard to be accurate. Your depth finder sometimes reads into mud, registering more depth than is there. And after you have kept all this—times ten—in the front of your mind all day, Owl & Company will present you with graphic and numerical printouts showing in hours, minutes, and seconds your headings and degrees, your rudder degrees, your engine r.p.m.s, your forward and backward speeds, your transverse velocities, your turn rates,

the action of your thrusters, the knots of wind you were working in, where you went, what you did, and everything you hit or
missed.

If an anchor moves along the bottom when you don't intend
it to, it is dragging. If you mean it to move, it is dredging. You
dredge the anchor, or anchors, to make a slow speed even
slower, to increase the precision of a maneuver, to do various
things you otherwise could not do, or to stop. The skippers on
the pond are now dredging. Andy, in Gilda, the model of a
tanker of a hundred and twenty-five thousand deadweight tons,
puts out a shackle and a half to swing on his starboard anchor
and make what he describes as "a tight turn in a hairy place." A
shackle is a shot is ninety feet or fifteen fathoms or twenty-seven
metres of anchor chain. Approaching Pier F in the rain, Andy
puts out two and a half shackles on either side and dredges both
anchors as if he were snowplowing skis. That is what dredging is,
Philippe says. The anchor acts as a plow in the ground. Your
chain length should be one and a half times to twice the depth
of the water. Keep a constant strain on the chain. Forget kicks
ahead: they can break your chain. The anchor prevents the ship
from making too much headway. It moves the pivot point forward, and gives you better control with the rudder. The ship
will turn more quickly and more sharply. After all, if a ship is
swinging on an anchor chain, the pivot point is the hawsepipe.
You can dock, if you have to, using only anchors.

Yvon drops two anchors to equal depth, goes hard to port at
forty r.p.m.; his stern swings to starboard, and his ship goes snug
against a pier. Andy is spectacular. He drops his port anchor with
several shackles and his starboard anchor with a short chain. This
helps him swing a hundred and eighty degrees and end up with
the dock ten inches from his starboard side. Philippe does not

entirely approve. He translates the scale. "Twenty feet," he says. "Don't try to come too close to the dock. Don't move too fast over ground; the anchor is bouncing."

Henry H. Hooyer, the author of the textbook "Behavior and Handling of Ships" (1983), called maneuvering on your own with dredging anchors "ship handling in its purest form." Hooyer, a Dutch master and pilot, was one of the first instructors at Port Revel.

All through the Cold War, Soviet captains came to Port Revel and learned ship handling in English—several hundred of them, from U.S.S.R. Morflot. About forty maritime countries have been represented here. The instructors place the Soviets only slightly ahead of Uruguayans and Koreans as skippers who, because of the language problem, have been difficult to teach. Cameroonians, Arabs, Greeks, and Indonesians have generally been more verbal and responsive. Japanese masters and harbor pilots are not involved in this comparison, because they never come here. Japanese pilots are retired Japanese skippers. First an old one takes you from the sea buoy, and then an older one takes you into the harbor. Many are in their eighties. Philippe says, "The pilot is so old he is almost feeling his way with a white cane." Pilots worldwide routinely board ships up rope ladders. Björn Grandin mentions a Japanese request that a ship in open waters near a sea buoy put out its gangway so that a pilot could use it to come aboard. This special, and not entirely safe, consideration had to do with the fact that the pilot was more than ninety years old.

Today the Port Revel merchant marine is going to practice meeting and overtaking in the Suez Canal. This is a replica of the southernmost four miles of Suez, and its bottom and bank effects are quite enough for one ship, let alone two. The bow wave, humping up between the bow and the bank, creates a bow cushion that tends to push the bow away if the ship runs too close to one side. Pumping water out from under the stern, the propeller lowers the pressure there. Bernoulli's principle also lowers pressure at the stern. Bernoulli's principle—where the flow is fastest, pressure is lowest—holds airplanes in the sky. Air flows faster over the top of a wing than under the bottom, because of the wing's shape. Water flows faster between a stern and a bank than on the other side of a ship. It has to, in the restricted space. Reacting to the lowered pressure, the stern is sucked in toward the bank. You try to anticipate suction and start compensating before it comes. In a bend in a narrow channel "suction steers the ship," according to Hooyer. To fight suction, you may have to go through a left-hand bend in the canal on hard-right rudder, scuttling along like a crab. Never depend on bow cushion to keep you from hitting a bank. The momentum of two hundred and fifty thousand tons can put you through any cushion and into the ground. In mid-canal the bow cushion and the stern suction are equal on the two sides. But the bottom is uneven. A canal pilot stays off the center line in order to know where the effects are coming from, like a basketball player keeping one hand on an opponent.

The greater your speed, the stronger the forces. With speed the bow wave builds up and pushes the bow off the bank and the stern into it. With speed the peripatetic pivot point moves forward, increasing the leverage of the stern suction. Both rotated and sucked, the stern hits the side of the canal. To prevent this, you try to compensate with rudder, but there is—written on the rudder—no guarantee. When SOGREAH was doing a study of the Suez Canal, forty years ago, the thought occurred to the engineers that they might learn more if they built manned, self-propelled models of real ships instead of a traditional towing tank. When masters and pilots saw the first model, they smiled derisively. In the words of Jean Graff, a SOGREAH engineer who is the director of Port Revel, "The smiles lasted half a day, and then they started sweating. They were screwing up. They had their talkie-walkies. They weren't even able to berth the ship. After ten days they agreed that they could extrapolate." They said they felt bank effects; they said that being in the model was much like being on a real ship in the real Suez Canal. Pilots and masters today are accustomed to doing ship-handling exercises on electronic simulators. "With a simulator you don't feel the ship," Graff continues. "Simulators are not scale models. Transient hydraulic phenomena around the rudder and the propeller are very difficult to translate into data." On an electronic simulator you could learn baseball strategy, but you could not learn to play baseball.

Kenny Lichtle has had less trouble going through the Suez Canal backward than forward. Trying it bow-first, he was all over the canal, hitting both sides. Later, after entering the canal stern-first, he backed through it all the way without so much as nicking a buoy. "It's much easier going backward than forward," he remarked offhandedly. "Great Lakes people do it all the time. Great Lakes people call the bridge the pilothouse. That's what it is." Like Scott Parker, Kenny works for Interlake Steamship, carrying iron ore, coal, or limestone, and backing up rivers to Great Lakes ports. He is a gentle hippie with a bald spot, and hair that falls to his shoulders. He has a graying beard and a golden sense of humor. When he saw me pissing in the Suez Canal, he drew himself up and said, "Have you no shame?" Kenny has six children and lives in Sandusky, Ohio, on Lake Erie. He was a deck-hand who rose to captain—came up the hawsepipe, as the expression goes, and, unlike the other skippers here, never attended a maritime academy. He is laid-back in manner and commands. As his ship heads into channels pocked with hazards, he leans on his arms, removes a cigarette from his mouth, and says, "Give me about ten right." I give him about ten right. Like all skippers on the Great Lakes, he says "half back" for "half astern" and "full back" for "full astern" and "dead stick" for "stop engines." The ore, coal, and limestone carriers of the Great Lakes are of a size with V.L.C.C.s—the very large crude carriers of the world's oceans, whose length is a thousand feet. The work he and Scott do is markedly dangerous. In swift-rising storms ore carriers have disappeared in thirty seconds. The Great Lakes captains mention their speed in miles per hour and call their vessels boats. The other skippers, watching Kenny and Scott here at Port Revel, and meeting them head-on in the Suez Canal, are developing a fresh reverence for ship handling as it is practiced in the middle of a continent.

In the canal all manage to meet head-on and pass without mishap. The combined width of two ships is more than half of the canal's channel. Two ships coming toward each other should each stay in mid-channel and go straight at each other until the right moment to veer. "You play chicken," Philippe instructs. "You play kamikaze." Many factors about the ships and the channel compose the right moment. If one ship moves over too soon—or if both ships move over too soon—there is great risk that the build-up of bow cushion against the banks will push the bows inward and cause a collision, as deep dents throughout the world fleet attest. "You play kamikaze up to a certain point, and then it's time to go," Philippe continues. "No problem with the meeting. No problem getting past one ship. If another is behind it, you could be in trouble."

A ship has a width of influence five times its beam, a depth of influence five times its draft. Two ships anywhere near each other are going to create discernible effects. A submarine passing three hundred feet under a V.L.C.C. is pushed down by the pressure of the ship. Passing ships repel each other at the bow and attract each other at the stern. You use rudder and you kick ahead with the engine to defeat the suction at the stern. In one class at Port Revel two ships in the Suez Canal were heading toward each other and intending to pass port to port. They diverged too soon. Both bows bounced off the bank cushion and swung sharply to the left. The ships crossed the channel in front of each other and passed unintentionally starboard to starboard.

As our dingless skippers listen to that story, they emit faint whiffs of immunity. They are already veterans of the model canal. And now they will re-enter it and practice overtaking each other. Passing a ship that is going in the same direction in a confined channel is difficult and perilous. In the Seine some years ago a freighter of ten thousand tons passed a small coaster full of grain. The coaster capsized, and all but the pilot died. Philippe says of overtaking, "We do it here to show you. But don't do it."

The model tankers Berlin and Grenoble are small enough for the exercise. Nearly all the others are either too large for the canal (the size known in the world fleet as Post Panamax) or come so close to filling it up that you wouldn't even think of trying to pass another ship. The Berlin model weighs 7,188 pounds and has a load draft of one foot five and one-eighth inches. The Grenoble weighs 7,761 pounds and has a load draft of a foot and a half. The model canal is two feet deep. The

Berlin is regarded here as "the pig of the fleet." She does not accept mistakes. She has a small rudder, very little stern power. A German skipper once said, "You should call her Paris."

In a canal channel the bow wave of an overtaking ship not only speeds up the overtaken ship by pushing it forward but also shoves the stern of the overtaken ship toward the bank, increasing bank suction on the stern. When the ships are side by side, the bow waves push them apart while mutual suction draws the sterns together. As the overtaking ship begins to draw away, its stern suction pulls the bow of the overtaken ship toward mid-channel and—at the stern of the overtaken ship—increases the suction from the bank. In other words, I pass you, I leave you screwed crosswise.

With two long blasts on his whistle and two short, Björn, in Berlin, asks to pass Andy in the canal. Long-short-long-short—Andy, in Grenoble, agrees to be overtaken. "Go slow, or dead slow," Philippe calls to Andy from the bank. "The greater the difference in speed, the smaller the problem." This problem is not small enough. Björn hits Andy. Andy "retaliates" as his bow is sucked into a second collision. Andy ricochets and goes aground.

Yvon is promoted to skipper of Grenoble. The two ships enter the canal again. Yvon blasts for permission to pass. In a few commanding words he anticipates and overcomes bow cushions and stern suction, bank and bottom effects: "Port twenty. Hard to port. Half ahead. Midship the wheel." Between the two ships is always daylight. Yvon says, almost somberly, "Nice, huh?" No little lagomorphs with long ears today.

Kenny, in the Berlin, with me as engineer, thinks he's going on the rocks. At least that is what he says. "Give me dead stick, full back, we're going on the rocks." Instead the bank effects steer the ship, and he collides with Scott. The two ships, veering out of the channel, plow the canal and block it. Kenny flicks a butt into the water, and Scott takes command of Berlin. Scott, who lives in Ocala, Florida, and commutes to the Great Lakes, was trained at Great Lakes Maritime Academy, in Traverse City, Michigan. Tall, with a dark and gyroscopic mustache, he is at least as keen as Kenny is informal. The two ships go around and re-enter the canal. Scott overtakes Kenny in the Grenoble. His commands are as crisp as Kenny's were casual. He counters the bow cushions. We draw even. We pull forward. Our stern sucks Kenny in. His bow hits our stern and sticks there as if it were welded. Downchannel the two ships lurch as one. Philippe cries out on his bullhorn: "Berlin is towing Grenoble! Like two dogs, you are stuck!" The entire enterprise is on the rocks.

"If you learn one thing here that helps you prevent an accident in the next ten years, we have succeeded," Joe Le Sciellour remarks. People who study at Port Revel ever after think twice about overtaking a ship in a narrow channel. For that matter, ramming piers, hitting the wave generator, or getting buoy chains tangled in their propellers tends to humble them too. These are captains who dream of ships. On the way to Port Revel in the van this morning, they told stories about dreaming of ships. Andy said he has had a recurrent dream for some years in which he tries to climb a mountain in a ship. He has the anchor out before him as piton. They dream of taking ships through the streets of cities, going hard to starboard at Thirty-fourth and Fifth. Kenny dreams of parking his ship in a mud puddle at a Kmart. And the van deposits them at Port Revel, which is beyond their wildest dreams.

Tight-Assed River

Pekin

The "Pekin wiggles" are halfway up the Illinois River, between the Mississippi River and Chicago. On the radio, other tows tell us how they are doing in the Pekin wiggles. During the forward watch, on this tow, the captain mentioned them when they were still three hours upstream. They would not be his to negotiate. Two in the afternoon and the pilot, Mel Adams, of the back watch, the after watch, is addressing them at the moment. He has made a sharp turn to the left followed by a bend to the right, and is now going into an even sharper turn to the left that will line him up with the Pekin railroad bridge of the Union Pacific. There is not much horizontal clearance under the Pekin bridge.

Mel is tall and lanky, fed in the middle but lithe in the legs. He has a sincere mustache, a trig goatee, and a slow, clear, frank, and friendly Ozark voice. He lives in southern Missouri, on Table Rock Lake, which has seven hundred miles of shoreline. The eight other people in the crew of this vessel all call him

"Male." They are from Kentucky, Tennessee, Oklahoma, southern Missouri, and southernmost Illinois. They work twenty-eight days per stint. When they report for work, they show up in Paducah and are driven in a van from Kentucky up into Illinois or anywhere else this towboat happens to be. Its name is Billy Joe Boling.

Overall, the Illinois is a fairly straight river, only ten per cent longer than its beeline, the fact notwithstanding that the bends at Pekin corkscrew like fishing line that has come untied. Mel understands monofilament. He is wearing shorts, sandals, a cap with the word "FISHING" sewed into it, and a T-shirt covered with fish. Each morning, before he goes off watch at five-thirty, he cell-phones his wife, Aurora, and gently awakens her. When he is at home, he routinely gets up at four-thirty, goes fishing, is off the lake by nine, and by nine-thirty has cleaned his fish and put them in the freezer. He says his personal best is a twenty-eight-pound flathead catfish. In his Bayliner Trophy 1703 with center console, he penetrates the bays and skims the shoals of that seven-hundred-mile shoreline, his touch grooved with experience.

A lot of good that will do him here. This vessel is no Bayliner with center console, and the Illinois River is not a big lake in the Ozarks. The mate Carl Dalton has gone up ahead with his walkie-talkie to serve as a pair of eyes for Mel in the pilothouse, near the stern. Carl is a tall guy who played Kentucky high-school basketball, but when he was halfway up the tow, near the break coupling, he was already a tiny figure, and now, all the way up at the head, he is an ant. This vessel is a good deal longer than the Titanic. It is thirteen feet longer than Cunard's Queen Mary 2, the longest ocean liner ever built. It is forty-four feet longer than any existing aircraft carrier. It is a hundred and five feet wide. And with Carl calling off numbers—"twelve wide on the port . . . two hundred below . . . twelve wide, a hundred and fifty below . . . eight wide on the port, a hundred and twenty-five below . . . seven wide on the port . . . six wide on the port"—Mel is driving it into the crossing currents of the hundred-and-fifty-foot gap between one pier and the other of the bridge's channel span. It helps that the railroad tracks have been raised. In their normal position, they are three feet lower than the Billy Joe Boling.

The Illinois River is in most places a little more accommodating. With exceptions here and there, the demarcated channel is three hundred feet wide. But you are not going to do a doughnut with this vessel. You are not going to do a Williamson turn. Both maneuvers describe closed three-hundred-and-sixty-degree circuits. This vessel is nearly four times longer than the channel is wide. The entire river in most places is about a thousand feet from bank to bank. Our bow wave quickly spreads to both shores. We could not turn about if we had all of the river to do it in. If we were ninety degrees to the direction of the channel, we would block the river solid and spill over both sides into the trees.

Among American rivers, only the Mississippi and the Ohio float more ton-miles of freight than the Illinois, a fact that does not seem to have done much to raise its national profile. People say, "The Illinois River? What's that? Never heard of it. Where does it go?" Actually, there are three Illinois Rivers in America, each, evidently, as well known as the others. One is in southwestern Oregon. One rises in western Arkansas, describes a vast curve through eastern Oklahoma, and goes back into Arkansas as a tributary of the Arkansas River. The autochthonous Illinois River begins not far from Chicago, at the confluence of the Des

Plaines and the Kankakee. From river town to river town, it draws a bar sinister across the state of Illinois—Marseilles, Ottawa, Starved Rock, Hennepin, Lacon, Rome, Peoria, Pekin, Havana, Bath, Browning, Beardstown, Meredosia, Florence, Hardin—descending two hundred and seventy-three river miles to Grafton, Illinois, on the Mississippi River forty miles up from St. Louis.

In the thousand feet in front of Mel are fifteen barges wired together in three five-barge strings. Variously, the barges contain pig iron, structural iron, steel coils, furnace coke, and fertilizer. Each barge is two hundred feet long. Those with the pig iron seem empty, because the minimum river channel is nine feet deep and the iron is so heavy it can use no more than ten per cent of the volume of a barge. The barges are lashed in seventy-six places in various configurations with hundreds of feet of steel cable an inch thick—scissor wires, jockey wires, fore-and-afts, double-ups, three-part backing breasts, three-part towing breasts. The Billy Joe Boling, at the stern, is no less tightly wired to the barges than the barges are to one another, so that the vessel is an essentially rigid unit with the plan view of a rat-tail file. In the upside-down and inside-out terminology of this trade, the Billy Joe Boling is a towboat. Its bow is blunt and as wide as its beam. It looks like a ship cut in half. Snug up against the rear barge in the center string, it is also wired tight to the rear barges in the port and starboard strings. It pushes the entire aggregation, reaching forward a fifth of a mile, its wake of white water thundering astern.

Carl Dalton, on the head of the tow, now says, "Six wide on the port, fifty below."

Mel, in the pilothouse, is grinning. He has come up to this railroad bridge many times before and evidently it amuses him.

"This place is so narrow you have to put guys out on the head to tell you where you are," he says, and laughs.

Where is he? Fifty feet from the bridge, and his head corner on the port side is lined up so that it should miss the nearest pier by six feet. He is steering the Queen Mary up an undersized river and he is luxuriating in six feet of clearance. Meanwhile— back here a fifth of a mile—the dry riverbank is ten feet behind the stern rail. The stern is so close to the bank you could almost jump off without getting your feet wet. Mel is not standing at a wheel. On this vessel, a wheel is a propeller. There is no wheel in the pilothouse. He is handling instead a pair of horizontal sticks—beautiful brass fittings with pearl handles, one for the steering rudder, one for the flanking rudder. He also has two throttles, one for each engine. Each throttle has a forward and a reverse position. If he goes forward on one and back on the other, he can walk the whole tow sideways.

Years ago, our captain—who is off duty and in his room sleeping—was a deckhand on a tow that hit this bridge and scattered all fifteen barges.

"Five wide," Carl says. Carl is five feet from the pier and has drawn even with it.

"That's perfect," Mel tells him. "That's all. I got 'er."

"Getting set" is vernacular for being moved sideways by current. When Mel is steering through less complicated reaches of the river, he will choose an object under a mile in front of him (an island, say) and another object (say, a church steeple) directly behind the first one and much farther away. If the steeple moves to the left with respect to the island, the tow is being set to the left. If the steeple moves off to the right of the island, the tow is being set to the right. He doesn't need any church steeples here. There is nothing subtle about the current under this bridge. We are about a third of the way through now and the current has begun to shove the head from the west side of the channel toward the east, skidding the whole big vessel from one pier toward the other. We started sixty inches off the west pier and—after moving forward eleven hundred and forty-five feet—we end up sixty inches off the east pier as the stern slides by it.

Mel aims the tow into a mile and a half of dead-straight river. Skyscraping grain elevators line the eastern bank. Beyond them, and behind a high levee, are the invisible streets of Pekin. "When we was going through the bridge, we had to favor the leg on the left side 'cause the current will push us over to the pier on the right side, so we had to favor the pier on the left side real close," he says. "You could feel the current catching the head, pushing it over towards the right. So we pushed it through about another two hundred feet, then let it run on straight rudder for a while. By the time we got through the bridge, we only had about five feet of clearance on the starboard side. That's how you take it through that bridge, especially when we got some current running, like we do now."

After lighting a cigarette, he adds, "There are seven different ways to run a river—high water, low water, upriver with the current on your head, downriver, daytime, nighttime, and running it by radar. Once you learn those seven ways, you can run any river. We made the Pekin wiggles in one try."

Open Sleeve

In this sort of journey, there is no real departure or precise destination. Its structure is something like a sleeve open at both ends. Several days go by, a couple of hundred miles, and then a machine in the pilothouse suddenly springs to life as if it were the tenth member of the crew. Staccato and syllabic, its voice blurts out, "You . . . have . . . ree . . . ceived . . . new . . . orr . . . derrs . . . Please . . . ree . . . view . . . them . . . as . . . soon . . . as . . . poss . . . ibb . . . bull." A printout comes forth like a tongue. Upriver in a day or so, we will be turned by the Ashley Lay. On the Mississippi River, a tow might consist of forty-nine barges in seven strings—a vessel more than fifteen hundred feet long and nearly two hundred and fifty feet wide. The diesels pushing it will develop as much as ten thousand five hundred horsepower. To enter the Illinois River and not plug it up forever, the numbers have to go down to fifteen barges and, say, thirty-six hundred horsepower, like the Billy Joe Boling. Nearing Chicago, the waterway becomes tighter and flatter (less current) and you don't need the Billy Joe Boling anymore. You want the Ashley Lay, twenty-eight hundred. Even closer to Chicago, where concrete walls close in on the waterway and bridges don't draw, "jackoff" boats take over. For dipping under bridges, their pilothouses go up and down hydraulically. They move six or eight barges at a time. On a boat with the power of the Billy Joe Boling, you go up the river until another crew turns you. You pick up their barges and go back down to the Mississippi, where, say, you turn the Edwin A. Lewis and the Edwin A. Lewis turns you. Then you go back up the Illinois.

Ours are Memco Barge Line barges. Memco moves upward of two thousand barges on Middle American rivers and is third in a very large field. When I called Memco not long after sending the company a formal request for a ride, Don Huffman, in St. Louis, said, "What day would you like to go?" It was as if I were talking to Southwest Airlines. Tows are moving about the country all the time. When and where would I like to get on one? I flew to St. Louis, and went up to Grafton, where the Billy

Joe Boling came along after a while and picked me off the river-bank with a powered skiff. Some five hundred miles later, the skiff would put me ashore in the same place. In an equal number of days (and by daylight only), I had ridden six times as far in Don Ainsworth's truck. Faster, certainly, but barge companies are committed to pointing out that a fifteen-barge tow like this one can carry what eight hundred and seventy tractor-trailers would be carrying on highways. This comparison is not without precedent. In 1805, barges on the Middlesex Canal, in Massachusetts, transported more than nine thousand tons of freight, and it was said that if the same freight had travelled on dry land fifty-six thousand oxen would have been needed to move it.

Six A.M. of the forward watch and Tom Armstrong—the captain himself—is at the sticks. The voice in the machine has been sounding off, and I am wondering about the changing of orders and the turning of tows. "How long do you usually know what's going to happen?" I ask him.

"Usually there's no usually in towboats," he answers.

He lights a Marlboro. He is thirty-nine—the fifth oldest in the crew of nine. His jeans are patched in the seat and he wears an aquamarine T-shirt lettered "GECKO HAWAII PRO SURF TEAM." Of medium height and strongly built, he has a precise, navigational mustache. He is left-handed, his hair is brush cut, his vision is 20/13. His eyes, remarkably bright, seem to project forward as horizontal periscopes. He has a constant, knowledgeable smile. "Towboating—it grows on you like a wart," he says. "See what I'm sayin'?"

Fond of that question, he repeats it many dozens of times per day. Phonetically, it emerges as "See what I'm sane?"

The sun appears above the trees, and Tom says, "Every day is a holiday, every meal a banquet. Got it made. Just don't know it." Another mantra. Another Marlboro. Sixteen years ago, he was a green deckhand on the lower Mississippi. He has held the rank of captain eleven years, working all rivers, mainly this one. His competence seems as absolute as his youthfulness seems indelible. Holding the sticks, he sits on his seat with his legs curled up under him, like anybody's grandson.

Captains all "come up through the deck"—the towboaters' equivalent of the merchant mariners' "coming up the hawsepipe." After working as a deckhand for two years, you can get a steering license. After you steer under a captain for eighteen months, you are eligible for a pilot license. You pass the physical, the radar training, and the simulator class in Paducah. A new, framed certificate appears on a bulkhead in a pilothouse somewhere: "William Thomas Armstrong . . . is licensed to serve as operator of uninspected towing vessels upon western rivers."

Tom is not hesitant to call the work stressful: "It takes good nerves to come down on a bridge sideways—I'm not sure I want to be out here driving a boat at sixty-five." He tells a story about a doctor who rode a towboat on the lower Mississippi to do stress tests on the captain. In the middle of the testing, the doctor was so stressed he asked to be taken off the boat. "One captain dropped out of medical school because his father died, and he came out here and was still here thirty years later," Tom goes on, in free association. I ask him how many skippers are women. "Two women worked their way up to the pilothouse," he says. "One of them is still out here, the other hit a bridge."

We are surrounded by glass in the pilothouse, large windows on all four sides. Our eyes are thirty-six feet above the water. The pilothouse smells like a bar under the old Third Avenue El. It is not a beer smell. Alcohol is forbidden and there is no evidence of it in sniff or behavior on the Billy Joe Boling. The pilothouse, which is swept and scrubbed clean every day, so reeks of tobacco smoke that the smell seems painted on the air. This is because Tom is a chain-smoker and Mel just smokes a lot. Between them, they are in the pilothouse twenty-four hours a day. Others in the crew are also present here for varying lengths of time. Seven of the nine are smokers. Gene Diebold, the chief engineer, comes up to the pilothouse in the evenings to sit and look at the river. The chief, as everyone calls him, is a round and pleasant man, about sixty, a onetime automobile mechanic who has developed hearing loss in his eight years on the rivers. A Missourian, he grew up in Benton, south of Cape Girardeau. He says he has "no high-pitched hearing left; if several people are talking, I can't understand a thing." Yet he generally ignores the large-cup ear protectors that hang on pegs outside his engine room, preferring inserted plugs. You see him in there with a blue-and-white towel wrapped around his head as if he were out here to hide from Homeland Security. The chief, as it happens, is allergic to tobacco smoke. But that does not alter his affection for the pilothouse and his evening contemplation of the river. By 9 P.M., Tom is past the second pack of his day. Tom says, "It's hard to find people who don't smoke these days. They tried to set up a boat that would be a non-smoking boat, but they couldn't find the crew members, see what I'm sane? Cigarettes aren't bad for your health—just ask the tobacco companies."

Mel and Tom, in the course of their watches, both dip snuff. They dip mint-flavored Skoal. They dip wintergreen long-cut Timber Wolf. Tom offers me some, and supplies instructions. I haven't smoked a cigarette in forty years, let alone dipped wintergreen Timber Wolf. I put it inside my lip and soon feel as if I've had a five-shot latte. Tom confides, "I dip snuff to try to cut down on cigarettes."

Six hours a watch is a long time for him and Mel to be up here, their hands on or close to the sticks. They can't leave and go below when they need to urinate. So a toilet is a part of the furniture in the pilothouse—open, unscreened. It's just there, in one corner, like the radar. At first I felt I shouldn't use it. For the skipper to pee in my presence somehow seemed politically correct, but not vice versa. I got over that in the first thirty-six hours, and have been peeing up here in the pilothouse as if the toilet were a bush on a fishing trip.

"There are two places in the world—home and everywhere else, and everywhere else is the same," Tom says, looking out at the levees, the miles of river, the willows, the cottonwoods, the silver maples, the roofs of small, concealed communities. Tom is from Cadiz, in western Kentucky. "Kay-diz," he says, his accent on the "Kay." "It's a two-stoplight town" less than twenty miles from Tennessee, on Lake Barkley of the Cumberland River. He went into the Army without finishing Trigg County High School, and out of the Army into towboats, on which he now makes sixty-some thousand dollars for working half the year. "I make pretty good money," he says. "Out here is a pretty good job. The money and the time off attract all of us. If we're not out here, we're not going to be no professor in a college, we're going to be in a factory five, six days a week. A factory worker, if his job is to put this screw in that gun, that's what he does all day every day for twenty years. Imagine how old that would get." Entrepreneurial, conscious of world money markets, schooled in the biographies of historic capitalists, Tom owns and rents out "a couple of dozen units" (rooms, houses, agricultural acreage), and additionally owns a hundred-acre farm with twenty beef cattle on it. While he is away on the Billy Joe Boling, his wife, Debbie, manages the property. Also a library clerk, Debbie is Tom's third wife. Separately and together, they have had no children. When Tom is at home, and is not making rounds on his motorcycle from one unit to the next, he is probably out on the Cumberland River piloting his ski boat.

Hennepin

We are two hundred miles up the river and approaching Hennepin, ninety minutes—seven more miles—upstream. This tow has about as much contact with the towns it passes as a tractor-trailer does on I-55. To the Hennepin Boat Market we have faxed ahead for food. We don't stop for much but navigation locks. Almost everything is brought to us by service boats as we drive on. However, we need to dock at Hennepin today to take on water.

The deckhands of the forward watch are straining at their cheater bars, revolving the ratchets that tighten the cruciate, interbarge wires, which are strung horizontally among timberheads and cavels, and in most places are only a couple of inches above the decks and gunwales of the barges. The deckhands are tuning the tow like a piano, and the work is beyond heavy. Closing pelican hooks, putting keepers in place, cranking ratchets, they make the wires so taut that if they stand on them the wires don't touch the deck. As we look down on the deckhands from the pilothouse, Tom takes a drag on a Marlboro, emits a gray cloud, and says to me, "If you didn't go to school and get a good education, you'd be out there working your ass off tightening them wires."

Rick Walker and Jason Beuke are the deckhands of the forward watch. Jason, of Paducah, is a two-tripper, this being his second trip ever on a tow. A wrestler when he was in high school, he weighs three hundred pounds. He carries it easily. Rick lives near Golconda, Illinois, close to the Ohio River. If you did not know him, you might say he has a demeanor that is vaguely sinister. If you did know him, you would probably say that he likes to give that impression. Thirty-four years old, fatless and wiry with dark bright eyes, he may not yet have met his first barber. An almost unceasing worker twelve hours each day, he is the Billy Joe Boling's second mate. Tom Armstrong refers to him as "the black-haired dude."

Rick is paired with Tom and Jason manning this immense vessel from five-thirty to eleven-thirty in the morning and five-thirty to eleven-thirty in the evening, the punctually observed hours of the six-to-twelve watch. If Rick is not out checking barges, tightening wires, or straightening up the captain's room, he is generally up here in the pilothouse polishing the windows inside and out, shining the metal surfaces, thickening the smoke. He takes note of my routines with unconcealed contempt, in part because I don't have any. I get up about when he does, a little before 5 A.M., awakened by knocks on my door from a deck-hand on the twelve-to-six watch. After a fast breakfast in the galley, I climb to the pilothouse, arriving usually as Mel turns the sticks over to Tom. Since there is nowhere to go—no long, Emersonian walks among the fifteen barges—I sit or stand in the pilothouse sixteen hours a day, staring at the river with an open notebook. Rick Walker makes clear that he looks upon this as idling in the nth dimension. One morning, he said, "Why don't you pick up a broom and do something useful?" At the end of my sixteen hours, when I stir to go below, he will say with incredulity, "Don't tell me you're going off to bed," accenting the "bed" as if it were a synonym for cowardice. Rick and Tom are not out of synch. When I mentioned that I have a fishing shack up a river somewhere, Tom said, "It's probably ten thousand square feet."

Meals are the bright punctuation of the day out here, never mind that dinner is at eleven in the morning, supper at five in the afternoon, and breakfast in the creeping dawn. The after watch eats at those hours and goes to work. The forward watch eats some minutes later and goes to bed—everybody sleeping and everybody working twice a day. Everybody but Bryan Velazquez, who is called upon when needed—mainly in navigation locks—and has to be available twenty-four hours a day. After a dinner of round steak, brown gravy, okra, hominy, green beans, and mashed potatoes, Tom remarked, "They feed us slaves like kings. Fish Friday, steak Saturday, chicken Sunday—towboat tradition." A sled dog would understand how long it takes us to finish. The galley is behind the engine room at the rear of the main deck and to get there you walk a narrow route along guard chains beside the river. You fill your plate and sit at a counter, all diners facing in the same direction. When I first sat down there, the cook, Donna Hobbs, told me to take my hat off when I eat.

Donna is highly regarded for smoking only behind the counter and not over the stove. Eighteen years on various rivers, she is from Paducah now, but she went to Jefferson High School in Rockford, Illinois. She wears flip-flops or thick-soled white running shoes, sweatpants, T-shirts, an embroidered square-neck short-sleeved cream blouse. Her hair is blond and she keeps it in a ponytail. If she is making cinnamon buns, her day begins at two-forty-five in the morning. No cinnamon buns, she gets up at three. On Sunday mornings at breakfast time, she is not in the galley. On Sunday mornings, she is allowed "to sleep in," and she gets up at 7 A.M. to prepare dinner. "I sleep in shifts," she remarked one evening at six when I lingered in the galley to talk to her. Finished for the day, she said she was going to take a shower and watch "The African Queen." The story is appealing on a towboat and she has watched the movie innumerable times. We talked about Bogart and the leeches, Bogart at the end in the reeds. She said it was amazing how fast he fixed that prop when he dinged it in the rapids. Donna is a quarter Cherokee. "You can see it in my high cheekbones," she said, turning sideways in her Kentucky Wildcats T-shirt, a gold cross hanging from her neck. She has a tattoo on her right arm—a dream catcher on a bear's claw around a bear's head. It filters out bad dreams. She was divorced in 1987, after which she lived with a man for nine years. She told him to do what he wanted when she was on the boat but not to run around when she was at home. He didn't.

Two buzzards circle the tow. Tom, steering, looking up at them, says, "They know who the cook is on this boat. They're waiting for one of us to die." This is outrageously unfair to Donna, and he knows it. "Some cooks are young," Tom goes on. "The company, they prefer the Fifty-five Club—fifty-five years old and fifty-five pounds overweight, see what I'm sane?" He mentions a regular cook on the rivers who is in her upper seventies. He also mentions Granny, whose real name is Mary. "There are fewer young ones than men cooks," he continues. "They call them in for an interview, see that they're young and beautiful, and she isn't hired. The company, it isn't their first rodeo, see what I'm sane? If she's young and beautiful, she has to be smarter than the average bear to survive. Good-looking woman, the men are like buzzards on a fence. If there's a young cook, the buzzards are sane, 'These are the best hot dogs I've ever eaten.' An old woman, she could serve them a six-course meal and they'd bitch."

Along the riverbank just below Hennepin, we pass two

dozen covered barges, loaded with grain at the Hennepin elevator and now moored in fleets waiting to be picked up. Some are tied to trees, some to massive chunks of concrete set in the bank. Old propane tanks serve as mooring floats. Wires from the moorings are tied to three bunched auto tires whose collective elasticity is neither too great nor too modest to control the wayward lurchings of two thousand tons of loaded barge. Chains large enough to anchor oceangoing ships in turn connect the tires to the concrete chunks in the bank or are looped around cottonwoods and maples. We tie up the tow, detach the Billy Joe, and run in to the Hennepin dock. Backed into a berth beside the dock is the Robert J., a condensed general store that is a small boat in itself, and ordinarily would come out on the river and attach itself to the running tow. Spectacularly varied, crowded with goods, it is stocked with everything a towboater might need or find attractive—a video, for example, called "Oral Orgasms" and subtitled "Carpet Munching Extravaganza." Close by "Oral Orgasms" are *Scientific American* and a 20-gauge shotgun up for raffle. Mark Judd, big and friendly, runs the Robert J. When towboaters telephone or fax ahead for something he doesn't have, he will go and get it—sometimes driving considerable distances—and he charges nothing for the service. He collects their prescriptions, goes off and fills them. If your tooth is aching, he will take you to the dentist. Heart? Liver? Duodenum? He will take you to a doctor. He went to a Wal-Mart once to buy Mel Adams a pair of glasses. He gives the towing companies a long rope. A towing company once owed him three hundred thousand dollars. Donna Hobbs, shopping in Mark's store, runs an eye over the porn shelves but does not bat it.

The Hennepin Boat Market, up the levee and into the town, is also owned by Mark Judd. It is the only bulk grocer serving the river's vessels in three hundred miles. The check-off shopping lists we get from them by fax say that Hennepin Boat Market "provides a 25-hour, 8 days a week, 53 weeks a year midstream grocery delivery." With Tom's permission, while he is taking on water and supplies, I walk a loop through the streets of Hennepin—a spread-out town of open spaces, with contiguous lawns, few sidewalks, and almost no fences, as if the houses were married quarters on a naval base somewhere, the dead silence of nine in the morning broken only by birds in the oaks and maples. Seven hundred people live in Hennepin, which is named for a priest who accompanied the Sieur de La Salle portaging out of Lake Michigan and into the Illinois River system in 1679. Father Hennepin, chronicler of the expedition, is described in James Gray's "The Illinois" (Farrar & Rinehart, 1940) as "a vain, pretentious priest who claimed the achievements of his betters" and "made love to himself on paper." I am late returning to the Billy Joe Boling, which has taken on its water, stowed its provisions, and for fifteen minutes has been ready to go. Tom, in the pilothouse, 9:30 A.M., supposes aloud that I have been to a bar. Add that to my ten-thousand-square-foot fishing shack, and I have suddenly become a rich alcoholic. Tom has had his wife, in Kentucky, check me out on the Internet. Now he says on the phone to her, "He's got a couple of daughters. Check them out, too. See if they robbed a bank or a liquor store."

Calling Traffic

When I told my friend Andy Chase that I was coming out here, he said, "The way they handle those boats—gad! They go outrageous places with them. The ship handling is phenomenal." The fact notwithstanding that Andy is a licensed master of ships of any gross tons upon oceans, he said he would envy me being here. This tow is not altogether like an oceangoing ship. We are a lot longer than the Titanic, yes, but we are a good deal lighter. We weigh only thirty thousand tons. Yet that is surely enough to make our slow motion massive, momentous, tectonic. Fighting the current with full left rudder and full left flanking rudder in the eighty-degree turn at Creve Coeur Landing, Kickapoo Bend, Tom Armstrong says, "I'm trying to get it pointed up before it puts me on the bank. There's no room for maneuvering. You can't win for losing. You just don't turn that fast. You just don't stop that fast. Sometimes we don't make our turns. We have to back up. The Illinois River's such a tight-assed river."

We are anything but alone. In addition to pleasure craft, other long tows are before us and behind us on the river, like a string of airliners on final in a long line to Newark—the Austin Golding, the Frank Stegbauer, the Martha Mac, the Tamera Pickett, the Starfire. With this difference: another succession of thousand-foot tows is always coming toward us in the opposite direction, sharing the same channel in the same small river. Tows moving downcurrent have the right of way. If you are headed upstream, you have to pull into a hold-up spot and wait for them to go by. Hold-up spots, in some parts of the river, are far between. Both Tom and Mel have their own copies of the "Illinois Waterway Navigation Charts," a publication of the U.S. Army Corps of Engineers. They have identified hold-up spots that will work under present conditions, and have marked them in pencil—places ample enough for putting the nose into the bank without blocking the river. When you are waiting for another vessel to pass, you literally stick your head into the mud at the edge of the river and hold there obliquely (/). Places are rare that are wide enough for two to pass while both are moving.

Trains run under centralized systems. These people are self-organized, talking back and forth on VHF, planning hold-ups and advances, and signing off with the names of their vessels: "Billy Joe Boling southbound, heading into Anderson Lake country. Billy Joe Boling, southbound."

This is known as "calling traffic."

"Billy Joe Boling heading down toward the Marquette Bar. Billy Joe Boling heading toward the Marquette Bar. Billy Joe Boling."

A deep-voiced acknowledgment comes into the pilothouse: "Billy Joe, Jon J. Strong." The captain of the Jon J. Strong has got the message.

"Billy Joe Boling heading southbound into Abe Lincoln. Billy Joe Boling."

For anyone within VHF range, this means that the Billy Joe Boling is soon to pass under Interstate 39's Abraham Lincoln Memorial Bridge. It means "I'm coming down, get out of my way." At Abe Lincoln, the river bends ninety degrees and soon goes under a second bridge.

Tom calls to another captain, "You'd better give them a shout down there before you get committed." In other words, before you proceed you need to know that the river is open to—and including—your next manageable hold-up spot. St. Louis to Chicago, Chicago to St. Louis, this is like jumping from lily pad to lily pad. It is also reminiscent of the way that airplane pilots in flight constantly study their charts, picking out airports where, if need be, they can make an emergency landing. "We don't try to plug up a hole and then try to get in the hole," Tom Armstrong says. "It don't make for a good day. We have to move from hold-up spot to hold-up spot and not think we're going to get in one when someone else is in it. On-the-job training is the only way to learn this."

On the job calling traffic—and in the interest of making time at the expense of others—some captains learn to deceive. As Mel Adams puts it, "They sometimes lie. They lie in both directions."

No one is going to be lying when two moving tows, in adequate water, are passing. The captains say to each other, "See you on the 1," or "See you on the 2." Passing on the 1 always means that both boats would turn to starboard to avoid collision. Two boats, meeting and passing on the 1, will go by each other port to port. Therefore, passing on the 1 in opposite directions is different from passing on the 1 when overtaking. Passing on the 1 when overtaking is to go by the other boat's starboard side. The stand-on vessel, nearly always the vessel heading upstream, maintains everything as is. The action vessel maneuvers. If you are learning this on the job, you may by now be up a street in Peoria. If you are still on the water, you may be feeling the hydraulic effect of the other tow sucking you toward it. One of my notes says, "The Mark Shurden with three barges carrying black oil passes us and sucks our stern, swinging our head toward the red buoys." The riverbank, variously wicked and benign, pulls us in or fends us off. Mel says, "There's a real fine line between bank cushion and bank suction. An extra five feet and it sucks you right over to it. You've got to stop and break the suction," while the Billy Joe shudders with cavitation.

Approaching a ferry, Mel on the VHF volunteers to drift while the ferry crosses the river. The ferryman says, "Keep her coming. I don't want to slow down the economy." The economy goes past the ferry doing four miles an hour. Tom says the tow moves more gracefully when it is going downstream: "It slides more, and is more dangerous, going down—at bridges, for example, with the current on your stern—but it's more graceful, and you have the right of way. Going upstream, it's easier to stop if you have to." Flanking is a downstream move. You slow your engines at a bend and let the current push the tow around. "Every bend is a challenge, though. You're pushing it to the max every day—pushing the drafts, toting the heaviest barges you can, going as fast as you can." Going deep is "steering as close to the outside of a bend as you can and still make the turn." It is what you would do in a canoe in a small stream, and this canoe is longer than the river is wide. "So shallow and so small, this river is more difficult to navigate than the Lower and the Ohio," Tom says. The Lower runs past Memphis, Vicksburg, and New Orleans.

They use the searchlight all night, a thousand watts, its beam a bright cylinder through the saturated air. It picks out green can buoys and red nun buoys—reds on the right going north. Not all the buoys are always in place. Picking his way in the dark across the seventeen broad miles of Peoria Lake, Tom describes what he is doing as "an Easter-egg hunt." The white beam is galactic with bugs—enough mayflies, it seems, to feed all the trout in the Rockies. Elsewhere on the river, missing buoys have been dragged away by tows. "This is like driving a car with your damned eyes closed," Tom says. "If you run aground, try to be going slow enough so you can back off." The Coast Guard buoy tender *Sangamon* passes us, pushing a small barge. On the deck, lined up like naval ordnance, are row upon row of new green and red buoys.

The swing indicator in the pilothouse measures the degrees to port or starboard that the tow is turning. Also close around the person at the sticks are the fax, the cell phone, the computer, the radar, the AM-FM radio, the tape player, the Qualcomm, two depth finders, two VHF marine radios (in order to monitor two channels), the G.P.S., the searchlight controls, and the general-alarm switch. There is no need for a compass, heaven knows, and—given the swing indicator—no need for a gyroscope. Knotted rubber cords hold back the books on the shelves under the fax. This vessel will wait a long time to ride its first swell, but when the Billy Joe Boling goes around a bend and its stern gets close to the bank and the wheel wash strikes the rudder, the vibration could sift a silo.

Coming up in the evening for his look around, the chief engineer says we are burning about twenty-four hundred gallons of diesel fuel a day. Not bad. We are getting nearly two hundred feet to the gallon. As a rule of thumb, a towboat burns one gallon per horsepower per day, but—at thirty-six hundred horsepower—that's not our thumb. The Billy Joe Boling has a tank capacity of sixty-two thousand gallons. We do not need anything like that amount of fuel but we fill her up anyway because we prefer not to "burn light." Tom says, "The lighter the boat gets, the sloppier it steers." It is best that the tanks not be less than half full. Putting that another way, diesel fuel is in use as ballast. As the barge industry is always ready to point out, in fuel consumed per ton-mile a tow is about two and a half times more efficient than a freight train, nearly nine times more efficient than a truck.

There are five dams on the Illinois River, none very high. Some are weirs, really, consisting largely of steel-and-timber wickets that can be lowered in high water so that tows can ride right over them, ignoring the navigation locks off to the side. In its two hundred and seventy-three miles, the river drops about ninety feet, indicating that the state of Illinois is almost as flat as it looks, its state-crossing river dropping down to the Mississippi six inches per mile.

At the higher dams, the navigation locks lift us or lower us about ten feet. "Locking through," the term that has described the process since the sixteenth century, is not, on this river, a simple matter of drain valves and filling valves. The locks consist of a "short wall," aligned with the current and standing in the river, and a "long wall" (or "guide wall") running along the bank. The short wall is rounded off at each end, a configuration known as the bull nose. The barges, three abreast, have five feet of clearance between the short wall and the long wall. The lock is six hundred feet long. Our vessel is nearly twice that. What to do?

Gingerly, you inch your thirty thousand tons up there past the bull nose. If you are heading downstream and you come in at too much of an angle, your head can become wedged between the short wall and the long wall while your stern is swung around by the current, with the result that your vessel becomes a lever prying at the navigation lock until masonry breaks, wires snap, loose barges are draped all over the dam, and your Billy Joe Boling, whatever it may be called, is hanging on the brink and listing.

You inch your tow up the long wall until nine barges are in the lock, and then you cut your vessel in half. You undo the wires at the break coupling. With the aft six barges, you back out. A door closes, sealing off the lock chamber. The drain valves are opened. The nine barges are lowered. Another door opens, and a mule—a wire on an electric winch—hauls the nine barges down the long wall to timberheads, where they are moored. The lock is refilled to receive the rear half of the tow. When it rejoins the front half, deckhands start leaning into their cheater bars at the limits of their strength, in all seasons and weathers, turning the ratchets that tighten the wires and restore the vessel to its complete integrity. You don't do this in ten minutes. We spend hours in the locks, and more hours near the locks waiting our turn. For smaller tows, there are rearrangements like the knock-out single and the set-over single that pack all components into the lock at one time, but we are vastly too large for that. The term for what we do is "double lockage."

Of Peoria Lock, Mel Adams says, "This is a tough lock to get into southbound when it's running some water. You get your head in there and it wants to suck you over towards the dam, bad. If they're running more than three feet of water through the dam, get a tug. The tug puts the head end up against the wall, pins it on the wall, lets you get your head inside the bull nose, and you can get your stern in with your engines. If you don't have the tug, you can get wedged in, and the current takes the stern around and the barges break up and go into the wickets."

Below the lock at LaGrange, and close to it, the rush of heavy water through the wide-open tainter gates of the adjacent dam is creating an eddy, which Mel—northbound here—calls a whirlpool. It turns clockwise, swinging around from the foot of the dam and running into the bull nose. Mel is inching up there, pushing his port head toward the long wall, his starboard head toward the bull nose. He could get over on the long wall, catch a line on the port lead barge, and rub this footprint aircraft carrier up the long wall, but that does not seem to be his default mode of ship handling. Maybe he can just go in there in one shot, and if he gets lucky he won't have to catch a line. The mate, Carl Dalton, will not have to humiliate him by throwing an assistive rope around a timberhead.

Carl is on the port head as the tow moves upriver. Mel says to him on the walkie-talkie, "They're all out at the dam. It won't be lookin' purty when I get up there."

Carl calls off distances, long and short. Distance from the

long wall. Distance from the lock gate. Distance from the bull nose. "Two hundred and fifty to the bull nose."

"I have to have the head on the wall to get it inside the bull nose," Mel mutters to himself. "You don't want to wedge in there. You could tear up barges, tear up the gates on the lock." But nobody needs to catch any lines as the huge vessel slides by the thundering rapids, absorbs the shock of the eddy, and aims for its five feet of clearance between the two walls.

"One hundred to the bull nose."

"Fifty to the bull nose."

"Even with the bull nose."

The tow, having smothered the whirlpool, now moves up between the walls and into the lock chamber.

When it stops there, Carl says, "The head never got more than a foot off the wall."

Mel says, "Sometimes you just get lucky."

Starved Rock

Off Mayo Island, Ottawa, in pitch darkness, the Ashley Lay turns us and we turn the Ashley Lay. If we were in the Hudson River and had started at the mouth, we would be in the Adirondacks. The six strings of barges lie abreast, and the Billy Joe Boling keeps them in place, its light beam aimed at the bank and holding steady on the trunk of a tree. Mayflies—fewer here—go through the beam like comets. A heron goes through like a stork. In a curious ritual, the Ashley Lay picks up our head gear—running lights, flagpole, heavy nylon lock lines—and carries it to the head of our new tow. We hand over their groceries. They give us a wad of cash. We take their head gear with us to the upstream end of the strings, where we drop it off, then wire up to the new tow, facing downstream toward the Mississippi.

In the thousand feet of barges we now have before us are grains for export, corn for Baton Rouge, and coke for Kentucky. We brought twelve thousand tons of coke up the Illinois River and now we are pushing fourteen thousand tons of coke down the Illinois River. Tom Armstrong, coming on watch at 5:30 A.M., takes this in, and says, "One day they'll figure it out and put us out of a job." Asphalt barges sometimes meet us, or pass us. They carry fresh asphalt from Wood River, on the Mississippi, to Chicago. Asphalt must be kept heated from the plant where it is made to the road where it is laid. So asphalt vessels carry diesel fuel to heat boilers which heat the asphalt all the way, including seasons when air temperatures are well below freezing.

In 1836–1848, a canal was dug between Lake Michigan and the Illinois River. In 1830, the canal planners had sketched two paper cities, meant to spring up as beehives of American commerce beside the two bodies of water connected by the Illinois & Michigan Canal. Near the south end was Ottawa, named for an Algonquin tribe whose name in turn meant "trade." The planners called the other town Chicago. In Washington Park, in Ottawa, in the summer of 1858, Stephen A. Douglas and Abraham Lincoln held the first of their seven debates. Ten thousand people were there to listen. Lincoln, as a riverboat hand, had first seen the Illinois in 1831, when he was twenty-two. On his way to New Orleans, he came down the Sangamon River and into the Illinois at Beardstown with live hogs, barrelled pork, and corn. Beardstown is eighty-eight miles above the Mississippi and is protected today by a concrete floodwall that would not look amiss on the Yangtze. Mississippi floodcrests sometimes back water up to Beardstown. The floodwall includes an immense white patch where an oil barge failed to make the Beardstown bend and rammed the city. When he was twenty-seven, Lincoln surveyed the town of Bath, upstream of Beardstown, and returned to Bath in 1858 to repeat his speech on the "house divided." Bath, rising toward prosperity, attracted numerous showboats with names like Goldenrod, Cotton Blossom, Majestic, and French's New Sensation, stopping off on their way to Peoria, fifty miles upstream. In 1850, twelve hundred steamboats called at Peoria, then as now the biggest town on the Illinois River. Modern Peoria has an areal population of three hundred and fifty thousand, a modest number that nevertheless quantifies it as Illinois' third-largest population center. Beyond its fountained waterfront and antique sternwheelers, Peoria presents a cityscape you can see from the water, its buildings too tall to be screened by levees. These include, on both sides of the river, some of the pillars of Caterpillar and the rye distilleries that made Peoria famous when Caterpillar was still in its cocoon. In 1901, the *Peoria Journal* audaciously invited the temperance agitator Carry Nation, breaker of bottles with hatchet, to be editor for a day and to publish anything she cared to about rye whiskey. Editor Nation—according to Gray's "The Illinois"—criticized the whiskey makers for not letting employees drink on the job. That day, at least, she was more interested in labor than liquor. She asked her readers, "What would you think of a dry goods concern that would not allow its employees to use what they make?" Those distilleries today make ethanol.

All day long as I look out from the pilothouse I can't help thinking, and thinking again, that this river is as natural as a railroad track. Its corridors are framed in artifice. The pool above the dam at LaGrange is eighty miles long. The State of Illinois and the U.S. Army Corps of Engineers have accomplished such extensive alterations that restoration is beyond reason. It would be easier to declare Manhattan Island a roadless area and raise the money to make it so. With wooded islands and bordering lakes—passing glimpses over fields to bluffs and ridges—the river does now and again recall the natural world. Yet within its straightened sides it is really a canal, and it has been a route of freight transportation since Colonial times. In 1745, after storms ruined crops in French Louisiana, French habitants in Illinois sent four hundred thousand pounds of flour down the river in deerskin sacks. By the eighteen-thirties, steamboats full of New Orleans sugar and "Dupont's powder" were serving the Illinois River towns. Pirates not infrequently boarded them, killed the crews, and lit off with the cargoes.

Navigational dredging began in the eighteen-fifties, but the rearrangement of nature did not really become earnest until the eighteen-nineties and the early twentieth century, when many hundreds of miles of levees were constructed not only along the river but also around segments of its floodplain—those bottom-land lakes, ponds, marshes, and sloughs—which were drained by a system of ditches and pumps, "reclaiming" acreage for agriculture. Between 1890 and 1928, a hundred and eighty-seven thousand wet acres were turned into farmland.

There was, withal, a military consideration. In the eighteen-sixties, it was thought possible that British warships would use the Great Lakes to join battle on the side of the Confederacy. Even after the war had ended, Brevet Major General James H. Wilson went on urging the government to expand the dimensions of the Illinois & Michigan Canal so that American gunboats could come up the Illinois River, go into the Great Lakes, and destroy the Royal Navy. Still thinking about it in 1888, the U.S. Congress called for a waterway from Chicago to St. Louis capable of handling naval vessels for "defense in time of war." The dam and lock at LaGrange were constructed in 1889. After the First World War, the State of Illinois continued the development of the Illinois Waterway but ran out of money, and the project was finished by the U.S. Army Corps of Engineers in 1933. During the Second World War, submarines that were built in the naval shipyards of Manitowoc, Wisconsin, did not dare go out to the North Atlantic past Montreal and Quebec because German submarines experienced in predation were waiting at the sea buoy and would destroy them before they could shake down. So the Wisconsin submarines slipped out of Lake Michigan at Chicago and into the Illinois River on their way to further preparations in the Gulf.

Louis Joliet—travelling north from the lower Mississippi in canoes with the black-robed Jacques Marquette—had foreseen, even in the seventeenth century, the possibility of a canal that could initiate a water route from the Great Lakes to the Gulf of Mexico, or even the Pacific Ocean. The portage linking Lake Michigan to the Des Plaines River and the Illinois River system was not strenuous. You went up the Chicago River, a minor stream that emptied into the lake, and went over a low divide into the drainage of the Des Plaines. The relative elevation of the divide was only about nine feet. In times of high water, Indians paddled right through the swamps there. A few years after Marquette, the thirty-seven-year-old René-Robert Cavelier, Sieur de La Salle, a Jesuit from Rouen, came down Lake Michigan from the north and made a comparable portage to the drainage of the Kankakee, paddling on into the valley of the Illinois in his quest for a water route to the Orient, a Midwest Passage. He eventually found the mouth of the Mississippi.

An open-water route from the Great Lakes to the Gulf was

actually how nature had laid things out. When the Pleistocene glaciation came, gouging and broadening stream valleys to make the basins of the future lakes, the ice was a thousand feet thick at Chicago. Rocks, stones, boulders, and sands pushed ahead of the ice were left as moraines when the ice melted back, and very large meltwater lakes formed between the moraines and the retreating glacial snouts. Now and again, the glacial lakes burst through the moraines, and catastrophic floods tore through the country to the southwest.

When the sheet ice had been younger and larger and was still spreading, it had relocated the Mississippi River, roughly shoving it about a hundred miles westward to its present route between St. Louis and Minneapolis. Now the great Kankakee Flood and related outbursts from the meltwater lakes cut a groove southwest into Illinois and found the ancient bed of the Mississippi, going down past future Peoria, Havana, Beardstown, and Meredosia to the new Mississippi at Grafton. Off and on for about ten thousand years, the Illinois River came out of Lake Michigan and its waters flowed on to the Gulf, but, as the continental crust slowly rebounded from the weight of the ice, drainages were altered, the Chicago outlet permanently closed, and the Lake Huron outlet took over to the east. This happened in historic time. When Father Marquette came up the valley, he found plenty of fish, plenty of game, and therefore plenty of Indians. He wrote in his journal: "We have seen nothing like the river that we enter as regards its fertility of soils, its prairies, and woods; its cattle, elk, deer, wildcats, bustards, swans, ducks, parroquets, and even beaver. There are many small lakes and rivers."

Four miles down from Ottawa, we approach Starved Rock. Now I am looking around with unusual interest. Those meltwater floods not only breached successive moraines but also were so voluminous and powerful that in some places they cut down through the glacial overburden and incised the bedrock below. This is one of those places, and the result of the excavation is a landscape that must be as dramatic as any in Illinois. Off the right bank, a long ridge of sandstone rises about a hundred feet, and on the left bank Starved Rock soon appears, a freestanding sheer-sided butte a hundred and twenty-five feet high. Behind it are bedrock bluffs in which eighteen streams have cut eighteen narrow, hidden canyons. La Salle built a fortress on Starved Rock to protect the Illini. He called it St. Louis. There are waterfalls in the canyons, and water dripping down walls of wet moss. There are red cedars, white cedars, white pines, white oaks, black oaks, red oaks, hickories, black huckleberries, and prickly pear cactus. There are wood ducks, vireos, catbirds, yellow-bellied sapsuckers, indigo buntings, red-tailed hawks, chickadees, nuthatches, cedar waxwings, scarlet tanagers, ospreys, and blue herons. In my excitement at the passing scene, I ask Tom if he has noticed where the eighteen streams come out, so veiled are they in vegetation, in creases, furrows, fissures in the trees. He says, "I concentrate on those red buoys on the left and those green buoys on the right."

I tell him I'm actually a roving investigator from the Marine Safety Office and I look for ways to distract captains.

He says, "Keep trying."

Toward Starved Rock Lock & Dam we are moving down Starved Rock Pool, and beneath us on the bottom of this artificial lake is whatever remains of the tribal Kaskaskia, where four hundred and sixty houses stood and seven thousand people lived in long wigwams with thatched roofs. From our left to our right, the dam comes away from the high cliffs, its tainter gates controlling flow, then a powerhouse flanks the guide wall, across the pit from the long wall, which lines the river's right bank. The pit is filling, getting ready for us, and the strong draw of water in its direction sucks us toward the bank. Manipulating the sticks, Tom is trying to walk us to port—without exceptional success. We are close enough to the bank to study ants. Tom says, "Sometimes you have very little control, you're just at the mercy of the Lord. When they're filling the pit, it sucks you that way. When the dam is running four and a half feet, it sucks you the other way."

In the course of my lifetime, I have made two journeys in river towboats, and twice have run aground. The first was the U.S. Army Corps of Engineers' towboat Mississippi, longer and stronger than the Billy Joe Boling, and, like a tractor without a trailer, accustomed to travelling "lite." Red-trimmed and cream-hulled, it pushed nothing but the program of the Corps. Its broad flat front was a wall of picture windows faced with cream-colored couches among coffee tables and standing lamps. It was making an "inspection" trip on the lower Mississippi and Atchafalaya rivers, holding hearings on board, and carrying as passengers regional people the Corps wished to sway. We were on the Atchafalaya and running wide open when the towboat Mississippi came to a sickening, shuddering, completely unexpected, and convulsive stop, breaking the stride of two major generals and bringing state officials and levee boards off the couches and out to the rail.

Standing in the Illinois River near some bridges and most locks are protective cells, which, in shape and function, are super-magnified versions of the bumpers in pinball machines. They are meant to guide if not deflect errant tows, and right now Tom could use their help. Engines aroar, wheelwash erupting, pilot-house shaking with seismic vibrations, he is trying to get away from the bank and close enough to the nearest cell to catch a line on a timberhead there. Ten years ago, during the first trip Tom ever made as a pilot, he saw a twelve-barge tow hit Starved Rock Dam and break into thirteen pieces. An inch at a time he draws nearer to the cell. Jason Beuke, three hundred pounds, is on the gunwale of a barge, holding a considerable length of heavy nylon line. To qualify for deck work, you have to be able to lift a hundred pounds. Jason can lift six hundred and forty pounds. He set the deadlifting record at his high school. He was a defensive lineman, too. And as a wrestler he "almost went to state," but in a meet in St. Louis "a big dude" pinned him, and he didn't go to state. Jason is just under six four. The dude was six six. "He was a big son of a bitch. He fucked me up." Blond, crew cut, of gentle disposition, Jason is usually articulate enough to seem like an intern sent to the tow by some college. The gap is slowly closing, and he is about to get his chance with that heavy line. He throws. He misses. In the pilothouse the vibrations seem to rise. Jason recovers the rope. He throws again. A loop goes over a timberhead, catching the line. Tom, pivoting on it, lines up the tow with the lock.

Environmental Movement

The Illinois & Michigan Canal lasted fifty-some years. Its fifteen locks dropped or lifted barges about a hundred and fifty feet. Along its towpath, canal boats were towed by horses and mules, the antecedents of the Billy Joe Boling, just as canal boats on the Erie Canal, the C. & O. Canal—the whole network of Eastern canals—were towed by horses and mules, with a memorable exception. In 1839, Henry David Thoreau and his brother, John, horse and mule, towed their own boat up and down the Middle-

sex Canal and the Union Canal, flanking the Concord and Merrimack rivers.

With the coming of the Illinois & Michigan Canal, an all-
water route from Canada to Mexico went right through the
Illinois River towns, and they rose for a time to national
significance. By the turn of the twentieth century, the Illinois
River was second only to the Columbia among commercial
river fisheries in the United States. In 1908, twenty-five hundred
Illinois fishermen caught ten per cent of the entire U.S. riverine
catch. They averaged fifteen million pounds a year. Some used
winch seines nearly a mile long. Some used traps baited with
cheese. Catfish, German carp, crappies, and black bass were
shipped in ice to Boston, New York, Philadelphia, Atlanta,
Memphis, and Chicago. For one abundant species, according to
some histories, Illinois became known as the Sucker State.

From the lakes and ponds on the floodplains of the river,
professional hunters annually harvested tens of thousands of
ducks. Mineable coal was everywhere. And with the discovery of
mussel beds, in the eighteen-nineties, numerous button factories
appeared in the river towns—four in Meredosia alone. The age
of plastics was fifty years away, and meanwhile buttons were
made from the mother-of-pearl that lines the shells of freshwater
mussels. Twenty-six hundred mussel-fishing boats were on the
river.

Havana, with its bars, gambling houses, and "four floating
fish markets," may have been, as it claims to have been, "the
most important inland fishing port in the United States." It got
its name because an island in the river there was said to be
shaped like Cuba. Opposite the island is the Spoon River, which
comes down from Modena past London Mills and Seville before
turning southeast to debouch at Havana. Naples is an Illinois

River town, as are Florence, Rome, Marseilles, Liverpool, and Bath. Not to mention Pekin. As pronounced in Marseilles, Marseilles rhymes with Car Sales. Des Plaines is Dess Planes everywhere along the Des Plaines. The word "Illinois," for that matter, was coined by the French who followed Marquette into the Illini country. The French are not responsible for Ill Annoy any more than the Egyptians are responsible for Cairo at the bottom of the state, which every sophisticated schoolchild in America knows to rhyme with Pharaoh. The steamer Belle of the Night is tied up dockside in Havana—yellow, with white balusters, its five concentric decks piled up like a wedding cake, its paddlewheels encased. Belle of the Night is a defunct restaurant with a Noachian gangplank but no customers—a floating symbol of a community whose parabola of prosperity went up through fish and ducks to buttons and down to casinos owned by Al Capone. What happened?

First, engineers reversed the Chicago River. As Chicago developed in the second half of the nineteenth century, there was cause for alarm that Lake Michigan, the city's repository of human and industrial wastes, was also its source of potable water. So the height of land on the Illinois & Michigan Canal was excavated into bedrock and gravity began moving water out of Lake Michigan and on to the south, bearing two hundred tons of Chicago wastes per day. That was not a large amount in comparison with the flushes that were coming after engineers completed—in 1900—the Chicago Sanitary and Ship Canal. Rendering the older and longer route obsolete, the Chicago Sanitary and Ship Canal went up the bed of the old Chicago River, cut even deeper into the bedrock of the portage divide, and went down through locks to the Des Plaines at Joliet. Now the Sanitary District of Chicago could draw down as much as fourteen thousand cubic feet per second from Lake Michigan, but the average over decades to follow was eighty-five hundred. Where I often fish in the upper Delaware, the river is two or three hundred feet wide, and if you are looking at eighty-five hundred cubic feet per second you are looking into a lethal torrent close to the threshold of flood.

By 1918, the State of Illinois had developed a formula for the dilution of raw sewage: 3.3 cubic feet per second could scatter the industrial and organic by-products of a thousand people. Thus, seven thousand cubic feet per second could flush a city of 2,121,212. Chicago's population in 1910 had been 2,185,283. In 1920, it would be 2,701,705, requiring only the adjustment of some valves in the city's anal orifice. Meanwhile, the second most prosperous river fishery in America had largely been destroyed. In a southward march of some sixteen miles a year, the river waters were becoming anoxic. Surviving fish below that line now tasted "gassy," not a good selling point in Philadelphia. River towns were hollowed out as five thousand jobs disappeared. Swimmers in Havana developed rashes.

With the influx of Lake Michigan water, Illinois River levels of course went up. Even in summer, levels at Peoria were seven feet higher than before. Surface waters doubled in the countless floodplain lakes and sloughs in the two hundred and thirty miles from Starved Rock to the Mississippi. Trees were killed, habitats erased, as fifty-six thousand previously dry acres were flooded. This was in comedic conflict with the state's drainage program that was on its way—with its levees, pumps, and ditches—to "reclaiming" tens of thousands of acres by changing lakebeds into farms. Eventually, the drainage program brought the surface waters down to a hundred and twenty per cent of what they had been before the Chicago River was reversed.

Chicago began treating sewage in 1922. In 1930, the U.S. Supreme Court ordered the city to reduce the diversions from Lake Michigan to fifteen hundred cubic feet per second. In 1955, the American Society of Civil Engineers named the Chicago Sewage Disposal System one of the "seven modern civil-engineering wonders of the United States."

In 1858, a farmer on the Illinois about thirty miles up from the Mississippi wrote in his journal that the river water was "very cold and as clear as crystal." The Clean Water Act of 1972 has done even more for the river than the treatment plants have, but nobody's journal is going to be using the word "crystal" in 2058. The river is not foul, as it once was, but it has a permanent tan, a beige opacity from agricultural runoff. Tom Armstrong says, "I wouldn't say it's ever blue. Ship pilots think they're blue-water people, and we're brownwater people." The Billy Joe Boling throws nothing intentionally into the river. The scraps of the galley are preserved in a freezer.

Empty Pockets II

Mel Adams is at the sticks in a long straight stretch of the river. A white cabin boat is in mid-channel directly in front of us, about three thousand feet away. It is not moving. We cannot see people aboard. For Mel, there is no possibility of maneuver, no possibility of stopping. Surely the cabin boat will move. Referring to our blunt head end, three barges wide, Mel says, "When they see a hundred and five feet of steel coming at them ten feet high, they'll get out of the way."

They do not. Mel, with binoculars, thinks he may have glimpsed a swimmer's head in the water, but that could have been a trick of the eye. As we bear down to two thousand and then fifteen hundred feet, the cabin boat stays where it is, dead in the water, less than two minutes from destruction. Mel gives it five short blasts, the universal statement of immediate danger. At just about the point where the cabin boat would go into our blind spot—the thousand feet of water that we in the pilothouse can't see—people appear on the cabin boat's deck, the boat starts up, and in a manner that seems both haughty and defiant moves slowly and slightly aside. We grind on downriver as the boat moves up to pass us port to port, making its way up the thousand feet of barges to draw even with the pilothouse. Two men and two women are in the cabin boat. The nearest woman—seated left rear in the open part of the cockpit—is wearing a black-and-gold two-piece bathing suit. She has the sort of body you go to see in marble. She has golden hair. Quickly, deftly, she reaches with both hands behind her back and unclasps her top. Setting it on her lap, she swivels ninety degrees to face the towboat square. Shoulders back, cheeks high, she holds her pose without retreat. In her ample presentation there is defiance of gravity. There is no angle of repose. She is a siren and these are her songs. She is Henry Moore's "Oval with Points." Moore said, "Rounded forms convey an idea of fruitfulness, maturity, probably because the earth, women's breasts, and most fruits are rounded, and these shapes are important because they have this background in our habits of perception. I think the humanist organic element will always be for me of fundamental importance in sculpture." She has not moved—this half-naked maja out-nakeding the whole one. Her nipples are a pair of eyes staring the towboat down. For my part, I want to leap off the tow, swim to her, and ask if there is anything I can do to help. We can now read the name on the transom behind her: Empty Pockets II.

This is happening between Brushy Lake and the Six Mile

Slough, if you see what I'm sane. Pleasure craft are anywhere, everywhere up and down the river. We traverse a reach in Peoria through the Cedar Street Bridge and the Bob Michel Bridge and the Murray Baker Bridge among at least two dozen pleasure craft spread over the river and framed between the arches. Pontoon boats, jet boats, powerboats—they go into the locks behind us, ahead of us. At the 89 bridge, Mile 218, a marina is on one side, a boat launch on the other, and twelve pleasure craft are visible, eight coming toward us, and who knows how many we can't see. Pleasure craft are like the bugs in the searchlight beam. On Peoria Lake, some of them are under sail. Southbound, a three-deck cruiser called Bewitched comes down on the Marquette Bar. "See you on the 2 whistle," says Bewitched, as if he were a thousand feet long. Above the Marquette Bar, forty-some pleasure boats are beached along a sand strip like white walruses. A boat crosses in front of us dragging two small kids on a tube. When pleasure-craft numbers get really high, a deckhand is sent to the head of the tow as lookout.

The wheel wash of the Billy Joe Boling goes out astern like a No. 10 rapid in the Grand Canyon, which "cannot be run without risk of life." The class of the rapid counts down, of course, with distance from the stern, and jet boats and jet skiers, playing in the wake, flirt their way forward through the rising levels of risk. If some macho jet skier were to cut in close to the stern, he would fast become soggy toast. Pleasure craft constantly cross in front of us, too, and when that happens Tom Armstrong will say, "He has a lot of faith in his engine, doesn't he."

Slow as tows are, they sometimes hit pleasure craft, although it is usually the other way around. A skier or boat that comes in from the side to jump the wake can be sucked into and through the propellers. If a water-skier falls a thousand feet in front of the tow, the skier has sixty seconds to get out of the way or the skier can go under the entire tow and into the propellers. As a pleasure boat passed us one day dragging a small boy on a tube, Mel said, "If the line broke, that little boy would be sucked right into the wheel wash." While Mel was crossing Peoria Lake a few years ago, a boat with a water-skier disappeared under his head and reappeared without the water-skier. Then the boat turned around, disappeared again, and reappeared dragging the skier out of the way. A day or so ago, we came down on a fisherman in a flatboat with an outboard motor, fishing in the middle of the channel. Mel, with binoculars, saw him tugging and tugging at his starting rope. Another fishing boat threw him a line and saved him. "People dropping skiers right in front of us, people falling off their jet skis right in front of us—it's enough to make a nervous wreck out of me," Mel has said. "Pleasure boats sometimes raft together, drinking beer, paying no attention, drifting down the channel. Get too close to 'em, you put a suction on 'em and pull 'em right to you. I get so dang worried that I'm going to run one of them over, kill someone. I couldn't live with myself."

If the head end is running a notch or a spike, a pleasure boat coming up behind us with intent to go around us can be lethally surprised. A notch is one missing barge. A spike is a barge at the head of the center string with notches on either side. Tom tells of an accident in which an intoxicated man was letting his kid drive their boat and the kid raced up the starboard side of a tow that appeared to him to be four barges long. Sharply rounding the fourth barge, swinging to his left to cut in front of the tow, the kid suddenly—and too late—saw a fifth barge, a spike, at the head of the center string. After crashing into its side, father, son, and boat were plowed under the starboard string. Of the operators of pleasure boats of all sizes, Mel says, "They are ignorant, ignorant, ignorant."

The crew of the Billy Joe Boling is always mindful of pleasure craft, in no small measure because they are forever hoping for "tit shots." This, I think, was the first towboater term I learned after coming aboard. It bounced off the windows of the pilothouse from dawn until dark every day. But nothing happened. From each of many hundreds of pleasure craft, there was nothing even suggesting a tit shot. I thought the captain and the crew were fantasizing, on their way to hallucinating, and probably should be committed. Now, though, Empty Pockets II, which slowed up as she drew abreast of us, puts on a burst of speed and curls around our stern and through our wake. Coming back to us on the starboard side, she picks up even more speed, and races down before us on wings of white spray.

I say to Mel, "I thought that was just a myth—that it didn't happen."

Mel says, "It happens all the time."

Call Me Tom

Another clear, warm day, and Carl Dalton is painting the tow knees with Doug Gable. The tow knees are two flat columns of steel—taller than Carl or Doug—that stand on the towboat's squared-off bow and butt up against the barges it is pushing. Mel Adams, steering, looks down from the pilothouse, thirty feet above, and communicates with Carl by walkie-talkie. He is telling him, inning by inning, how the Cubs are doing against the White Sox. Carl, the first mate, is in equal measure strong, responsible, funny, and upbeat, always greeting with evident pleasure the gruelling physical day that begins at midnight and includes two six-hour watches. Doug, from Granite, Oklahoma, his face a ten-o'clock shadow, his teeth not altogether present or accounted for, his longish hair flowering behind his red baseball cap, suggests the legacy of the Western mountain trapper. Fourteen days off, twenty-eight days on, he used to take a Greyhound from Oklahoma to Kentucky to report for work, but for this trip he bought himself a car. He dropped out after two years at Western Oklahoma State and worked as a driller and blaster in rock quarries before becoming a deckhand on towboats. The phone rings in the pilothouse.

The crew dispatcher in Paducah asks to speak to Carl Dalton. Mel relays the word to Carl, who leaves the main deck and climbs the interior stairs to the pilothouse. Mel turns off the baseball game. Carl says hello to the crew dispatcher and listens as the dispatcher asks him in some detail about a guy he hopes to sign up as a deckhand. After listening for at least three minutes, Carl says, "He's over thirty years old and he sleeps with a nightlight." There is an extended silence in the pilothouse as the dispatcher continues to speak to Carl. Then Carl says, "He's not much on the working thing." An even longer silence follows as Carl patiently listens to Paducah. Then Carl says, "I don't want him on here."

The crew dispatcher works for B&H Towing, which leases its boats from Memco, which then charters the boats; and that, in the words of our captain, "is how they busted up the unions out here." The hunt for willing-and-able deckhands is a difficult one for the dispatcher, as Carl—third-ranking person on the Billy Joe Boling and invaluable himself—is much aware. When guys are riding to Paducah for their fourteen days off, the company will call them in the van to see if they want to go at once to another boat. Carl lives in Wickliffe, about thirty miles from Paducah. He played his basketball at Ballard Memorial High School, where he dropped out in 1980, he says, "like a fool." He knows everybody. At breakfast one day, he told me, "There's not that many blacks in Wickliffe, but we're all kin."

The work is hard on deck anytime, he said, but especially in winter. The tows punch and punch again at the ice to break a trail. Sometimes at dusk they can look back and see where they started at dawn, while the deckhands tighten wires in snow or freezing rain. "You go out there to jerk up a ratchet, you fall, slip, the deck is so slick." The ice on the river may be eighteen inches thick. Sometimes a trail is broken with one barge while the fourteen other barges—each tied to the next—follow the towboat "like a train on a track." Danger may be highest in winter, but it is always present. "Duckpond" is the towboaters' term for any open space among the barges where a member of the crew could fall in. The ends of some barges are squared and vertical, the ends of others bevelled, trapezoidal, raked. The rakes are for streamlining at the head and stern ends of the tow, but they may be anywhere in the assemblage, and if rakes abut in the middle of a tow they form a duckpond:

Some "oddball barges" are not quite as long as the others—a cause of additional duckponds. On the subject of hazards to deckhands, Tom Armstrong says, "Lines break, slice 'em in half like a damned banana. Or a nineteen-year-old kid falls off a head barge, goes under, and dies." The Billy Joe Boling has not had a lost-time accident in two years. What happened? "A guy was homesick. He really wasn't injured. He said he had a sprung back. Once he got off, he sprung back to healthy."

Of most deckhands, Tom says, "Even if they're sick, they get up there and do it." For their twelve-hour days, deckhands start at eighty dollars a day ($6.66 an hour). They work their way up to a hundred and nineteen. Resourceful, hardworking, in a class by themselves, they remind me of people I knew in Alaska, with the difference that many of the towboaters are more than a little apologetic about themselves, variously confessing their small towns and calling themselves hillbillies. The Alaskans I'm thinking of saw themselves as a class apart, meant for a different geography, without much interest in the place they called the Outside. "We may not all have come over on the same boat, but we're on the same boat now," Tom Armstrong says. And Rick Walker remarks, "There's a lot of kids out here right out of McDonald's, and they'd be better off if they'd stayed at McDonald's. But if you can handle this work, you can make fifty to eighty thousand a year without a college education or even a high-school diploma."

Tom, owner of beef cattle and rental properties, spends a part of each day meditating upon incomes higher than a captain's—how large a part of each day only he would know. The part he shares is on the cassettes he plays in the pilothouse, listening to a narrator who says, "In just a few moments, I'm going to give you the formula for getting rich," and goes on to ask, "Whose drum are you marching to, even assuming you're marching to anyone's?" Repeated reference is made to "the gold mine between your ears" and to "M.S.I."—"the great key"—multiple sources of income. "Five ideas a day is twenty-five a week—that is, if you don't think on weekends." The tapes refer to "America's results coach," and they quote Oriah Mountain Dreamer in praise of people who "refuse to die with their music still in them." That is, they cause it to pour forth before it is too late. He listens to Dan Millman quoting Ashley Montagu on Bertrand Russell and the pursuit of happiness. Among Tom's favorite books—present on a shelf in the pilothouse—is "Think and Grow Rich," by Napoleon Hill, the book that resulted after Andrew Carnegie prodded Hill to study five hundred successful people. Impulsively, Tom will start up the tapes at any moment of the day or night between six and twelve. Steering the Billy Joe Boling from light to light in the dark, he listens to "Discover the Value of Lifelong Learning" and "Twenty Minutes That Can Change Your Life." On the VHF, he advises the captain of another towboat to put cattle on land that the other captain owns near Pekin. "Then it's a farm and a tax write-off," Tom explains. "That's the way to go, brother. Money ain't in the cows, it's in the tax deduction."

Doug Gable and Mel Adams are the only crew members who went to college, and Mel—with a degree in computer science and marine biology—is the only graduate. In the pilothouse, he listens to National Public Radio. When he is holding up—tow head near the bank, waiting for another tow to pass—I have more than once found him standing over the chart-book-and-radar cabinet, slowly turning pages, taking notes. He is in deep study and appears to be plotting some sort of course, but he is actually compiling an order from a Bass Pro Shops catalogue. The threadfin shad and the brook silverside are forage fish in Table Rock Lake—that is, the white bass eat them. Mel reads to me from an article he has saved on lure colors: "In clear water, use blue-and-chrome, black-and-chrome, black-and-gold, and anything that looks like a threadfin shad. In stained water, chartreuse." His selections include the Bandit Deep Diver, the Excalibur Fat Free Shad, and some Norman Deep Little N crankbaits in gel-coat colors: sun-green shiner, sun smoky shad. Mel grew up frog gigging, crappie fishing, and noodling—catching catfish by hand from nests in the bank ("It was risky. What if a big cat bit you or the nest included water moccasins?").

Mel has a tattoo on his right arm: a skull and wings. He says, "Actually, that's a six-pack of Mickey's barrel-mouth." In the Navy, aged twenty-two or so, in San Francisco, he drank the Mickey's barrel-mouth and went in for the skull and wings. On his other arm is an island sunset, pricked on Guam. He regrets both tattoos. "It's all the go now—that and body piercin'. Back then, if you had a tattoo you were a biker or a sailor." Mel was a chief petty officer. He sailed on ships of many kinds—guided-missile cruiser, fast combat supply ship, aircraft carrier. He was six years on Guam, six in Hawaii. Aurora, his wife, is Filipina. She grew up near Olongapo, a Death March site on the Bataan Peninsula, where her parents had a fish farm. Her father was a shipwright at Subic Bay. Mel and Aurora have three teen-aged kids, one on her way to becoming a registered nurse, another a performing musician hoping for Juilliard.

Mel once piloted a tow from Corpus Christi to suburban Chicago carrying eleven thousand tons of black oil. He went sixteen hundred miles up the Gulf-coastal waterways, the Atchafalaya River, the Lower, the Upper, and the Illinois River to Lemont. And now, after one more night on the Illinois, dawn appears. He calls Aurora and awakens her. Two miles out of Peoria Lock, he is southbound, approaching Clark Dock, on the right bank, four miles up from the Pekin wiggles. The Billy Waxler, with two barges, is tied to the Clark Dock, so Mel, in his words, is "favorin' them red buoys" along the left side of the channel to give himself plenty of clearance as he passes the other tow. Having come up to the pilothouse before breakfast, I have been here since we left the lock a few minutes after five, in ample time for the next event.

This is the next event. At 5:25 A.M., the Billy Joe Boling and the fifteen barges instantly lose a hundred per cent of their momentum and come to a sickening, shuddering, completely unexpected, and convulsive stop. This eleven-hundred-and-forty-five-foot vessel has not just been sliding in mud; it has run aground hard. The port wing wire has snapped, and, as we will learn soon enough, seven other wires have snapped, too. The port wing wire runs from the last barge in the port string to the Billy Joe Boling itself. Now, ghastly, that barge and the one in front of it begin to drift slowly away. Grain and corn excluded, half a million dollars' worth of barges are taking off on their own for Baton Rouge. Tom Armstrong appears in the pilothouse like a genie. It is, after all, five-thirty in the morning and time for him to relieve Mel and take over the hapless sticks. Simultaneously, Tom and Mel reach for the general alarm. Tom raises its red plastic cap. Mel throws the switch.

Every crewman is on the deck anyway, at the changing of the watch. The gap between the grounded vessel and the two loose barges widens. Fifteen feet. Twenty feet. There may be a chance to catch a line. Doug Gable, who has disappeared from the main deck, reappears with a bright-white brand-new line, a large eye at one end. Coils in one hand, eye in the other, he heaves the line, attempting to lasso a steel, sausage-shaped cavel on the barge. He has time only for the one throw. The line falls into the water. The barges drift farther away.

Mel, inspired, reverses the throttle of the port-side engine and gives it full power. The reversed wheel wash drives a No. 10 rapid upstream at the side of the Billy Joe and into the escaping barges. Slowly, magically, the runaway barges forget Baton Rouge, go back upstream, and return exactly to their original positions in the port string. Mel says, "Those barges, when they hit, looked rared up—you know, pushed up in the water. Anybody says they never ran aground on the Illinois River it's because they never ran the Illinois River."

In the space of a few minutes, Rick Walker, second mate, lays twenty feet of frayed and broken wing wire across a wire cutter and trims it back with a sledgehammer. He picks up the intact new end, curls four feet of it into a new eye, splices it, and leaves a foot of protruding tail. He lays the new eye over a cavel on the stern port-string barge. The additional wire has come off a winch like fishing line off a reel. Rick with steel cable can make loops like an angler. The winch tightens the new wing wire. Up the tow, Rick and others replace the three fore-and-aft wires and four breast wires that also broke. The port lead barge remains stucker than a postage stamp. Knocking keepers off pelican hooks with sledgehammers, deckhands detach the port lead barge so that Tom will be able to back up the rest of the tow and, with a lock line, yank the port lead barge free.

"There's one aground every day up here," Tom says. "It's not a deep river. If you can't back it off, you have to take the barges apart and dig it off. All it costs is time."

Mel, turning at the head of the stairs, has a parting word for me. He says, "When you write all this down, my name is Tom Armstrong."

Five Days on the Concord and Merrimack Rivers

On the thirty-first of August, 1839, John and Henry Thoreau—brothers, aged twenty-five and twenty-two—set out from their home in Concord, Massachusetts, in a small skiff on the Sudbury River. They were bound for Hooksett, New Hampshire, about fifty-five water miles north. The boat was fifteen feet long, styled like a dory, and new. They had made it in a week. They carried two sets of oars and a sail. On the thirty-first of August, 2003, with a college roommate who has long lived in Concord, I set out in a sixteen-foot Old Town canoe at a put-in site on the Sudbury which is Thoreau scholars' best guess as the place where the Thoreaus took off. It is now the back yard of a couple named Kate Stout and Pete Funkhouser, who live at the intersection of Thoreau and Main. Across Main is the house where Henry David Thoreau died. He and John grew up in a now long-gone dwelling thought to have been very nearby. John was his brother's best friend, perhaps his only close one. After nicking himself with a razor, John died of tetanus at the age of twenty-seven. "A Week on the Concord and Merrimack Rivers," Henry's first book, rehearses their journey as a species of memorial, the fact notwithstanding that Thoreau never mentions his brother's name.

On August 31, 1839, as the brothers prepare to launch, "a warm drizzling rain" rains all morning, so the Thoreaus delay their departure until the "mild afternoon." On August 31, 2003, a cool and sunlit day, we were on the Sudbury soon after breakfast. In addition to houses with sloping lawns, Concord Academy was off to our right. Henry Thoreau founded an earlier Concord Academy, in 1838. John taught there. Across a swamp on the left was Nashawtuc Hill, but in 2003 we could see neither school nor hill from the tree-screened Sudbury. The water was slow and smooth. In half a mile, we came to Egg Rock, an outcrop of diorite, as impressive in its size as in the words inscribed in the rock: "On the hill at the meeting of these rivers and along the banks lived the owners of Musketaquid before the white men came." The rivers Sudbury and Assabet join at Egg Rock to form—as Thoreau tells us in the first words of his book—"the Musketaquid, or Grass-ground River." It had been renamed Concord River, but "it will be Grass-ground River as long as grass grows and water runs here," he says, suggesting a viewpoint not widespread in his time. Far into his text, he recalls boatmen, in low water, mowing the grass of the Concord River as if it were a hayfield, the better to deliver their freight.

Under light, steady current, the bent river grass pointed us downstream, and through the oaken pilings of the Old North Bridge. On the right bank—the British side of the bridge as the redcoats faced the Colonial militia—was an obelisk dated 1836. Off the other end, in bronze, was the Minuteman sculpture by

Daniel Chester French, whose sitting Lincoln sits in the Lincoln Memorial. Inscribed below the Minuteman was the least obscure stanza of Ralph Waldo Emerson's "Concord Hymn," which Thoreau quotes and then follows with a couple of pages of his own verse. The "Concord Hymn" was first performed in 1837, when the obelisk was dedicated. Henry Thoreau was in the choir, singing. He was a senior at Harvard, days away from his graduation. John was in all likelihood present as well. The choir sang:

> *By the rude bridge that arched the flood,*
> *Their flag to April's breeze unfurled,*
> *Here once the embattled farmers stood*
> *And fired the shot heard round the world.*

The Thoreaus carried guns and fired them to signal their departure from town. In his book, Thoreau refers to Emerson—his mentor, his model, his benefactor, his employer—only as "a Concord poet." In Thoreau's wanderings north of the Moosehead—which resulted in "The Allegash and East Branch," the first recreational American canoe trip reported to the future—Edward Hoar, a Concord neighbor, was with him all the way, and in nearly ten thousand words was mentioned only as "my companion" or "my friend." This was, of course, not churlishness on the author's part but a diffident custom practiced in his time, as if it were ordered by "The Concord Manual of Style," or, for that matter, in the way that the modern *New York Times* seems to insist that the first-person pronoun be swaddled as "a visitor." In "A Week on the Concord and Merrimack Rivers," John Thoreau is immortalized as "the other," although it is not always clear who "the other" is. At dusk on the day they reach Hooksett, "one of us" goes up the bank to look for a farmhouse "where we might replenish our stores" while "the other remained cruising about the stream, and exploring the opposite shores" for a place to stay the night. It's always "one" or "the other," never "me" and "my brother." But this time Henry is trapped in his own terminology, as, in the past tense and from the author's perspective in the rowboat, "the other voyageur returned from his inland expedition," and we know that it was John who replenished the stores, getting precious little credit for it.

Not being as mannerly as Henry David Thoreau or the *Times*, I don't mind telling you that my companion on the Concord River was Dick Kazmaier, who, after that first day, bid me farewell, yielding his place to my son-in-law Mark Svenvold, who went up the Merrimack with me to Hooksett. The Thoreau brothers reached Hooksett on September 4th, as did we, but along the way we stayed in different places than they did. Their first campsite was on an island in Billerica seven miles from Concord. At the end of the second day, they pitched their tent in Tyngsborough, on the Merrimack, a short distance below the ferry there. A short distance below Tyngsborough Bridge, where the ferry was, we slept higher up the bank, in a resort hotel called Stonehedge. On September 2nd, they rowed upstream into New Hampshire and on to the mouth of Penichook Brook, a little north of Nashua, where we arrived a full day ahead of them, taking out at Nashua's Greeley Park on September 1st. The difference was caused by an altered structure of the journey. The Thoreaus were travelling not only on two rivers but also on two commercial waterways. At the falls of Billerica, eleven miles below their home, they intersected the Middlesex Canal, which ran from salt water in Boston to the Merrimack at Middlesex (now part of the city of Lowell), "and as we did not care to loiter in this part of our voyage, while one ran along the tow-path drawing the boat by a cord, the other kept it off the shore with a pole, so that we accomplished the whole distance in little more than an hour." The whole distance was six miles, and by 2003 it included, among other things, the multi-petalled cloverleaf where I-495 crosses U.S. 3 and also connects with an interstate spur. On the Billerica side of that cloverleaf, north and south of Brick Kiln Road, you can walk nearly two miles through deep woods along the old canal, which has aged there for a century and a half untouched and unrestored, thirty feet wide, water still in it, but low under green algal scum. White pines are there, tall enough to be the masts of ships. Honeysuckle, huckleberries, birches, oaks. In the low and distant hum of internal combustion, the quiet path is precisely the one the brothers used with their cord and their pole. In Lowell, nearing the Merrimack, the canal emerges from woods and, conjoining Black Brook, becomes the water hazard that divides the second and third fairways of Mount Pleasant Golf Club, John and Henry all but visible hauling their skiff from the second tee and the third green to the second green and the third tee among the putting golfers, the swinging golfers, the riding golfers in their rolling carts.

Mark Svenvold and I—on September 1st—started out early in the day on the Merrimack in Lowell, directly opposite the place where three stair-step locks, in the afternoon of the same date, lowered the Thoreaus into the river. If we had it easier than they did, skipping over by necessity the Middlesex Canal, they had a softer time of it in New Hampshire. In 1826, a dam was built at Pawtucket Falls, in the heart of Lowell, Massachusetts, and, as Thoreau reports, "the influence of the Pawtucket Dam is felt as far up as Cromwell's Falls," in New Hampshire, five miles above Nashua. (The word "falls," then as now, was applied not only to free-falling water but also to rapids.) The Thoreaus bypassed Cromwell's Falls by means of a canal-and-lock system on the west side of the river. In the eleven miles between Cromwell's Falls and Amoskeag Falls, in Manchester, the Merrimack ran (and still runs) on its post-Pleistocene gradient, white in its bouldered rapids. Above Cromwell's and below Amoskeag, the heavier falls were circumvented by seven lock systems collectively known as the Union Canal. The Thoreaus, of course, whisked their boat upstream through the whole of the Union Canal, rowing, yes, against the currents of the pools, but everywhere relieved of the rigors of the rapids. Things would not be so for us. The Union Canal is rubble. Scouting our trip by car in midsummer, I felt discouragement looking down into the massive boulderfields laced with white water in all those miles approaching Manchester. I doubted that we could make much progress there.

Scarcely a quarter of a mile below the Old North Bridge, the Concord River enters the Great Meadows, which, in Thoreau's words, "like a broad moccasin print, have levelled a fertile and juicy place in nature." Part floodplain, part swamp, now on one side of the river, now on both, the moccasin print is six miles long, looks essentially as it must have in 1839, and is now Great Meadows National Wildlife Refuge. Kazmaier, paddling in the bow, noting plants on the banks, said, "You can tell that fall is coming when you spot the purple loosestrife." Kaz is less well known as a naturalist than as a businessman whose Kazmaier Associates has seemed to have a tentacle in every aspect of most known sports, from the international licensing of basketball broadcasts to the manufacture and sale of baseball uniforms and football helmets. There was a time when the coming of fall would have been signalled to him by a little more than loosestrife. In the decades since 1945, he is one of four recipients of the Heisman Memorial Trophy who did not go into professional football. Instead, he earned an M.B.A. at Harvard Business School. The stiff-arm trophy is on a bookshelf in Concord, looking underattended in an acreage devoted to dogs, hens, roosters, goats, dressage rings, stables, and horses of his youngest daughter, Kristen, a professional equestrian, who lives next door. Routinely, he does "night barn" for Kristen—goes out in the late evening, fills buckets with water, and flips leaves of hay to the horses.

In a couple of Administrations, Kazmaier had been chairman of the President's Council on Physical Fitness, but he didn't have to work hard on this placid river. Thoreau compares its "scarcely perceptible" current to the character of people in nineteenth-century Concord. He also says the river's "wild and noble sights" are "such as they who sit in parlors never dream of."

We passed two fishermen in a boat, and asked how they were doing.

"One fourteen-inch pickerel. Last week, I caught a thirty-inch northern."

Drawing away, we heard the man who had responded to our question explaining to the other fisherman that a pickerel is crafty and "lies in ambush."

In this same reach between Ball's Hill and Carlisle, the Thoreaus pass a bank fisherman with a silver-birch pole, and that sets Henry off into his classic and digressive set piece—four thousand words if it's a syllable—on fish and fishing: the passage in which the pickerel, "motionless as a jewel," waits to swallow "at a gulp . . . a brother pickerel half as large as itself," and "sometimes a striped snake, bound to greener meadows across the stream, ends its undulatory progress in the same receptacle";

the passage in which he tells us that he lovingly massages fish with his hands in the water; the passage in which he tells us that "he who has not hooked the red chivin is not yet a complete angler"; the passage in which he counsels the American shad, blocked in its runs by ever more dams, to "keep a stiff fin" and hope for a better world.

Another mile, and we watched a young guy on a granite outcrop pull a young pike from the water. It was two feet long. Where Thoreau heard "a faint tinkling music" of distant bells, we heard the tinkling of a motorcycle, but it was the only such sound to come over the river on this day before Labor Day. Hearing it, too, were a man and a woman rowing on the river in a four-oared shell. The Thoreaus' first overnight was on the west side of an island seven miles below Concord, four miles above the falls at Billerica, and we stopped there for lunch. This was probably the same island. Thoreau mentions two, close together, and only one distinctly remains. We drank sweet bottled tea, and voluminously ate oatmeal cookies, fruit, potato chips, and ham and turkey sandwiches. For dinner in that first campsite, the Thoreaus had—make of it what you will—"bread and sugar, and cocoa boiled in river water." They also drank the river cool. They heard foxes on the island in the night.

Obscured by the trees on the left bank was a Billerica subdivision called Rio Vista—its houses, bungalows, and cottages dating from the nineteen-twenties, its entrances flanked by concrete pillars raisined with spherical stones. I had wandered around in Rio Vista two months before, ingesting information. Billerica is pronounced as if he were one of three brothers named Ricka. John Ricka. Henry David Ricka. Bill Ricka. Rio Vista has a street named Thoreau, and I wondered how the residents pronounce that. Thoreau scholars generally accent the first syllable of his name. Elizabeth Witherell, the editor-in-chief of The Writings of Henry D. Thoreau, had told me that people around Concord seem to say "THERR-oh," as in "I gave it a thorough cleaning." I knocked on the door at No. 22 Thoreau. Two slats of a Venetian blind came slowly apart. A woman of upper-middle years informed me that she was not about to open the door. I shouted back through the glass, asking about an island in the river behind her house. "I never heard of one!" she shouted back. Would she mind telling me how she pronounces the name of her street? "Thor-OH!" she shouted, with a bold stroke on the "OH."

"A name pronounced is the recognition of the individual to whom it belongs," Henry Thoreau says, near the end of "A Week on the Concord and Merrimack Rivers." "He who can pronounce my name aright . . . is entitled to my love and service." His name is everywhere in Thoreau country. At the foot of Lock Street in Nashua you approach the Merrimack through Thoreau's Landing, a spread of nature-colored condos—handsome, homogenous, extensive.

Sunday morning and "the air was so elastic and crystalline that it had the same effect on the landscape that a glass has on a picture. . . . We were uncertain whether the water floated the land, or the land held the water." In 2003, the Concord was similar for us that Sunday afternoon. Blue herons lined it like gargoyles. Who knows what pious thoughts they were thinking. Thoreau says that on this day "the fishes swam more staid and soberly, as maidens go to church," and "the frogs sat meditating, all Sabbath thoughts, summing up their week." Like the Thoreaus' dory, our canoe moved through flat-calm water that reflected the surrounding world. Thoreau says, "It required some rudeness to disturb with our boat the mirror-like surface of the water . . . for only Nature may exaggerate herself." The water we rudely broke with our paddles was as clear as the air and the reflection. Moreover, in eleven miles on the Concord we saw one beer can (afloat), one orange-and-white plastic barrel (in the alders), and no other flotsam or jetsam. The Clean Water Act of 1972 was among the highest legislative accomplishments of the twentieth century. It owed more than a little to thought set in motion by Henry David Thoreau.

Just as he describes it, the Concord narrows dramatically and shallows out over a "yellow pebbly bottom" as it approaches the falls in Billerica, where the Thoreaus went off on the Middlesex Canal and where Kaz and I were to rendezvous with my wife, Yolanda Whitman, in her Odyssey. To let her know that we were in Billerica and when we would be landing, Kaz produced a cell phone, waved it in the air, and said, "Henry David couldn't do this!"

In the last quarter-mile, where the river ponded widely above a dam, we homed in on a small rock island with a single tree, and on a very old brick factory that had been built beside the dam forty-one years after the Thoreaus went through. Helen Potter's Mill Mouse Gallery was in the bricks now, Colleen Sgroi's Gallery and Art Classes, and the law office of Margaret Loranger Sweeney. The Middlesex Canal had crossed the Concord River here, drawing from this high point the water that filled the canal to the north and to the south. In a boulder on the left bank we saw a big iron D ring. It had held one end of the canal's "floating bridge," which supported horses hauling the commercial traffic. On Faulkner Street, the brick factory and a concrete bridge from 1930 occluded the route of the Thoreaus.

———

Where the brothers entered the Merrimack, whatever is left of the three locks that took them down to the river is buried beside Advance Auto Parts, 1-800-Rent-a-Car, the Tandoori Grill, and the Asian Pacific Buffet. The remains are under the Sterling warehouse for North American Van Lines and the rails of the Boston & Maine. Across Broadway from all those historic places is Hadley Field, with its baseball diamond, its children's playground, its skateboard park, and its low stone marker as the route of the Middlesex Canal. Coming through the park, the canal went right through the warehouse and stair-stepped down to the river.

On September 1st, at seven-fifty in the morning, Mark Svenvold and I started off in a light rain, due west up the Merrimack. Starting up the Merrimack, Thoreau says, "We now felt as if we were fairly launched on the oceanstream of our voyage," and he compares the village harbors in that reach of the river to the harbors of Venice, Syracuse, and Rhodes. The Merrimack there is a thousand feet wide and subject to the winds if not of an ocean, at least of a good-sized lake. I hate fighting headwinds, so I was grateful for the calm gray overcast, the rain that diminished to mist. We would be paddling upstream about forty miles, at least twenty-five per cent of it with no help from the pooling influence of dams. Mark is six feet three, in his middle forties, athletic. In this endeavor, I preferred him to his wife or, certainly, my wife. This wasn't my first rodeo. Mark also has the high fluency and ironic humor of someone else who went up this river, long ago. He is a poet and the author of "Elmer Mc-Curdy," a nonfiction book in which he easily bests the challenge that his central figure is a corpse.

Lowell, which had more than a hundred thousand people by 2003, already had twenty thousand in 1839. For Thoreau, this was not a wilderness trip; these were not the woods of Maine. It was a journey up a minor American Ruhr, partly developed and partly under construction, ever more nascent with miles north. On the riverbanks, rails were being laid as he rowed. In his book, when he calls Lowell "the city of spindles and Manchester of America" he is not referring to the ambitious village thirty miles upstream. Nor is he above a borrowed thought. In his duffel, he had John Hayward's "The New England Gazetteer" (published earlier in 1839), which describes Lowell as "the American Manchester."

The red bricks of Lowell and neighboring Chelmsford had come down the Merrimack in canal boats. Mark and I passed a four-story factory in whose tall windows about half the glass was not present—an empty brick shell of a bygone New England. "CHELMSFORD MILLS FOR LEASE." The Merrimack is formed in central New Hampshire by the conjunction of the Pemigewasset and the Winnipesaukee (Thoreau's Winnepisiogee) and flows pretty much due south to the Great Bend at Chelmsford, where it turns east for Lowell and the ocean. The Thoreaus, taking their "nooning," sat on sand under an apple tree and ate wild plums "opposite the Glass-house village" here at the Great Bend.

We turned the corner, headed north, and before nine in the morning were entering the channel behind Tyng's Island—the Pennacook Confederacy's phonetic Wickasee, Thoreau's Wicasuck, "a favorite residence of the Indians," home of the sachem Wannalancet, son of Passaconaway. Thoreau repeatedly brings up the history and predicament of Native Americans from the seventeenth century forward, and what has become of their possessions, as he does here. Yet he might have been slow to understand the scene we came into now: men riding in little carts and seeming to kill things on the ground. In the mouth of the channel, paddling, we watched them, to our left, approach and putt on the third green. This was Vesper Country Club, dating from 1875, where Harry Vardon, who would win six British Open Championships, slept in a tent in 1900, got up, and set the course record. Joe Kirkwood played here. Walter Hagen played here. Vesper's first champion (1895) was Austin Chadwick, destined to become president of the Lowell Five Cent Savings Bank. The fourth hole, par 3, plays over the channel, its green on the mainland. As we went by, the golfers we had been watching were teeing off. A guy hit a shot into the water right in front of us, as if he were shelling a frigate. Running three-quarters of a mile before rejoining the main river, the channel was generally a hundred and fifty feet wide. Crossed by two small bridges, it resembled a canal, which it had once been, when the dam in Lowell was less high and a lock lifted boats circumventing the rapids on the far side of Wickasee Island; but that was before the Thoreaus' time. In Henry's book, they row straight up the silenced rapids.

On their fifth day, above Amoskeag Falls, in Manchester, the brothers pass a ten-foot obeliscal monument to the family of Major General John Stark. It "commands a prospect several miles up and down the Merrimack," Thoreau reports, and goes on to say, "It suggested how much more impressive in the landscape is the tomb of a hero than the dwellings of the inglorious living." Then, in purest hermitspeak, he asks, "Who is most dead,—a hero by whose monument you stand, or his descendants of whom you have never heard?" Five hundred feet up the bank, the monument is still there, veiled in vegetation and not visible from the river.

Stark died in 1822 at the age of ninety-three. While Thoreau notes that Stark "commanded a regiment of the New Hampshire militia at the battle of Bunker Hill; and fought and won the battle of Bennington in 1777," Thoreau seems not to have been aware that every automobile in New Hampshire would bear on its license plates the first four words of this apothegm from the General: "Live free or die; death is not the worst of evils." In any case, Thoreau does not quote it. Instead, looking up at the Stark memorial, he smolders with indignant irony, saying, "The graves of Passaconaway and Wannalancet are marked by no monument on the bank of their native river." That is no longer strictly true. In Litchfield, on the east bank of the Merrimack about halfway between Nashua and Manchester—where the Thoreaus saw acres of elms and maples six inches high—is Passaconaway Country Club.

As the Thoreaus rowed past Wannalancet's Wickasee, in 1839, a couple of men asked them for a ride off the island, which Henry and John, freighted low, declined to provide. "As we glided away," Henry would recall, "we could still see them far off over the water, running along the shore and climbing over the rocks and fallen trees like insects." Or golfers.

At their campsite below the Tyngsborough ferry, they "hung a lantern to the tent pole," spread their buffalo hides on the grass, and read the gazetteer, "our Navigator, and from its bald natural facts extracted the pleasure of poetry." They carried potatoes and melons: "We threw our rinds into the water for the fishes to nibble." Above Nashua at the mouth of the Penichook, they had more boiled cocoa for supper. At Coos Falls, below Manchester, they inadvertently pitched their tent in a trail used by masons who were working on the lock there. Early the following morning, while they were rolling up their buffaloes, the masons came by on their way to work. This was the only instance, Thoreau says, when anyone saw them in any of their campsites. Try that in century twenty-one. In Hooksett, when "the other" went to the farmhouse for food, he came back with "a loaf of home-made bread, and musk and water-melons for dessert." In Tyngsborough, when Mark and I went up the bank to the Stonehedge Inn, leaving behind the Thoreau brothers with their melon rinds and cocoa, we perused a menu that included, sans punctuation, "Herb Crusted Cod with a Organic Baby Vegetable and Wild Rice Casserole Maple Smoked Bacon Reduction." I had one of those. The wine list was only a little shorter than the Boston area telephone directory, and might have appealed to a British banker. You could have a 1996 Meursault for $176, a 1997 Gevrey-Chambertin for $240, a 1984 Robert Mondavi Reserve for $245, a 1953 Château Mouton-Rothschild for $1,585, a 1947 Château Latour for $3,400, or a 1945 Margaux for $3,600. Laid down in the Stonehedge cave were ninety-six thousand bottles of wine. In the center of the dining room was a glass tower of recumbent wines that may have been an architectural reference to the glass column of visible books in the Beinecke Library at Yale. Under the Stonehedge portico was a lingering black Jaguar, evidently a prop.

"We occasionally rested in the shade of a maple or a willow," says the younger Thoreau, "and drew forth a melon for our refreshment, while we contemplated at our leisure the lapse of the river and of human life." One night, "by a deep ravine, under the skirts of a pine wood," a high wind arose. "The pines murmured, the water rippled, and the tent rocked a little, but we only laid our ears closer to the ground, while the blast swept on to alarm other men. . . . Long before daylight we ranged abroad with hatchet in hand. . . . Then with our fire we burned up a portion of the loitering night, while the kettle sang its homely strain to the morning star." Thoreau had difficulty in his search for a publisher for this book. He eventually published it himself. After seven hundred and six copies were returned to him unsold, he said, "I have now a library of nearly nine hundred volumes, over seven hundred of which I wrote myself." From the Penichook campsite, after the wind subsided, he and John took off upstream in the dark at 3 A.M. in an enveloping river fog.

At the Tyngsborough ferry, the Thoreaus see "a gig in the gray morning, in the mist," and "children with their two cents done up in paper." The children's fare was two cents. Off the west end of the modern bridge is the Henry Farwell House, dating from 1705, where English proprietors serve cheese scones, crustless mini-sandwiches, and, in bone china, teas that come out from under cozies. Farwell started the ferry service in 1809. The old town hall across from the Farwell House was five years old when the Thoreaus went by, in 1839. Neighboring houses, still there, date from 1808 and 1790.

Svenvold and I went under the Tyngsborough Bridge soon after nine in the morning, hoping to complete the stretch from Lowell to upper Nashua by nightfall. We underestimated what we could do. At ten, we came to a sign on the right—"Welcome to Hudson, New Hampshire." A few more strokes and I looked over my shoulder. Nothing welcoming there. Massachusetts didn't care whether you died free or lived in California. The river was peaceful, mostly silent, secluded. From time to time, we heard the surf of highways we could not see. We saw kingfishers along the Merrimack, and blue herons, the fisher kings. Eight Canada geese came in, splat, for belly-flopping crash landings—the only kind of landing they can manage. We saw a shopping cart, a truck muffler, a dolly, dead sweepers full of Styrofoam debris. A sweeper is a tree that is still connected to the shore but has fallen into the river. Current moves flotsam into the sweeper, which collects the flotsam. The Merrimack had its share of foul sweepers, but, over all, the river was remarkably clean, the sight we now came to notwithstanding.

Far ahead and near the west bank, a small geyser was shooting white water straight upward in the otherwise flat river. The eruption was only a couple of feet high, but in that apparently motionless riverscape it had the focal effect of a natural phenomenon. It drew us toward it—the ultimate orifice of the Nashua Wastewater Treatment Facility, spinning great concentric swirls of white foam on the river, like half an acre of cappuccino. This hideous sight was enough to frighten a shipful of Vikings, as Mark Svenvold was prepared to affirm. The discharge smelled like laundry detergent and chlorine, nothing worse, but in this place more than anywhere else—including all the rocks and rapids to come—I preferred that the canoe remain upright. The effluent seemed to disperse quickly and the water downstream had been clear as we approached—peculiarly, the signature of Thoreau and the environmental movement. In communities along the river, some three hundred thousand people drink the treated Merrimack.

Passing under a pair of high bridges, we came to the mouth of the Nashua River not long after noon. Turning into it, we pulled up the canoe on a sandy beach among boulders, and, under red maples, ate Stonehedge-prepared club sandwiches laced with avocado. The Nashua was clear, smooth, and fast—not white water but a firm current coming down through a railroad bridge whose bowstring trusses enhanced a lovely scene. The Nashua River, near its mouth, bisects the city, flourishing three oxbow bends before debouching into the Merrimack. The Thoreaus, after passing under a covered bridge and arriving at the Nashua, were not much interested. Henry praises the tributary for its "elm-shaded meadows" at Groton, but says that "near its mouth it is obstructed by falls and factories, and did not tempt us to explore it." It tempted Mark and me, and we took off for the public library, digging hard against deceptive currents. A week earlier, for training purposes, we had gone a mile and a half against the upper Delaware at a stage near flood. But this was more difficult, possibly because the Nashua was shallow and we were not poling. Working off the avocado, we got around a meander bend and under the 101 bridge, almost a mile up. Then we came to a small island, beyond which were another railroad bridge and a dam. On our left was the spire of St. Casimir's Catholic Church, dark-red brick, 1857. St. Casimir's is on Temple Street near Scripture. Scripture is one-way. On our right was a brick mill, fourteen years old when the Thoreaus went by, with three large arches standing in the river, framing a pitch-black watery cavern. We fought up past the arches to the top of the island, where we decided to let the Nashua return us to the Merrimack.

A two-mile digression is not a rarity in Thoreau. He is, to a fare-thee-well, an author with the courage to digress. In this same reach of the Merrimack, while slicing his midday melons, he mentions that they are "a fruit of the east," and his thoughts go off, his pencil with them, to "Arabia, Persia, and Hindostan, the lands of contemplation and dwelling-places of the ruminant nations." He visits a lot of ruminant nations—their faiths, literatures, and philosophies—and returns reliably after a detour of six thousand words. On the Sunday morning that he hauls the dory through the Middlesex Canal, he passes a church, close to the Merrimack, whose congregation pours out as the brothers go by. This triggers five thousand words on comparative religion before the dory is lowered to the river. Had he been a candidate for employment in the pulpit of that church, the congregation might not have been eager to hire him. "Absolutely speaking, *Do unto others as you would that they should do unto you* is by no means a golden rule, but the best of current silver," he remarks. Jesus Christ "taught mankind but imperfectly how to live." "The church is a sort of hospital for men's souls, and as full of quackery." On the Merrimack approaching Tyngsborough, he refers to God as "the Scene-shifter."

One of his consultations with "The New England Gazetteer" gives rise to six thousand words of literary theory. "Books of natural history aim commonly to be hasty schedules, or inventories of God's property, by some clerk," he writes. Literary criticism is "the art of navigation by those who have never been out of sight of land." You can all but hear a student shout, "Go, T!"

Some of his digressions repay in brevity whatever the long ones may have borrowed. Paddling under an overhanging tree a few miles below Nashua, he goes into a high-density set piece of two hundred and thirty-five words about the species *Tilia americana* (American basswood), from which people have made matting, ropes, shoes, nets, cloth, roofing, bucklers, baskets, paper, cradles, sugar, medicine, gunpowder, and the "sounding-boards of piano-fortes." The wood is remarkable for its "toughness and flexibility," he says, and, withal, for being unusually light—as Mark and Kaz and I could testify after moving our canoe fifty-some miles with Shaw & Tenney basswood paddles in our hands.

In the dense fog above Penichook, Thoreau on the river cannot see a mountain he knows to be there, so he describes instead, in four thousand words, a mountain-climbing hike he once made in the Berkshires near Williamstown, with allusions to the Catskills thrown in. The pitted rocks of Amoskeag Falls inspire in him five hundred words on the notable potholes of New England, and they in turn lead him to outline his understanding of geomorphology, which somehow leads him into the ramifications of Roman history. The scholar Linck Johnson calls these patterns a "complex weave." The first image that came to my mind was a string of lights—or any linear structure with things hanging on it, like a heavily loaded clothesline. In the magisterial Emerson, Johnson finds the aptest image. Emerson described the narrative of "A Week on the Concord and Merrimack Rivers" as "a very slender thread for such big beads & ingots as are strung on it."

Thoreau's structure would be almost pure free association were it not for the river reeling him back in. The book seems something like a carnival midway, or a hall full of convention booths, or an aisle in a flea market. Thoreau invites you to linger at one of his tables, booths, or sideshows, a characteristic for which he surely deserves to be forgiven. This writing is commentary, editorial, philosophical, homiletic—defying generic assignment. Now he is John Muir, now he is Joseph Campbell, now he lingers in the doorway between psychiatry and religion. Near Reeds Ferry, he remarks, en passant, "We are doubleedged blades, and every time we whet our virtue the return stroke straps our vice."

By rough word count, "A Week on the Concord and Merrimack Rivers" is ninety per cent digression and ten per cent narrative. Near the end, the ratio is even more lopsided. Thoreau seems anxious to be done with the rivers, to get the geography out of the way and bring the piece of writing to its oblique but cardinal purpose: a nine-thousand-word final digression, on friendship. Elizabeth Witherell, whose Thoreau publishing project was once on the Princeton campus and is now at the University of California, Santa Barbara, has pointed out to me, "John died in January, 1842. His younger brother decided to memorialize him in a book in which he would combine an account of the trip with philosophical observations and meditations." And she went on to say that "Thoreau looks first at and then through the landscape"; he is demonstrating "the timelessness at the heart of change." Thoreau is in such a hurry going south that he seems to have enhanced the distance he travelled. In a two-day return voyage of fifty-four miles, he indicates that he went fifteen miles one day and fifty the next—a twenty per cent exaggeration, not an unheard-of inflation in recollections ten years old.

Thoreau did not begin writing "A Week on the Concord and Merrimack Rivers" until 1845. That is what he was doing in his wee house at Walden Pond, which he built on Emerson's land. He also began "Walden" there, which he published in 1854. These were his only two books to appear in his lifetime. In 1839, he had not rowed to New Hampshire with intent to write a book. In the fourteen volumes of his journal, three pages derive from the trip on the rivers when he was twenty-two. After he died, at the age of forty-four, pieces he had contributed to *Sartain's Union Magazine*, *Putnam's Monthly Magazine*, and *The Atlantic Monthly* were collected by Ticknor & Fields as "Cape Cod" and "The Maine Woods." "Typically he would make a trip, write a lecture, lecture again, making changes, and eventually publish the lecture in a magazine," Witherell says. "There is no notebook from the Concord-Merrimack trip. He did write some things on the trip, because he says so."

———

In a light but steady rain, Mark Svenvold and I started out from Greeley Park, Nashua, around nine in the morning on September 2nd, six hours later than the Thoreaus, on September 3rd, left their nearby campsite at Penichook Brook and rowed off in the pitch-black fog. The banks of the Merrimack characteristically rise sheer for ten or so vertical feet before levelling out and then rising again steeply to a second terrace. Just about where the Thoreaus camped, a bit downstream from the mouth of the brook, we saw two small concrete tombstones, scarcely a foot high, on the shelf between the terraces. Mark somehow got himself up the ten feet, and read the inscriptions from the metal plates on the tombstones: "HENRY 85–95," "RILEY 86–95." Henry? An Airedale, possibly. A cat. A gerbil. A parrot. A python. In the windless rain, we proceeded on, where Thoreau, on this "calm and beautiful day," saw potato fields, pastures, corn, rye, oats, and "few houses." From the Merrimack, "the country appeared much more wild and primitive than to the traveller on the neighboring roads. The river is by far the most attractive highway." He could say that again in the twenty-first century. High behind the Merrimack's western flank was Route 3—north-south, like the river—a plastic strip mall running from one New Hampshire city to the next, a fast-food industrial complex. We rarely heard it and never glimpsed it. The Merrimack, bordered in its densities of trees, was a discrete world.

About two miles above Penichook Brook we came to Cromwell's Falls. The impoundment of water behind Pawtucket Dam, at Lowell, is now said to extend to Reeds Ferry, five miles up from Cromwell's Falls, but I would not describe as impounded a riffle of water gurgling over a ledge. It was an alluring sight at last to see the real river with its clothes off. There was

nothing small about it—eight hundred feet wide, with a cluster
of islands on the eastern side. Near the west bank was the massive stonework of the lock and canal that the Thoreaus and the
floating freight carriers of their time had used to circumvent the
ledge. Completed in 1815, it is one of the two best-preserved
components of the canal-and-lock systems on the Merrimack.
Others are little more than big perches of cut stone strewn along
the edge of the river. The lock doors, of course, were wooden
and perishable, but some of the remains include hinges. The
guide wall stood on the easterly side. Opposite was a large part
of the long wall that led boats to the lock, just as the long walls
of the Ohio, the Illinois, the Tennessee, the upper Mississippi
lead thousand-foot tows past the bull noses of guide walls and
into locks today. In boulders along the Merrimack we saw iron
rings, where canal boats, in the heavy traffic, were tied up to
wait for their turns in the lock. The drop at Cromwell's Falls is
about six feet in something over half a mile—enough to make us
work, and more than enough to make us wonder about the multiple rapids ahead. Once again, the rain was turning into mist.

"We passed Cromwell's Falls, the first we met with on this
river, this forenoon, by means of locks, without using our
wheels," Thoreau says. They had brought a set of wheels from
Concord to help them get around the rips of the Merrimack,
but they never needed them. Reading "The New England
Gazetteer," Thoreau learned that Cromwell was a seventeenth-
century trader whose dishonesty made a poor impression on the
natives and they resolved to murder him. "This intention was
communicated to Cromwell, who buried his wealth and made
his escape," said the gazetteer. Locally, Cromwell's buried wealth
gave rise to as much legend as a Spanish galleon under the Straits
of Florida. Thoreau rehearses various tales about farmers who

may or may not have plowed their way to Park Avenue, and concludes with a remark that could have founded the Republican Party: "The truth is, there is money buried everywhere, and you have only to go work to find it."

"These falls are the Nesenkeag of the Indians," he points out. "Great Nesenkeag Stream comes in on the right just above." The "keag" in "Nesenkeag" is pronounced "keg," as is the same syllable in "Amoskeag." Just above Cromwell's Falls on Route 3, very close to but not visible from the river, is a Budweiser brewery that has a production average of eighteen thousand kegs a day.

Several canal boats were present; the Thoreaus had to wait for the locks, for they were now "fairly in the stream of this week's commerce." In 1839, commerce was what the river was about, the purpose toward which it had been altered. Some years before, the bricks of Lowell had been clay in the ground five or six miles above Cromwell's Falls, and now the bricks of Manchester were coming downriver to Amoskeag from Hooksett, much in the way that the Empire State Building would come to New York from bedrock near Bloomington, Indiana. A canal boat—seventy-five feet long, nine and a half feet wide—could carry sixteen cords of wood. It could carry sixteen thousand bricks. The Middlesex Canal and the canals of the Merrimack falls had opened the way to market for the commercial freight of northern New England. Dams, pools, locks, and canals had urbanized Passaconaway's river and implied the future of other rivers. Thoreau is lyrical on the working life of the river boatmen, whose outdoor existence he ranks extremely high. At Cromwell's, the brothers talk with one, "a rude Apollo of a man . . . in whose wrinkles the sun still lodged, as little touched by the heats and frosts and withering cares of life, as a maple of the mountain." Two such men crewed each boat, often barefoot.

Upcurrent, they used poles about fifteen feet long with iron tips. They jammed the pole into the river bottom and then strained against it, the same way you pole a canoe. Downcurrent, they steered—an oar at either end. Horses drew them the twenty-seven miles on the Middlesex Canal. A horse, just walking around, can carry roughly two hundred and fifty pounds. A horse dragging a canal boat could move fifty tons.

When the Thoreaus were small boys, the steamboat Merrimack, with a hundred and fifty people and a brass band, went up the canal from Boston and fifty-some miles into New Hampshire. Occasionally, in their boyhood years, a canal boat would come up the Concord River "silently as a cloud, without noise or dust." They marvelled that the "vessel would float, like a huge chip, sustaining so many casks of lime, and thousands of bricks, and such heaps of iron ore, with wheel-barrows aboard."

On the Merrimack in 1839, they would hang on to a canal boat, drift back with it, chat with the boatmen, and make use of the company water jug. Rowing north, Henry seems to have developed an opinion of the canal boats themselves that hovered closer to hate than to love: "A canal boat, with its sail set, glided round a point before us, like some huge river beast, and changed the scene in an instant; and then another and another glided into sight, and we found ourselves in the current of commerce once more." He describes them "creeping stealthily up the side of the stream like alligators." Elsewhere, "with their broad sails set, they moved slowly up the stream in the sluggish and fitful breeze, like one-winged antediluvian birds." The railroad was about to kill all these creatures. Writing his story in the eighteen-forties, Thoreau said, "The locks are fast wearing out, and will soon be impassable."

A mile or so above Cromwell's Falls, Thoreau climbed the always isolating bank and the steep river terraces above it to a point where he could see the precursory Route 3 "a quarter or half a mile distant, and the particolored Concord stage, with its cloud of dust, its van of earnest travelling faces." A mile upriver were Thornton's Ferry and Naticook Brook, which the Thoreaus drank. Matthew Thornton's is one of the three New Hampshire signatures on the Declaration of Independence. Had the Thoreaus climbed the banks and terraces there, they would have seen his homestead, which still stands, a door away from Dunkin' Donuts.

At the mouth of the Souhegan, which comes in a mile and a half above Thornton's Ferry, Thoreau digresses into a story about a hostile band of Mohawks who were there almost precisely as many years before Thoreau as Thoreau was before us. We digressed into the clear currents of the freestone Souhegan, as Thoreau evidently preferred not to do, and went up past its confluence with Baboosic Brook and on maybe half a mile before we were stopped by a calendar scene: water spilling white over a thirty-foot mill dam framed in the arch of a bridge.

Another mile up the Merrimack, the Thoreaus stop for lunch, as did we, on "a large island . . . with steep banks and scattered elms and oaks." The island is a couple of thousand feet long, and where they stop is not reported, but this is what they do for lunch: they notice a flock of passenger pigeons filling up the trees, and Thoreau bursts into song about the "greater travellers far than we" and the "wiry winnowing sound of their wings" and "their gentle and tremulous cooing." Running out of ode, he says, "We obtained one of these handsome birds, which lingered too long upon its perch. . . . It is true, it did not seem to be putting this bird to its right use, to pluck off its feathers, and extract its entrails, and broil its carcass on the coals; but we heroically persevered, nevertheless, waiting for further information."

Under a red maple near the north end of the island, where

driftwood trees were piled high, Mark and I ate tuna-salad sandwiches, and, in lieu of boiled cocoa, finished them off with bittersweet chocolate. On the mainland, a cell-phone tower, its head above the trees, watched over us. In the sand at our feet were two golf balls—each a Strata zero. The Thoreaus would go on to camp on the west bank above Coos Falls, but we elected to stop at Reeds Ferry and spend some time in the late afternoon assessing the Union Canal.

Frankly, it seemed impossible. Along the riverbanks leading into Manchester are precious few places—among all the industrial parking lots, airport approach roads, and dead-end streets—where you can get close enough to the river to have a look at the rapids, but from the Granite Street Bridge and the long Amoskeag River Walk at Arms Park we saw tumbling cascades that were even more rock than rapid. Through dense trees in Londonderry, near the airport, we glimpsed Coos Falls, fifty vertical feet below us and not much farther away. The water wove itself in white strands through massive black boulders. In Litchfield, farther south, we walked half a mile on a trail through high grass and along an abandoned trolley line in forest and down to Moore's Falls, longest of all, about a third of a mile—a beautiful riverscape in white, black, and green, the fact notwithstanding that it called to mind a quarry.

From Moore's Falls to Amoskeag Falls, a distance of about nine miles, the river least resembles what the Thoreaus saw, not only because a city of a hundred thousand has arisen where they entered a growing village whose population in 1830 had been eight hundred and seventy-seven, but, as noted, because they ascended the falls in locks and passed them in canals. We faced not only the sequence of rapids but the boniest rapids you would ever see, and we were facing them in the wrong direction. What to do?

At nine in the morning, we set off from Reeds Ferry and paddled up toward Moore's Falls, scarcely half a mile. From downriver, the rapids seemed to be a high New England stone wall across the end of a field, an illusion to be repeated all day. After landing on the east bank, we set the canoe's center thwart, which was shaped as a carrying yoke, on Mark's shoulders, and we climbed in two hundred yards the sixty vertical feet that got us to St. Francis of Assisi Church, on the river's highest terrace, among parochial schoolchildren aswarm on a playground. There we met Yolanda and the Odyssey, put the canoe on top, and further portaged a third of a mile to a cul-de-sac where an empty house with a real-estate sign hovered over the river. It was a form of portage I came, marginally, to regret, but the Thoreaus had two wheels, never mind that they didn't use them, and we had four. They had a two-thousand-foot canal down there and two locks to lift their boat a total of ten feet; we had the ruins. Moreover, Moore's Falls is not only the longest rapid in the river; it is also the shallowest, suggesting Lexington Avenue in a heavy rain. With a fifty-foot rope, we lowered the loaded canoe down the precipitous incline, and from the lip of the bank lowered it again, the ten-foot drop to the river. You can't hurt an Old Town Penobscot 16.

Quoting "The New England Gazetteer," Thoreau says, "We reached some rapids called Moore's Falls, and entered on 'that section of the river, nine miles in extent, converted, by law, into the Union Canal, comprehending in that space six distinct falls.'" Aimed at the next five, Mark and I continued upriver. Having no idea what sort of progress we could make, we had decided to give eight hours to the Union Canal, see how far we could get, and then find a way to remove the canoe from the river. We thought of Stark Landing, in the middle of the city, about three hundred yards below the Granite Street Bridge, but that was wishful thinking. Above Moore's Falls was a mile of flat water, or almost flat water. It was moving right along, but it was nothing like our training pitch on the upper Delaware. Thoreau describes "rowing incessantly" through here and how pleasant it was to ease over into a canal and "lock ourselves through . . . for commonly there was no lock-man at hand,—one sitting in the boat, while the other, sometimes with no little labor and heave-yoing, opened and shut the gates, waiting patiently to see the locks fill." A few lines later, he says, "We rowed leisurely up the stream," and in places it was like that for Mark and me as well. It wasn't all heave-yoing. It wasn't all stiff current coming around boulders. There were swirling eddies, where current locally turned upriver. There were some deep, long pools.

On this date (September 3rd), the Thoreaus camped on the west bank just above Coos Falls—a name pronounced in New Hampshire with two syllables, like "chaos," and in Oregon with one syllable, as in "goose." As we approached Coos, we were again confronted by the chimeric stone wall, making the river look impassable. At each big rapid, a wing dam had been a component of the engineering—an oblique arm sticking far up into but not all the way across the river, its purpose to divert water through the canals and locks. The wing dam at Moore's Falls had been thirty-two hundred feet long, at Coos twenty-five hundred. That's a lot of rock to pile up. Now scattered through the rapids, it appears from a distance to be as integral as it once was, and from nearby to be the rocks of a riverbed on Mars. The Coos canal had been framed by the east bank and an island, and now consisted of two small pools separated by isthmuses of high dry rock. It was certainly no thoroughfare, but it seemed preferable to the souse holes, standing waves, and growling water that reached across the river from the west side of the island. We carried the canoe up and over the first isthmus, paddled the second pool, and carried the canoe across the boulders to the north end of the island. There was still a lot of white water in front of us and no way to paddle it, so I walked upcurrent with the fifty-foot rope and, when it was straight, turned and pulled the canoe up to me. Three good pulls and it came on its own, or so it seemed—just picked its way around the boulders, up ledges, and through the little rips until I had to stop it with my hand. Mark came up and held the canoe while I made my way upstream another fifty feet with the rope. I turned and pulled. That got us to the pool above Coos Falls.

Soon we were at Goff's Falls, where the Thoreaus found "a small village, and a handsome green islet in the middle of the stream," and we found New Hampshire's largest city. The United States Geological Survey has a gauge at Goff's Falls, and on this day (as we would learn later) it was registering 3.25 feet, the river running at fourteen hundred and sixty cubic feet per second. A week before, it had been running at twice that volume. Four days later, it would be doing so again. There was a big iron bracket—like a staple, in cross-section two inches square—at the base of Goff's Falls. Mark tied the canoe to the iron for a while, to let it calm down before we lined it up the rapids.

The next rapid was just downstream of the bridge where I-293 completes a link from its parent highway to the Everett Turnpike, on the west side of the river. The trucks looked down into the Class 3 chaos of Short's Falls, the whitest water avoided by the Union Canal, with a central drop of seven feet in eleven yards. The roar of the river swallowed the sound from the bridge. We couldn't hear the trucks. We got into the river and walked the canoe, shoved it up sluices and hauled it over ledges.

Mark later asked me what I had liked best about this day, and I said, "The way the canoe came up through the rips, following so readily when you pulled on the rope. It seemed to want to get up there as much as we did." In Short's Falls, though, there wasn't much of a chance to pull rope. Hanging on to the canoe, letting it support us as we moved against the currents, seemed the more sensible thing to do. A given piece of white water can be both softer than you think and less forgiving. It can let you walk through it, and it can pin you to a rock for the rest of your life. There were times, in holes, when I was up to my armpits, but that could not be called dramatic. Among armpits on this planet, mine do not imply great depth.

Four hundred yards above the interstate bridge, we came to Carthagina Island, standing in a flat-water pool. Thoreau doesn't call it by name, but he describes it as "a large and densely wooded island . . . the fairest which we had met with, with a handsome grove of elms at its head." Carthagina Island is more than two thousand feet long. The American elms seemed to be gone, as you might expect; but there, sitting on a big rock in the river near the head of the island, was the icon American bird—a bald eagle, which appeared to have enjoyed a lifetime in which it had eaten extremely well. The Merrimack, even in Massachusetts, had been well attended by kingfishers, sandpipers, and eagles in the air. But this big eagle on the rock seemed in no hurry to move, seemed to have shed whatever ambition it once had. It looked lazy, fat, accomplished, interested mainly in its investments.

Less than half a mile above Carthagina, at Griffin's Falls, where a twenty-five-hundred-foot wing dam had deflected water toward the east bank of the river and into a canal, the wing dam was, as usual, strewn through the rapids, but the canal was in beautiful condition. On its two sides, the big perches of windlassed granite were close in appearance to what they would have looked like when masons finished them in 1811. With Cromwell's Locks, this was the best relic of the Union Canal. Beside the top of the east wall was flat ground, a filled-in piece of the steep riverside, where the lockman's house must have been. Water was racing through the canal and lock, the doors, of course, long gone, and we would have put the canoe up through there had a large fallen tree, five or six feet in circumference, not been lying across the foot of the canal a few inches off the water. So we had to go around the lock, shoving and lining the canoe up the rapids and back into the canal at its upper end.

We decided to stop for lunch, Griffin's being a lovely place. If you are familiar with necropolitan Manchester, it is just down the bank from Pine Grove Cemetery, a mile below the Queen City Bridge. We had beached the canoe, spread our provender on the rocks, and were drying out a little when I happened to glance upward. My wife was studying us through the trees. All morning, she had been tracking us from byways and bridges, a feat so difficult in an automobile that she had failed to catch up until now, never mind that she was cleverer than I had been in finding places to get at the river, such as this one. We offered her lunch, and she accepted.

We shoved off. There was some tumbling water near an island half a mile up, and it seemed to be making sound befitting a big falls. I thought, That little rapid sure makes a lot of noise for something that is scarcely more than a riffle. What we were hearing, through a cuff of trees, was the combined Everett Turnpike and I-293, which go through downtown Manchester tight to the west bank of the river. In Thoreau's words, "The trees made an admirable fence to the landscape, skirting the horizon on every side."

Against the somewhat stepped-up current, we went under

the Queen City Bridge and past the mouth of a tributary stream. Or, as Thoreau tells it, "Not long after this we saw the Piscataquoag, or Sparkling Water, emptying in on our left, and heard the Falls of Amoskeag above." The falls of Amoskeag were two miles upstream, and mighty they had been, but now—in 1839—they had long since been eunuched by the dam that was providing water for Manchester's power canals, not to mention the thousands of feet of boat canal on which the Thoreaus would cruise through town. What the brothers were hearing from the mouth of the Piscataquog, as they soon discovered, was not Amoskeag Falls but the outlet of the power canals. Growing there as the Thoreaus went by was a solid mile of brick buildings, rising in four long tiers above the river—far and away the largest collocation of cotton mills in the world, and destined to make Lowell the Second City of spindles.

> Just above the mouth of this river we passed the artificial falls where the canals of the Manchester Manufacturing Company discharge themselves into the Merrimack. They are striking enough to have a name, and, with the scenery of a Bashpish, would be visited from far and near. The water falls thirty or forty feet over seven or eight steep and narrow terraces of stone, to break its force, and is converted into one mass of foam.

In September, 2003, no roaring water was falling down the terraces of stone, no exotic tourists were present, and there was nothing much to see on the river but forty seagulls in conference. Soon, we came to Stark Landing—farther up all the rapids than we had thought we'd ever get. Yolanda and the Odyssey had not arrived to meet us. The canoe, once again, had been faster. An elderly fisherman was sitting in a folding chair, flipping his lure into the river with no apparent interest in what it might encounter. He asked us what time it was.

"Two-thirty."

Mark and I looked at each other. We had been on the river less than six hours.

The stem of the canoe never touched the landing. Instead, it swung left, and headed for Amoskeag Falls. Quickly, we came to the rapids under the Granite Street Bridge. We crossed the river below them, and went up a few chutes on the west side, before paddling became impossible. We poled a little, but gave that up, jumped into the river, and walked and lined as before. To tell you the truth, it was easier hauling upstream than it would have been going in the other direction and clunking against all those rocks. It was actually a lot of fun—reading the river, picking the river, shoving the boat up the *fil d'eau*, using the tongues of water, walking the eddy walls. So why did we cross the river to go up the western side? To mitigate embarrassment, among other things. This was Merrill's Falls, Manchester, at the city's central riverfront, where—from Arms Park, on the eastern side—a virtual amphitheatre of granite steps descended to the river. In bed at night for three or four months, I'd been listening to Manchester laughing—a chorus of Mancunians sitting on those steps convulsed by us on the way uphill with our canoe. If they had laughed at the Thoreau brothers, they would surely laugh at us:

> We locked ourselves through here with much ado, surmounting the successive watery steps of this river's staircase in the midst of a crowd of villagers, jumping into the canal to their amusement, to save our boat from upsetting, and consuming much river water in our service.

Through boulder gardens and bygone weirs, we gained on Notre Dame Bridge, passing Arms Park, the granite steps, and a completely indifferent Manchester—an all but empty River Walk, a chorus of zero. Overhead were a great many quarter-inch cables, perpendicular to the currents, a gridiron in the air. From the cables, during kayak competitions, slalom gates are hung, touching the white water. I found three golf balls in Merrill's Falls. One was from a driving range who knows where, and one carried the logo of Intervale Country Club, two miles above Amoskeag Dam. Gradually, we got to the northern side of Notre Dame Bridge, and for us the end of white water. But not the end of stiff current. We climbed back over the gunwales, settled in, and to stay above the rips were paddling with all we had when the cell phone rang in the canoe. Someone closely related to us was calling to congratulate us, but we were paddling for all we were worth—really working at it in a muscle-aching way—and were in no position to take an adulation break, so, rudely, we didn't take the call. Glancing across the river, we could see the caller on the Amoskeag River Walk.

As Thoreau notes, "The descent of Amoskeag Falls, which are the most considerable in the Merrimack, is fifty-four feet in half a mile." That will give you a rapid to reckon with, and at this thunderous place Native American people immemorially convened. Thoreau says that "Amoskeag" means "great fishing place." R. A. Douglas-Lithgow's "Native American Place Names of Maine, New Hampshire, & Vermont" says it also means "One takes small fish." Be that as it may, Wannalancet kept a house nearby. We gained momentum and went on up the west side of the river in the tailrace pool of the dam, past the bare and truly mountainous beds of the dead cascade. The boat canal had required nine staired locks to get above it, when the thunder ceased.

On a small sandy beach just below the dam, Mark and I gave each other a high ten. Then we carried the canoe up an extremely short, extremely steep trail—those fifty-four vertical feet—and into the parking lot of a Ramada, where we were checked in.

This was storied Amoskeag, where the spray curled up like smoke, and where Indians and Colonists, in an annual rite of the spring migrations, danced, feasted, fished, and wrote treaties. In 1739, a hundred years before the Thoreaus' journey, the preacher Joseph Seccombe, who called himself Fluviatulis Piscator, delivered a sermon here that was later published as "A Discourse Utter'd in Part at Ammauskeeg-Falls, in the Fishing-Season." Nine known copies exist of this first American publication on sport fishing, which Fluviatulis Piscator resonantly defended before his racially mixed outdoor congregation. A copy was sold at auction in 2001 for eighteen thousand dollars. That would surely impress Thoreau, in various respects: in 2003, you could still buy an original cloth first edition of "Walden" from theworldsgreatbooks.com for only twelve thousand five.

Just above the dam, we launched the canoe at nine-fifteen in the morning, in water, on this fourth of September, 52.8 feet higher than the water we had left the afternoon before. After scraping nine miles over bedrock and boulders, we were all but disoriented by the depth. It felt aerial. "Above Amoskeag the river spreads out into a lake reaching a mile or two without a bend," Thoreau writes, and this expansive reach among shore-front condominiums and broadcasting towers is where he thought the canal boats, sailing on ahead of him, were like a flight of one-winged antediluvian birds. Two miles north, at the first bend, we passed Intervale Country Club in a light steady rain, the calming, cooling sort of weather that had followed us all through the trip. We were outrun by a golf cart rolling along a fairway with a large umbrella open overhead, making it appear to be a rickshaw from NASA. Aiming now for the big piers where I-93 crosses the river, we passed private homes in the trophy range, with tessellated riprap like fortress walls, and elaborate stairways, balustered white, descending the riprap in stages to dual-consoled cockpit boats tied up below.

Making good time on the motionless water, we had soon covered more than five miles, were back in the wooded isolation characteristic of the river, and were looking up a straight shot of two and a half miles to a small distinctive mountain, or, in Thoreau's words, "We could see rising before us through the mist a dark conical eminence called Hooksett Pinnacle." After passing under three bridges, two of them abandoned, we would come to the end of our trip at A. J. Lambert Riverside Park, Hooksett Village, below Hooksett Dam—a spectacular scene colluding natural white cascades with water falling over the dam and plunging from the powerhouse. We would meet the Odyssey there, not to mention Yolanda, who would drop down from the interstate past the corrugated structures of "HOOKSETT SELF STORAGE—RECORD PROTECTION."

The Thoreaus had not rowed that far. They had stopped for the night—September 4th—somewhere close to the beginnings of the last long reach toward the Pinnacle, where we were now. This was where John went to the farmhouse for provisions and came back with "a loaf of home-made bread, and musk and water-melons for dessert." Then the brothers crossed the river, to the east bank, and found a "convenient harbor"—the mouth of a small stream—where they could hide their boat. This was as far north as they travelled on the Merrimack River, the place from which they went off on foot and by stagecoach for seventeen pages in the White Mountains—their week within a week—and then returned to find the hidden boat and head downstream for home. Mark and I found the mouth of a brook coming in from under a railroad track through a very long cylindrical culvert, which we could look through as through a telescope, seeing verdure at the far end, H. D. Thoreau framed in cameo.

"We had come away up here among the hills to learn the impartial and unbribable beneficence of Nature," he says of this moment, but while he was waxing philosophical one of his melons drifted away. He had put it in the mouth of the creek to cool, and it took off. "In pursuit of this property," the brothers jumped into their boat, chased the melon downstream, and, "after long straining of the eyes, its green disk was discovered far down the river, gently floating seaward." They had cut a tap out of the melon to hasten the cooling, yet the melon had stayed upright, and, in the unbribable beneficence of Nature, no water had gone into the tap.

Out in the Sort

In an all but windowless building beside the open ocean in Arichat, Nova Scotia, a million lobsters are generally in residence, each in a private apartment where temperatures are maintained just above the freeze point. In a great high-ceilinged room known as the Dryland Pound, the lobster apartments are in very tall stacks, thirty-four levels high, divided by canyonlike streets. The size of the individual dwellings varies according to the size of the inhabitants; and there in the cold dark, alone, they use almost no energy and are not able to chew off their neighbors' antennas or twist off their neighbors' claws, as lobsters will do in a more gregarious setting. The cold water comes down from above and, in a patented way, circulates through the apartments as if they were a series of descending Moorish pools. Beguiled into thinking it is always winter, the lobsters remain hard, do not molt when summer comes, and may repose in Arichat for half a year before departing for Kentucky.

They belong to a company called Clearwater Seafoods,

which collects them from all over the Maritime Provinces, including the Cape Breton region of Nova Scotia, where Arichat is, on an island called Madame. Clearwater has a number of off-shore licenses, its deep-sea trawlers fifty to two hundred miles out, tending mile-long lines of traps and enhancing Clearwater's catch of lobsters that weigh three to fifteen pounds. A twenty-plus-pounder is rare but not unknown.

Sixty people work in the Arichat plant, sometimes around the clock. The manager is a big rugged guy named David George, who was wearing an N.Y.P.D. T-shirt when I met him and who summed up his operation by saying, "We go through a shitload of lobsters in a two-month period." From Clearwater's headquarters in Bedford, beside Halifax, I had driven up to Arichat with Mark Johnson, manager of Clearwater Lobster Merchants, New Covent Garden Market, Battersea; Dominique Bael, of Clearwater's La Homarderie, Quai des Usines, Brussels; and Marc Keats, the company's chief of European lobster sales. Lobsters were arriving at the rate of a hundred thousand a day, and each acceptable newcomer—its antennae waving, its carapace glistening—was given discrete space on a conveyor belt designed to advance its journey toward someone's distant mouth. The sensitized, computerized belt was, among other things, weighing the lobsters and assigning each by weight to one of sixteen grades. Lobsters graded "select" weigh between two and two and a half pounds. Chix all weigh just over or under a pound and are graded as large chix, medium chix, and small chix. A large quarter is a pound-and-a-quarter lobster that is an ounce or two on the heavy side. A small quarter is a light one. A large half weighs a little over 1.6 pounds. As the lobsters fly along the conveyor belt, computer-brained paddles reach out and sweep them variously left or right off the belt and into chutes that lead to large trays partitioned to accommodate lobsters of their exact heft. Biologists hover around the belt. The lobsters have a long way to live.

Clearwater once shipped lobsters to a Nobel Prize dinner. The company's delivered price was cheaper than the price of Swedish lobsters. Now and again, a lobster with claws the size of bed pillows goes to Japan to be featured in a display, but what the Japanese want in steady volume are chix. The world at large wants chix and quarters. Americans, almost alone, want the big ones. Clearwater lobsters go weekly to Guam. They go to Tel Aviv, Bangkok, Osaka, Los Angeles, Sioux Falls, Phoenix, Denver, Missoula, Little Rock, Brooklyn, and Boston. Lobsters are to Christmas dinners in France what turkeys are in America. On the eve of Christmas Eve, planes heading east for Paris have almost infinitely more lobsters in them than human beings. In annual consumption of lobsters, France is No. 1 in Europe. Clearwater has two customers in France, and is not looking hard for a third. An impression seems to be that the French are cheap and they want cheap lobsters. Moreover, when invoices go out it's a long time to the first euro. You will not find an ad for Clearwater in *Cuisine et Vins de France*. Christmas is also lobster time in much of the rest of Europe, and even in Asia. Lobsters are routed from the Dryland Pound to Louisville to Anchorage to Seoul. They go to Mexico, Turkey, Germany, Italy, Switzerland, and Spain. By the truckload, they go to Maine!

Four hundred thousand pounds a year pass through Clearwater's reservoir in New Covent Garden, Mark Johnson remarked, while we watched three-pounders and four-pounders scrolling by on their way to Las Vegas. In England, he mainly sells large quarters. Marks & Spencer is his biggest customer. Second is British Airways. On a *Restaurant Magazine* list of the fifty finest restaurants in the world, thirteen were in England, and six of those were customers of Clearwater lobsters.

The rationale of the Dryland Pound is to make hard, healthy lobsters available to the market year round, overcoming the impediments of Clearwater's short fishing seasons and nature's cyclical shrinking of lobsters' internal meat. The Clearwater harvest takes place for a couple of months in springtime and again in November-December. The harvest in Maine takes place all year. When a lobster becomes so fully meated that it begins to overcrowd its carapace, it molts—generally in summer. First, its meat shrinks radically and is softened by absorbed water. The shrivelled and softened flesh is able to come out of the shell. In Halifax, these rudiments were reviewed for us by Sharon Cameron, a biologist on the faculty of Clearwater's Lobster University, whose students were company personnel and customers on visits to headquarters from around the world. Recovery—the regrowth of flesh and the hardening of the new and larger shell—requires two months. As lobsters age and grow—five to seven years for each pound—years can go by between molts. The premium, tenderest lobsters are within a few months of their recovery after molting. Clearwater harvests only hard lobsters. Since there is no way to tell if a hard lobster molted three months ago or three years ago, chefs undercook the big ones, because they are tenderest when raw.

Professor Cameron slipped a needle into the belly of a lobster, drew blood, and squeezed it into a refractometer. The more blood protein, the longer you can store the lobster, she said. Clearwater's harvests take place when blood protein is highest. "The U.S. fishes mostly in summer, when blood protein is lowest. Convenience is the reason. They're not doing it for lobster quality. They're doing it for their own convenience."

Lobsters in the Arichat Dryland Pound lose all inclination to molt. They are like orange juice at Tropicana, frozen in massive blocks so that Tropicana can cover the whole of the calendar year although the Florida harvest runs for only seven months. To make sure that there is no summer in the Dryland Pound, the ocean water descending through the apartments is maintained at thirty-four to forty-one degrees Fahrenheit, and in one way or another, in and out of brine, Clearwater keeps its lobsters about that cold until a UPS package car drops them at somebody's door.

Long-distance travel will stress a lobster and affect it physically. Among other things, it loses weight and accumulates ammonia. This can happen on a smooth highway, let alone in giddy turbulence at thirty thousand feet. If a lobster succumbs, the ammonia will detonate as a shaped olfactory charge. The next time your quarterback is sacked unconscious, put a dead lobster under his nose and he'll stand up ready for action. If lobsters are going to travel the globe, they need rest at strategic places en route— they need to "float," in the language of the trade, for recuperative periods. Accordingly, when Clearwater became aware that UPS was building a new air superhub in Louisville, Clearwater decided to go there, establish a rest-and-rehabilitation reservoir close to the airport, and cause Louisville to become the flying-lobster capital of the United States.

Every five or six days, an eighteen-wheel reefer with a red cab and a silver-white box loads up at Arichat, pulls away dripping, carefully circumscribes Isle Madame on roads scarcely wider than it is, passes white lobster boats in arms of the sea framed in black spruce over massive shelves of bedrock, and picks up speed for Kentucky. It goes through St. John, and on down New Brunswick 1 to Calais, Maine, where United States Customs X-rays the truck's entire box, which can be carrying as many as thirty thousand lobsters. Dropping six gears, the truck climbs Day Hill on Maine 9, locally known as "the Airline," crossing the ridges of Washington County. The Day Hill gradient in winter weather sometimes causes tractor-trailers to slide backward while their powered wheels go on spinning forward. At Bangor, the lobsters connect with I-95 and follow it down into New Hampshire and on nearly to Boston, swinging southwest on I-495 and—to save ten minutes—taking I-290 through Worcester. Steve Price is one of the drivers. Dennis Oickle is often paired with him. Steve says they "eat on the fly." He brings food from home, keeps it in the truck's mini-fridge, and heats it in the microwave. Steve—brush-cut hair, trim avuncular beard—is the father of three. He says that Dennis, "being young, eats junk." Stops are so few that Dennis, for the most part, has to bring the junk with him. They both live in Sackville, Nova Scotia. At work, they don't see a lot of each other. While one drives, the other sleeps—four hours on, four off. They hold the Clearwater record for the run—Arichat to Louisville in twenty-seven and a half hours. Most trips take at least twenty-nine hours, some as many as thirty-two. They cross the Hudson at Newburgh, the Delaware at Port Jervis, the Susquehanna on I-80 at Mifflinville, Pennsylvania. At a Bestway truck stop not far from State College, they spend seven hundred dollars and upward for fuel, but they wait to take a shower on the deadhead leg home. Over and under their crates of lobsters in the box are layers of corn ice as much as a foot thick. On the interstates, the dripping water leaves a trail behind the truck. Since the sole decoration on the box is the company's simple blue-and-red logo— "CLEARWATER"—other drivers will now and again call on the CB radio and, typically, tell them, "Hey, you're losing your load." On the interstates of Ohio, the lobsters have to slow down to a crawl—fifty-five m.p.h., a strict state law—to Akron, to Columbus, to Cincinnati, with ammonia levels rising. The truck has a global positioning system. Ross Wheeler, Clearwater's truck manager in Halifax, tracks the journey on his computer, as do Mike Middleton, Tim Wulkopf, David Brockman, and Dave Joy, in Louisville. From time to time, they all e-mail the truck. Clearwater is a collection of mainly young and exuberant people, so informal that their worldwide directory is alphabetized by first names. There are two hundred people in the Lobster Division.

The truck comes into Louisville on I-264, gets off near the airport at the Poplar Level exit, goes south about a mile, and turns onto Produce Road—8:05 P.M. this time, a spring evening, twenty-nine hours and forty minutes from Arichat. Dennis is asleep, unable to defend himself about the junk food. A forklift takes two hours to unload some ten thousand pounds of lobsters—a light load, variously in crates and in Dryland system trays. A "truck map"—the sort of cargo chart that would be familiar to the first mate of a merchant ship—helps blend the arrivals into the reservoir, where strings of crates are suspended on ropes, and more than fifty thousand pounds of lobsters can chill out at two degrees Celsius in brine made with Kentucky branch water and sea salt in bags from Baltimore. The new arrivals soon appear on the "reservoir map," from which orders in the sixteen different grades can be filled. Housed in one unit of a commercial tilt-up, the reservoir is four feet deep and close to ninety feet long. Arriving crates are randomly opened and inspected before they are immersed. En route, the lobsters have lost about three per cent of their weight. Looking for "weaks, deads, and rots," Dave Joy is not for the moment finding any. He peers down into the bottom of the crates for signs of bleeding, which takes experience, since lobster blood is clear. He examines shells for cracks.

Gripping a thorax, he lifts up a lobster, wet and shining. It splays its claws like a baby bear. Now he takes hold of each claw and lifts the lobster by the arms like a human child. Its tail forms the letter C. The odds on this creature ending its travels in a Palm restaurant are extremely high. It is full of life and weighs five pounds. Long before midnight, the truck departs for Canada, loaded with empty crates. In bed in the back of the tractor, Dennis has slept through the whole of the stop in Louisville.

Clearwater's over-all mortality rate was once as high as twelve per cent but is now under five per cent, despite the fact that lobsters characteristically lose their energy fast. To demonstrate, Mike Middleton, Clearwater Louisville's chief of operations, holds one up horizontally. Its tail extends stiffly. Its claws spread out. It seems ready to fly. Within ten seconds, though, the tail has gone down like a bad dog's. If you pick up a lobster and the tail droops from the get-go, the lobster is probably verging on death. Lobsters that are weak and dying are sold to Asian buffets. Dead lobsters are probed with an electrode. If the tails curl up, the lobsters are frozen instantly and sold for stock and bisque. If the tails do not curl up, the carcasses are catfish bait. Middleton says he grows "huge pumpkins" over moldering lobsters. He also takes home an occasional robust giant. After parboiling it, he splits it longitudinally from head to tail and completes the cooking on his outdoor grill.

Middleton, Wulkopf, and Brockman have learned their lobsters in Kentucky. Dave Joy, on the other hand, grew up on St. George's Bay, between Port aux Basques and Corner Brook, in Newfoundland. With Clearwater almost from its inception, in 1976, he bought Newfoundland lobsters for the company for a decade before moving to its headquarters in Nova Scotia. Later, he took two years off to get a degree from Fisher Tech, in Corner Brook. When UPS drew the lobsters to Kentucky, he was drawn, too, and intends never to leave. He is the plant manager, in charge of the rez, as everyone calls it, and supervisor of the packing. Short and compact, in a blue T-shirt and blue warmup pants with white stripes, he picks up a big lobster that is stopping over on its way to Los Angeles. Does the tail come up? How fast does it come up? "It's a quick decision by the packer," Dave says. "He's only got a few seconds to make up his mind." Claws akimbo, tail flat—sold! With subzero gel packs, the lobsters go into standard thirty-pound Styrofoam boxes logoed "CLEAR-WATER," "HARDSHELL FRESH," "VIVANT." Thirteen selects are about all that will fit into one of these boxes—thirteen "pieces," as whole lobsters are called. If the customer wants chix, the box will hold twenty-seven or twenty-eight pieces. Even if they are well chilled by the gel packs, lobsters can be out of water no more than forty-eight hours before mortality steeply rises. After-noons and evenings, the clock starts ticking as they go into the Styrofoam boxes. At 10 P.M., a brown UPS "moose," a step van somewhat larger than the standard package car, backs up to the Clearwater dock. The driver is wearing brown shoes, brown socks, brown shorts, a brown polo shirt, and a brown headband—Susan Badger. On a typical Monday or Thursday evening, UPS will pick up about three thousand pounds of lobsters, but this is a Wednesday and the net load is somewhat shy of six hundred. Badger starts off for the UPS air hub, five minutes away.

She is carrying about two hundred and seventy lobsters tick-eted for a spray of destinations, including the Cranberry Tree Restaurant, in Skagit County, Washington, sixty miles north of Seattle; Bosackis Boat House, on a lake in northern Wisconsin; the Ho-Chunk Casino, in Baraboo, Wisconsin; the Rainbow Casino, in Nekoosa, Wisconsin; Elden's Food Fair, in Alexandria, Minnesota; Jane's Tavern, on the Middle Loup River, in Rockville, Nebraska; a Keg restaurant in Chandler, Arizona; the Useppa Inn & Dock Company, in Bokeelia, Florida; the Ione Hotel, in the Sierran foothills of California; a private home in Put-in-Bay, Ohio, on an island in Lake Erie less than ten miles from Canada; Estiatorio Milos, a Greek restaurant at 125 West Fifty-fifth Street, Manhattan; and Mountainside Lodge, near Old Forge, New York, in the Adirondacks.

Of course, none of those are from that truckload just in from Nova Scotia. The new arrivals are beginning their required rest, but, in Tim Wulkopf's words, "the turnover is two weeks tops and out of here." Most of that truckload is gone in a few days—for example, Next Day Air to Manhattan Beach, California, left at someone's front door at nine-twenty-six in the morning; to the Horseshoe Casino, in Robinsonville, Mississippi (fourteen hours out of the rez); to an e-customer in Pasadena, Texas; to Spinnaker's Restaurant, in St. Joseph, Michigan; to a Palm in Denver; to a Ruth's Chris restaurant in Lafayette, Louisiana; to the A&B Lobster House, in Key West. Wulkopf says, "Between e-commerce and wholesale, I can't think of a state we don't ship to. Montana, Maine, West Virginia, Missouri, New Mexico, North Dakota, South Dakota, Georgia, Hawaii, Alaska. We have customers in Puerto Rico." Of Clearwater's air shipments, about seventy-five per cent go west. But Clearwater's Canadian lobsters are also flown back east from Kentucky to Connecticut and New Jersey. Online, people will order as many as fifty or sixty pieces, but mostly fewer than ten: two to New Castle, Delaware; two to Hackensack, New Jersey; two to Barre, Vermont. The lobsters go by moose to the UPS hub as living passengers e-ticketed on the eleventh-largest airline in the world, arriving at the UPS air terminal to be screened and scanned and sorted and to ride up escalators and on horizontal belts toward heavy aircraft nosed up to gates.

UPS once leased old gas stations, furnished them with sawhorses under four-by-eight plywood sheets, and used the old gas stations as centers for sorting packages. Now they have the Worldport, as they call it—a sorting facility that requires four million square feet of floor space and is under one roof. Its location is more than near the Louisville International Airport; it is between the airport's parallel runways on five hundred and fifty acres that are owned not by the county, state, or city but by UPS. The hub is half a mile south of the passenger terminal, which it dwarfs. If you were to walk all the way around the hub's exterior, along the white walls, you would hike five miles. You would walk under the noses of 727s, 747s, 757s, 767s, DC-8s, MD-11s, A-300s—the fleet of heavies that UPS refers to as "browntails." Basically, the hub is a large rectangle with three long concourses slanting out from one side to dock airplanes. The walls are white because there is no practical way to air-condition so much cavernous space. The hub sorts about a million packages a day, for the most part between 11 P.M. and 4 A.M. Your living lobster, checked in, goes off on a wild uphill and downhill looping circuitous ride and in eight or ten minutes comes out at the right plane. It has travelled at least two miles inside the hub. The building is about seventy-five feet high, and essentially windowless. Its vast interior spaces are supported by forests of columns. It could bring to mind, among other things, the seemingly endless interior colonnades of the Great Mosque of Córdoba, but the Great Mosque of UPS is fifteen times the size of the Great Mosque of Córdoba.

Most packages enter the hub and leave the hub in "cans"—

aluminum containers in quarter-moon and half-moon shapes that fit the cylindroid interiors of the aircraft. The cans look something like domal tents, and in size could serve as back-yard gazebos. A can can hold well over a ton of lobsters, the bulk of the Styrofoam boxes notwithstanding. If a can loaded with ordinary packages weighs as much as two tons, one UPS worker can easily move it. The concourse floors are variously embedded with ball bearings and inverted caster wheels, causing a can to move lightly and a pedestrian to proceed at risk.

If no problem develops along the way, a standard six-sided package going through the hub will be touched twice by human beings: as it is unloaded on entry and as it is loaded into a can after its trip through what the UPS workers universally call "the sort." Some five thousand workers come nightly to the sort, but few of them ever touch a package, which is largely what the hub is about, as it carries automation off the scale of comprehension. After a package comes out of a can and is about to zing around in belts and chutes and into on-ramps and down straightaways as fast as an athlete can run, the first of the two handlers—package under eyeball—applies the live human factor, making a couple of crucial but not irreversible decisions: the package is to be placed on the correct choice among three adjacent belts, and the package is to go off on its ride label-side up. Sortation used to require a more complex application of human thought, but in the development of the UPS air hub the intellectual role of the workers "out in the sort" underwent a process of "de-skilling." "When they made the hub, they de-skilled a lot of positions," a UPS manager explained to me. "Label-side up. That's pretty much the extent of the training for these folks."

Those three initial conveyors are for six-sided packages, for "irregs" (parcels of irregular dimension, like automotive exhaust pipes), and for "smalls" (anything really modest in size but mainly the overnight and two-day-air envelopes with which UPS tries to nip the heels of FedEx). Triaged, the packets and packages ride up the concourse and into the core—the rectangular space with a footprint of twenty-eight acres where a package picks up speed as it moves from one to another set of east-west and north-south loops and is pushed, shoved, stopped, started, carried, routed, rerouted, diverted, guided, and conducted to belts that lead to belts that relate not only to the region, state, county, community, and neighborhood it is going to but also, in some crowded cities, to the street and block. A hundred and twenty-two miles of belts and monorails accomplish this in what is actually a more orderly manner than the rolled chicken wire that—as you gaze up into it—its compression suggests. You see packages in every direction moving on a dozen levels and two principal floors, which are perforated by spaces that allow the belts to climb to all levels and descend ultimately to the level of the airplanes. Over all, this labyrinth, which outthinks the people who employ it, is something like the interior of the computers that run it. Like printed circuitry, seven great loops, each a thousand feet around, are superposed at right angles above other loops. A fly fisherman would admire the proportions of these loops, which are like perfect casts, the two sides close and parallel, the turns at the ends tight. Unending sequences of letters and small packages zip around these loops, while the larger packages follow one another on the belts, each package tailgating the one in front of it but electronically forbidden to touch it. When a collision seems imminent where belts converge, the guilty package stops dead in its tracks and awaits its turn to move on. Collectively, the loops are like the circuits in the motherboards among the interface cards of a central processing unit wherein whole packages seeking specific airplanes are ones and zeroes moving through the chips.

Somewhere around each primary loop is one of three hundred and sixty-four positions where a given parcel will suddenly depart for another loop, where there are three hundred and sixty-four additional positions, at one of which the package will continue its quest to school up with like-minded packages. The first set of loops runs east and west, the second set north and south, and so on. It doesn't take a black-hole mathematician to see that the range of choice is not as wide as the universe but is getting there. If for some reason an exit position is not ready to accommodate an arriving small package, the package remains on the loop to make another circuit and another try. Under the most complex of circumstances, a package could travel several miles inside the hub before it boards a plane.

The core of the hub is not an infinite indoor space, of course. It is only a scant half-mile long, but it seems infinite because if you are in the vastness of the sort you can see only a short distance in any direction, including up. I was never left alone there, but if you were left alone there you would need a compass no less than you would if you were dropped into the forests of Gabon between Makokou and Mékambo. You make your way forward through the dense stands of columns—columns three inches square supporting conveyors, columns sixteen inches square rising to the roof—and you look up through grids and grates and through more grids and grates laced roundabout with six-sided boxes in skeins like fast-moving scarabs. There is also a density of sound—the hum of blowers, conveyors—and you pass illuminated signs, not all of which you find illuminating: "PRIMARY I—WEST INDUCT, AREA C"; "SORT EXCEPTION AREA—I"; "EMPLOYEE-RETENTION COMMITTEE"; "TORNADO

SHELTER AREA." The hub is still waiting for its first tornado. In two decades, the airport has been shut down only twice—by a foot and a half of snow in 1994 and on September 11, 2001. Some belts are color-coded—red belts for smalls, black belts for irregulars, orange belts for six-sided parcels—not that the color especially matters, since the packages know where they are going. The smalls, irregs, and six-sides each go into their own circuits. When a six-sided package reaches the position where it is meant to leave a belt, it is shoved off by chunks of thick black rubber known as "hockey pucks." The pucks at rest line the sides of belts and know in advance the length and weight of a package they are going to shove, so that a sufficient number of pucks slide out to do the shoving. Three hockey pucks slide out to shove a box of lobsters off a belt and down a chute.

UPS carries money in bags in the bellies of planes: Brink's money, Fort Knox gold, coins from casinos. Irregulars in the sort ride around in low-sided flatcars on monorails, roller-coastering from level to level. When an irreg in a cannister like a fire hydrant happened by, I asked what it was. Bull semen was the answer—on its way from Nebraska to Montana via Kentucky.

When the smalls come into the smalls loops, de-skilled workers place each envelope or small package label-side up on a tray that is scarcely eighteen inches long. On the loop, the trays are lined up two abreast, and if you climb a couple of ladders to look down on them from an open-grated observation platform, you see the two rows of tilt trays, as they are called, swiftly circling the long carousel loaded mainly with one-day or two-day letters. Completely surrounding the smalls loop at the bottom of a sloping apron of smooth wood are heavy canvas bags with open mouths. As a tray approaches the bag for which its letter is intended—a bag, say, that will be flying toward Oahu within the hour—the tray tilts to the outside, spilling the envelope onto the wooden slope. The weight of the envelope and speed of the loop and distance to the bag and friction on the wood all having been calculated as if by a Norden bombsight, the envelope slides forward and down, and drops into the bag, missing by a matter of inches the Tallahassee bag on one side and the Green Bay bag on the other. When a bag fills up, a worker closes and replaces it, and if an envelope comes along on its way to that bag it stays on the loop for another circuit. Dan McMackin, of UPS headquarters in Atlanta, once told me that people in the World Trade Center used to send UPS Next Day Air envelopes to people on other floors in the World Trade Center, because the packets would get there sooner than they would in the house mail. UPS is not so automated that it would send an overnight letter to Louisville and back to the sending Zip Code, let alone the same building. Next Day Air does not always require an airplane. A lot of Next Day Air parcels travel by tractor-trailer. UPS would send them by brown submarine if that was the better way to go.

Travis Spalding, whose office is elsewhere in Louisville, was the UPS supervisor who went everywhere with me and was the sesame of UPS security. For all that, he could lose his way in the jungles of the hub just about as readily as I could, and the two of us often had to ask directions. In a couple of million square feet of automation, a human voice giving directions is not easy to find, and we bushwhacked a good deal before coming upon someone like Jeff Savage, a manager of the small sort. After a crystal explanation that preprimaries decide which of three primaries are to follow them, preceding an advance to a Posisorter, which sets up the pucks and diverts packages to belts, he walked with us a considerable distance as if through dense and trackless vegetation, and eventually came to a mezzanine edge where you could see far down and far up through a cavernous vista of the core of the hub. This was the Grand Canyon of UPS. On each of ten or fifteen levels, packages were moving in four compass directions at the rate of one mile in two and a half minutes on a representative sampling of the seventeen thousand high-speed conveyor belts. Pucks were pushing packages to the left, to the right, including lobsters that raced into cylindrical spaces and whirled in semicircles as if they were on an invertigo ride with an "aggressive thrill factor," in the language of amusement parks. In no other place could you absorb in one gaze the vast and laminated space where, in the language of UPS, "automated sortation takes place." Travis Spalding said, "The technology is not new, but nowhere else in the world is it used on this scale, including Memphis."

Over recent years, FedEx, of Memphis, has been chasing UPS in ground transportation of packages with about the same intensity that UPS has displayed in competing with FedEx in overnight deliveries. FedEx is the world's seventh-largest airline. As the rivalry ages, the one comes ever more to resemble the other, like *Time* and *Newsweek*, which often seem to have the same cover, and sometimes do. The root criterion impelling UPS and FedEx appears to be that a healthy business grows, expands, and must go on indefinitely expanding, or it dies. The economist Kenneth Boulding once said, "Anyone who believes that exponential growth can go on forever in a finite world is either a madman or an economist." Nature's model for this paradox is *Homarus americanus*, the American lobster, which, almost indefinitely, expands and molts, expands and molts, growing an ever larger shell until it ends up on a bed of bamboo leaves in Japan.

If you own a Toshiba laptop and something jams, crashes, or

even goes mildly awry, you call 1-800-TOSHIBA and describe your problem. If the answerer can't help you, a brown package car shows up at your door with an empty padded box hollowed out in the shape of your laptop. UPS takes your computer overnight to Louisville, and keeps it there. Two miles south of the runways are six more UPS buildings, white and windowless in a spotless and silent landscaped campus, and covering, on average, more than three hundred thousand square feet. Your laptop goes in there—Building 6. Within a few hours— in a temperature-controlled, humidity-controlled, electrostatic-sensitive area—an electronic-repair technician who is a full-time UPS employee will have the innards of your Toshiba laptop spread all over a table. Computers, laid open, can be devastated by static electricity. There are eighty technicians. You visit them in gowns and slippers. They replace hard drives, main-system boards, liquid-crystal displays. In the process, they remove viruses as if they were whisking lint. In a day or two, your laptop takes a ride through the sort and flies in a browntail back to you.

UPS became interested in this kind of thing a few years ago when the company realized, as was explained to me, that it had "maxed out in the package-delivery trade and now needed to expand." Toshiba evidently could not care less whether customers know or do not know that UPS repairs its laptops. To UPS, Toshiba has also outsourced its buyer remorse. After new computers are returned to retail stores for credit—downloaded with who could guess what—the computers are gathered up by UPS and detailed in Louisville, flushed out and in every sense cleaned. With ninety-day warranties, the computers go back into the sales stream. In Building 6, NPR stands for New Product Return.

In Elizabethtown, Kentucky, half an hour down the interstate, is a seventh secluded warehouse—four hundred thousand square feet—where UPS shelves a variety of products including every last component of Bentley motor cars. Queen Elizabeth arrives at Balmoral in her Bentley. You can go to the Bronx in your Bentley for a hundred and sixty-five thousand dollars, the current cost of a Continental GT. There are more Bentleys in the United States than in England. In Zionsville, Indiana, is a Bentley dealership whose Web site tells you that it has the largest inventory of Bentley parts in North America. People in places like New York and Montana will truck their Bentleys to Zionsville for repairs. When they do, Zionsville relies upon UPS in Elizabethtown for parts. The Bentley factory in England has called Elizabethtown for parts. Carl Norris, three years out of Western Kentucky University, is an operations supervisor there. Leading Travis Spalding and me through the client zones of the vast UPS depot, he walked into a fifteen-thousand-square-foot space where bins and racking systems held everything from nuts, bolts, and gaskets to entire engines ready to fit into cars like bread into toasters. "This is the Bentley account," he said. "These engines are rated at two hundred miles per hour. They'll bust two hundred." Norris introduced us to Michael Mountain, locally known as Mr. Bentley, a well-built African-American who looked as if he also could bust two hundred. Michael Mountain took us through windscreens, wheels, and exhausts—irregs wrapped and ready for the hub— and on to transmissions, which were packed in wooden chests that would not have seemed unusual to Long John Silver. If your Bentley breaks down in the Steptoe Valley of Nevada, you may be there for the night, but a brown vehicle will soon show up with parts. "The GT can have a refrigerator in the boot," Mountain told us. "And this is a pollen filter." Pollen filter? "Yes—so your allergies don't act up while James is driving you around town."

UPS calls this relatively new part of its business UPS Supply

Chain Solutions. Bentley is among the oldest S.C.S. accounts. Another is Rolls-Royce, whose packaged V-22 Osprey engines were also sitting on the Elizabethtown floor. When a start-up shoe company was growing so rapidly that its trucks had nowhere to unload, UPS Supply Chain Solutions became the shoe company's principal warehouse. Not every client is as open about the relationship as are Bentley, Toshiba, and Rolls-Royce. Large areas of all seven warehouse floors are off limits to visitors, reserved for companies who would prefer that their products not turn brown en route. They have nondisclosure contracts. These include not a few of the household names in American commerce. They want you to think it all comes straight from them. Famous cameras from the Orient arrive in Louisville in bulk-shipment crates. UPS has the retail boxes waiting, and fills them with the famous cameras. UPS repairs certain printers. They refurbish certain cell phones.

One afternoon not long ago, I bought a printer through Amazon.com and, being me, clicked the box for free shipping—promised to be at your door within two weeks. The printer actually arrived before ten the next morning. I was puzzled speechless at the time but have since come to know that my e-commerce order caromed from Amazon to UPS, and quite soon the printer was rolling from a UPS warehouse to the hub. When I told this story to Howard Strauss, a digital savant who worked for NASA on the Apollo program before coming to Princeton University, he said, "In my business, people are always saying it's easier to move bits than atoms. Bits move at the speed of light. Atoms move at the speed of a 747, if you're lucky." My transaction travelled both ways, and a good deal faster by binary digit.

The Elizabethtown warehouse owes its existence to the dotcom orogeny, when UPS Air swelled into the e-commerce trade. When the bubble burst, some dot-com clients abruptly vanished—here today, gone forever—and UPS did not even know where to send the leftover goods. One that stayed solid was Jockey.com. In nine thousand boxes in six rows of bins—each row two hundred feet long and organized by something like the Dewey decimal system—UPS keeps Jockey panties and Jockey shorts and Jockey bras and Jockey shirts and Jockey nightgowns and Jockey socks in the warehouse in Elizabethtown. Jockey is in Kenosha, Wisconsin, but this is the nexus of Jockey.com, and when you order your next pair of briefs UPS will find them on a shelf in Kentucky, wrap them, and send them through the sort. Carl Norris said, "A company that is concentrating on marketing and sales doesn't have a lot of time to worry about distribution problems. That's where we come in. We become a partner with the companies. We run these businesses like they're our own."

We moved out of Jockey space and into thirty-seven thousand square feet of veterinary cat and dog food, fuel for the Royal Canin company's "Innovative Veterinary Diets"—to be found only at clinics and never at Wal-Mart. If your cat has a sensitive stomach, use Hi Factor Formula, said instructions on the palleted bags and cans. Eating Royal Canin, your pet will, on average, live a little longer, but you have to buy the product throughout the life of the dog. Or cat. There was venison-and-potato dog food, vegetarian dog food, potato-and-whitefish dog food, and green-peas-and-rabbit formula for the "nutritional management of gastrointestinal disorders" in cats. There were foods for feline urinary syndromes, foods for feline inflammatory bowels. Lending credence to Royal Canin, its allotted space at UPS smelled like a vet's office.

While Jockey came to the hub from Wisconsin and Clearwater from Nova Scotia, Hillerich & Bradsby was already there.

By the front door of 800 West Main Street in Louisville, close to the Ohio River, is a baseball bat that weighs sixty-eight thousand pounds. This is Hillerich & Bradsby's company sign—the ne plus ultra Louisville Slugger—and for Hillerich & Bradsby UPS Air is the premier supply-chain solution. Suppose Derek Jeter runs low on bats and sends an anxious message to Louisville. At 800 West Main, a big ash dowel goes into a machine that was made in Italy and is programmed for Jeter's personal slugger— a thirty-two-ounce, thirty-four-inch P72 with a regular knob, a twenty-nine-thirty-seconds-inch handle, and a two-and-eleven-thirty-seconds-inch barrel. In sixty seconds, starting at one end, a bat emerges from the dowel. It is dipped in lacquer for a Smith finish, which is black. A Smith finish is also sateen, like dancing pumps. Eleven more dowels go through the same procedure, and then a six-sided package is off to the sort and into a plane that is aimed at the New York Yankees, wherever they might be. On the Friday when Fred McGriff, chilling out in Durham, was called up by Tampa Bay, he needed new bats he had ordered, and a package of twelve was sent UPS overnight and delivered in Florida in time for Saturday's game.

About two-thirds of major-league players use Louisville Sluggers. When they need bats badly, they call Charlotte Jones, of the Pro Bat Department. Other employees travel around among the teams, while Jones spends her days taking orders on the phone. Ken Griffey, Jr., calls her Mom, as do a great many major-league players. She routinely asks them if there are adjustments they would like to make in their existing profiles. Would you like to try a flared knob this time? Would you like your bats cupped? A cupped bat has been scooped out at the fat end to lighten the swing. Usually, a player's interest in adjustments is in inverse ratio to his batting average. In considering new dimensions and characteristics, he has more than six thousand choices. The ballplayers call Mom up from everywhere, and they don't always get through. "Bret Boone," she says, "if he's not getting the pop out of his bats, he's likely to pick up his phone at all hours of the night." Her published number is 1-888-444-2287, and her home telephone is unlisted. Players say to her, "I want that special number." They don't get it. Mom is actually a grandmother. Her phone is upstairs and she sleeps downstairs. She likes to quote Yogi Berra, who said, "There can't be anything wrong with me—it has to be the bat." If players pay for their own bats (ash, forty-two dollars; maple, fifty-five), they can sell broken ones to fans and get a fourfold return on their investment. If the ball club pays for the bats, the ball club sells the broken bats. After a century and a quarter, there is something left in baseball of the grubbing, gloveless era. When Ken Griffey, Jr., was nearing his five-hundredth home run, he called Jones often to buy more bats. Jones describes Griffey as "one of the best salesmen for Louisville Slugger," and says that in his profile preferences he is unusually consistent, faithful to his Jose Cardenal model C271C with a double dip of lacquer. The second dip makes the wood harder. Griffey, she says, quoting him, is not easy to reach, either, accepting phone calls in the clubhouse only from his wife, his parents, and "that woman from Louisville Slugger." At Hillerich & Bradsby, a unit is a six-sided package of two, four, six, or twelve bats. A major-league player goes through a hundred bats a year, and two hundred units a day go in brown package cars from West Main Street to the hub. On UPS invoices Hillerich & Bradsby in Louisville spends as much as thirty thousand dollars a week.

If you walk from New Jersey to California, you can replace your socks by Next Day Air, as at least one man has already done.

Aged sixty-nine when he started, he wore bar-coded T-shirts. On his arrival at each successive city, UPS scanned him, ready to call 911. His itinerary grew in the computerized tracking system, which starts ordinarily with a UPS driver's DIAD (die-add), the cumbersome "delivery information acquisition device" that looks like a safe-deposit box in the driver's hand and not only records pickups and deliveries but also initiates tracking labels. On the walker's seventieth birthday, he was still walking. UPS delivered the cake.

A package going through Louisville is scanned as many as six times in the hub alone. When you see a bright-red beam crossing a box, that was an infrared image sensor. The label is read, the weight and the dimensions are registered. The label is digitally photographed. If something is wrong, as is not infrequently the case, the system calls the package an "exception." Labels may be illegibly handwritten. Reused boxes may have two or more labels. Foot Locker boxes are reused so much that somebody's homemade cookies may want to go to three cities. A Zip Code may have a slipped digit or may simply not be there.

In the Telecode Office, a large room at the edge of the core, rows of telecoders bend toward computer monitors and study bad labels in digital imagery. Telecoders have twenty to thirty seconds to rectify the labels in an electronic way, which, usually, they are able to do, tapping at their keyboards. If they fail, nothing jams the loops, because the offending packages are swept away to exceptions. Down in a "sort exception area," a new label comes out of a machine and is stuck on the package by another human hand.

A large percentage of the people at the computers appear to be college students, and that is what they are. While automation has de-skilled the sort from the human point of view, shrinking the population around the belts, it is at the same time burning the midnight oil of college students in order to overcome its blemishes. Automation alone will not do everything for eight million packages a week, and UPS is so needful of reliable part-time employees that it has embraced the field of education as if it were a private university. It recruits students. It pays tuitions. It gives medical benefits and assistance with housing. It pays for books. It gives bonuses for passed courses. It adds fourteen hundred dollars to a baccalaureate degree. UPS is both the founder and the endowment of Metropolitan College, which has classrooms at the hub and also outsources its students to the University of Louisville, Jefferson Community College, and Jefferson Technical College. One semester at a time, the college signs contracts with the students, committing them to attend classes by day and work in the small hours for the UPS Next Day Air operation. Whether this is an academic bonanza or indentured servitude is in the eye of the scholar.

More students go to Metropolitan College than to Haverford. I met many of them at the hub and talked at length with three. Jamie Kjelsen (silent "j"), one of the telecoders, was a striking young woman with long dark hair, bright brown eyes, and mother-of-pearl polish on her nails. She had been a high-school senior in Brandenburg, Kentucky, five years before, when some "Metro reps" came to the school and set up a table. During a lunch break, she signed a card, expressing an interest in Metro that reflected concern for her family ("My parents are middle class and would have a hard time paying for my school"). She had started with UPS as a diverter clerk on a conveyor in the old hub, and when the new hub was finished she went into the Telecode Office ("That's where we sort unsmart packages"). Her nightly routine, she said, was to telecode from eleven-something until about three-thirty, then ride fifteen minutes on a UPS shuttle to her car, then drive home. Asleep by five-thirty, she would get up around noon if she had a class at one. When did she study? "After work, after class, during fifteen-minute breaks at work, and riding in the shuttle. If there's a twenty-six-page report due or an important test coming, I might take the day off." To make ends meet and do so on her own without help from her parents, she had a second job—Fridays and Saturdays at Champs Sports in the mall. Taking the second job had forced her to reduce her number of courses and thereby lengthen her education ("If you go part-time, it takes twice as long to graduate"). After five years in college, she was a junior. Aiming toward a bachelor of science degree in sociology from the University of Louisville, she would finish possibly in three more years—"when I'm twenty-six," she said, in a tone that faded with resignation. Could I have her e-mail address? "Sure—oceanrollie@ hotmail.com."

Amos Hammock was working in the shift, an air-operations term that refers not to hours but to the job of shifting cans. Big, beefy, brush-cut, and tackle-shaped, he was among those who, with one hand, could haul a two-ton can over the casters and ball bearings to a waiting airplane, making sure that the can stopped rolling beside the correct airplane. After a year on an outbound belt, he had risen to the shift, and was now managing the efforts of nineteen others. Around his neck was a blue-and-white woven lanyard that said "PIKEVILLE HIGH SCHOOL." Pikeville, on the Appalachian Plateau, is in eastern Kentucky, nearly two hundred miles from Louisville. Amos heard about Metro College on a radio commercial. He went to Hazard, Kentucky, to meet a Metropolitan College recruiter. He signed for "a hire-on bonus" of twenty-four hundred dollars, and a hundred dollars a month against rent—in addition, of course, to wages ($8.50 an hour). "You get paid," he said to me. "And they pay for your school. People would be about stupid not to take the chance." Now he was on the verge of an associate's degree in applied science from Jefferson Tech and, with diploma in hand, would be hoping for a job as an industrial mechanic.

Metropolitan College guides its students even while they are working in the dead of night. "College mentors are going around in the hub all the time," Amos told me, referring to college officers who are, all in one person, deans, course advisers, directors of studies, financial-aid representatives, counsellors, and confidants. At Oxford, they would be called moral tutors. They can also be fellow students, like Betsy Curtis—an eighteen-year veteran of UPS who had left the sort to raise children but decided to return to it specifically "to take advantage of Metro College." Separated from her husband, she had gone back to the hub and back to college when her third child was old enough for a preschool program. And now she was a Metro College mentor in the small-sort area, arriving for work at 10 P.M., moving from one to another of the hundred and fifty students in her charge, occasionally getting hit by a package that missed a bag, and with firsthand understanding of a job that computerization had made "simpler but more tedious." She said, "The loan is the only thing that relates to staying time—four years for eight thousand dollars." One night a week, she would sit in a break area, backlit by the food and beverage machines, telling students about loan programs, retro reimbursements, and milestone bonuses (thirty hours, six hundred dollars). And she was very much one of them in the sense that in the daytime she was taking classes, too—on the University of Louisville's main campus, past Churchill Downs, a couple of miles toward the river from the hub. "By the end of the week, I'm so tired I can't hardly . . . I don't get very much sleep at all," she said. "But I want to finish without owing a ton of money. I leave the sort between two and two-thirty." Driving south toward home around three—tapping her cheeks, the "windows open for air"—she has nodded momentarily at the wheel.

Only twenty minutes from the hub, Betsy lives in rural, rolling country, where the crops are tobacco, sorghum, alfalfa, and churches. Asleep by three-thirty, she is up at six-forty-five to take her sons to school, and soon she is off to the university and her logic class. For exercise, she walks up to four miles a day on the university track, then goes home to do housework and yardwork and (often) cut grass. She has two pastures and two horses and forty acres with a lot of grass. She "gets along on five hours' sleep" because "there's always something to do with the house, yard, and children through the afternoon and evening before going to work," doing her best, all the while, "not to be grouchy." Friday into Saturday, she has stayed asleep nineteen hours "playing catch-up—sometimes it catches up with me." She sings in her church choir and appears in the Christmas pageant. She goes to her son's basketball games. When her daughter, Jasamine, was on the North Bullitt High School dance team, Betsy would take a pillow and sleep in her car outside the school, asking to be awakened for Jasamine's performance. Jasamine would come out and wake her up. Some of Jasamine's friends from those days now work in the small sort and have come to understand why Betsy was so often sleeping. Of all workers in the hub, many are single parents, seventy per cent are female, and the median age is thirty-four.

Of her husband, Betsy says, "He is going through second puberty." She is blond, with a smiling and trusting face and mother-of-pearl polish on her nails. When I met Betsy, her sons were in the third and tenth grades, and Jasamine, a first-year student at the University of Louisville, had a twenty-month-old daughter named Hailey. Six months earlier, the baby's father had been hit hard by a drunk driver on Mud Lane near the Blue Lick Airport. Twenty-four years old, he was injured internally and underwent a hip replacement. After class, Betsy would stay with him until she went to work; then his mother would take over. With help from her own mother, Betsy also looked after the baby until spring. Now she had ten classes to go to gain her baccalaureate in marketing, and intended to follow that with a master's in secondary education. She hoped to teach high-school business classes in Bullitt County someday. So, to make it all possible, she said, "I'm out in the sort."

In a sequestered end of the core of the hub, an eight-foot chain-link fence, opaqued by blue plastic strips, surrounds an area reserved for United States Customs. If you get up close and peer through a break in the plastic, you see X-ray machines. You see packages with characters on them, packages with Spanish words on them. You see inspectors wearing badges and firearms. You do not see dogs, but they can smell you. As packages stream through the sort, Customs can query out anything it wants to. Tracking the tracking, it studies the software with software.

On one of my first approaches to the hub, through a guarded peripheral gate, a package of Fruit Breezers in my pocket set off a screech from a metal-detecting wand. I had already been asked for my tape recorder, returnable on departure. A terrorist who decides to send himself somewhere by UPS Air might have difficulty getting off the ground, let alone through the hub. Among the many moats and screens set up by the company in recent years is this one: "Dear UPS Air Cargo Customer: Individual pieces that weigh 150 lbs. or more, and which are large enough to contain a human being, must be tendered stretch- or shrink-wrapped and/or banded to be considered ready for carriage." In other words, Harry Houdini could send himself Next Day Air. Others need not apply. A human irregular might make it through the sort, but only mummies qualify.

Not much gets near the browntails, so it was faintly giddy to be cleared one day in a car driven by Travis Spalding and to be far out by a taxiway as an A-300 landed. Brown and white, shaped like a very large guppy, it could have crammed in some three hundred passengers and instead was carrying ten thousand boxes arranged about as tightly. Slowly we followed it into a bay past the high brown fins of other planes, until it docked at B-09, smelling like a camp lantern. About a hundred UPS planes touch down in Louisville on an average evening. During the Christmas season, one lands every ninety seconds. Two of the planes we went by had been previously owned. You could see the filled-in windows where passengers had once looked out. Most were bought new and seamless—especially the 757s and 767s. Two pilots soon descended from the A-300 and got into a van that would take them to their lounge at the hub's Air Service Center. Their deplaning passengers may have been just boxes, but the pilots were dressed to a standard at least as crisp as Delta's or United's: filigreed gold on their brown hats, gold-striped brown epaulets on their white short-sleeved shirts, brown striped ties, brown trousers, shining brown shoes. UPS brown was borrowed long ago from the brown of Pullman railroad cars, and, with Pullman long gone, UPS has trademarked the color. When sculptures of racehorses appeared recently on sidewalks all over Louisville (a semi-permanent civic promotion), UPS erected a brown Pegasus outside the hub— a winged horse with a brown saddlecloth, ridden by a jockey in brown silks. UPS vernacular is all but trademarked as well. A package car is never a truck, because the company wishes to distance itself from the scruffy connotations of the term "truck driver," never mind that UPS drivers are all Teamsters. By corporate fiat, the very initials of the company's logo stand for nothing anymore. Officially, they carry no meaning, unless you happen to know that they once stood for United Parcel Service.

The Air Service Center is an all-night hive, its tight spaces as crowded as a newsroom, full of dispatchers, meteorologists, crew schedulers, crew reschedulers, flight dispatchers, and global trackers. There were contingency people studying storms and choosing alternative routes. Surrounded by a ring of contingency computers was a dull plastic cylinder that closely resembled a dome light from the roof of a police car. Action would erupt if it were to light up red. It lights up red when a UPS airplane anywhere in the world cannot take off for mechanical reasons or cannot function for any reason. After the light goes on, a standby crew gets into a standby airplane and flies off to fill the gap. Every night around the network, UPS has something like thirteen airplanes and thirty-two crew members ready but unassigned. They sit and wait for trouble to arise, like pilots in the Swiss Air Force, whose planes are hidden inside Alps, always ready to emerge, in times of need, through camouflaged doors in the sides of the mountains. The UPS term for this is "hot spares." In Louisville or elsewhere, the light lights up, a siren goes off, and a loudspeaker says, "Activate the hot spare!" Hot-spare crews report to work each evening and go out to the ramp to pre-trip their plane. Then they wait. They arrive at seven and go home at three in the morning. If they are triggered by a call to "replace a mechanical" or "rescue that volume!," they have thirty minutes to get their plane off the ground.

The pilots' lounge at two and three in the morning is a sea of brown-and-gold epaulets, vans idling outside, pilot bags piled high beside the curb where pilots go out to smoke. The talk at the tables is of "seven fours," "seven fives"—747s, 757s—and of approaching "pull times," when blocks are pulled away from wheels and airplanes depart. A faint whiff of hauteur is in the ready room—like the ambience of surgeons in a cafeteria. Essence of pilot is even stronger than essence of UPS—an impression, it should be said, that seems to derive almost wholly from the male pilots.

Worldwide, the airline has about twenty-five hundred pilots. Many come from the military. To be employed by UPS, they need as many hours as they would need to be employed by Delta or United. Not by chance, the percentage of UPS pilots who are women is higher than the industry average. I spoke with Stacey Bie one day as she was waiting for a van. She told me that she had been a military pilot ten years back, and then had started with UPS as a junior second officer. She was now a senior first officer, the rung below captain. An Ohioan educated at the University of Texas, she was aviator trim, and uncommonly attractive, with alert eyes and dark-brown hair. She said matter-of-factly that she would like to be a captain, yes, she would like to do it; after all, that was the goal everyone had at the start. Captain was where the seniority arrow pointed. On the other hand, a new captain among captains draws the less desirable routes and the less desirable hours. As she put it, "Junior captains work all night, and get the worst of nighttime flying." Also, being a captain would reduce her time with her husband and her two children, in Cincinnati. She said goodbye, and went off to fly her 757.

Coal Train

"C" was for coal train, "TS" for power in the Tennessee Valley, and "BT" for Black Thunder Mine. CTSBT was the proper name of the train, in the way that Broadway Limited, Burlington Zephyr, Super Chief, and Florida East Coast Tamiami Champion were once the names of other trains. Five Florida East Coast Tamiami Champions could not have filled a track beside CTSBT, which was seven thousand four hundred and eighty-five feet long, on this January morning in Marysville, Kansas, and was actually running shorter than most coal trains. There were a hundred and thirty-three aluminum gondolas and hoppers and five diesel-electric locomotives—three in the rear, two of them deadhead. Replacing another crew, Paul Fitzpatrick and Scott Davis climbed into the lead unit, after sending me up the ladder before them. We had slept at the Oak Tree Inn, a motel under contract with Union Pacific, in rooms that Paul Fitzpatrick described as "darker than the inside of a football." The rooms had been quiet, too, heavily armored against sound and light so that train crews could sleep during any part of a day. For us, the protection had not much mattered. The company's call from Omaha—as always, ninety minutes before reporting time—had come at 5:05 A.M.

Heading north and northwest, we were soon going up the grade to cross the divide between the Big Blue and Little Blue rivers. Overnight, heavy ground fog had frozen in the trees, had frozen on every weed, wire, and bush, so that—two weeks after Christmas—Kansas appeared to have been sprayed white for Christmas. From horizon to horizon, the raking light of the sun shot forth through the ice. Fields were confectionery with thin snow. Our eyes were fifteen feet above the tracks and more than that above the surrounding country. We got up to forty miles per hour ascending the grade.

The train could go that fast because it was so light. It was empty. The five locomotives and the mile-and-a-half length notwithstanding, the entire rig weighed less than three thousand tons. And now Scott Davis, the engineer, said, "I'm going to air 'em out, Paul."

And Paul Fitzpatrick, the conductor, looked through his track warrants to see what restrictions may have been set up ahead. Then he said, "O.K., buddy, blow the dust out of 'em." Not that there was much coal dust left in those empties as we topped out at sixty going down to the Little Blue.

Winds that a train stirs up are not in the conversation with winds that can stir up a train. "If you're pulling empties, a north wind can take you from fifty miles per hour to eighteen," Scott said. In places like Kansas, Nebraska, and Wyoming, stiff winds have stalled trains. To wreck a train, you don't need a tornado. In Utah, between Salt Lake City and Ogden, winds coming out of the Wasatch canyons and crossing the tracks of the Union Pacific have knocked down empty ballast trains, empty coal trains, and double-stacked-container "intermodal" trains—events known collectively as "blowovers." In the Laramie Range, the Wyoming wind will shoot up a slope and lift a train from below.

"Tailwind, you get a little better speed, a side wind will slow you down," Scott said. From behind the cab windows of a diesel-electric locomotive, wind is difficult to assess. It can be blowing hard and you don't really see it, let alone feel it. "You're making fifty, then you're struggling to make forty-seven. You think, What's the reason? Wind? Or some problem with the train? Your curiosity is wondering why." Passing through towns, Scott looks for flags. He looks for wind socks at airports. But mainly he looks for the sweep of weeds in the ditches, for the legible motions in trees, and, if the weather is dry, for the speed of moving dust. We came to the state line and left Kansas for Nebraska.

Paul said, "Your intelligence goes up ten points when you cross that line. Back there, you go barefoot, screw your cousin, and try to steal something."

Paul and Scott are from North Platte, Nebraska, where Paul was born. Scott was born in Ogallala, fifty miles west. In the language of the railroad, their "turn" is North Platte to Marysville and back. They make the run at least ninety times a year—now and again, but randomly, together. They know every siding, every crossing, every movable-point frog, every rising and descending grade. Train crews don't just go off in all distances and directions, like the pilots of corporate jets. Train crews work locally on memorized track and terrain. To get a coal train from, say, northeast Wyoming to central Georgia, you would need at least eleven different crews. The central figure in such an odyssey is not an engineer, a conductor, a dispatcher, or a trainmaster—

the multiple, replaceable, and redundant human beings—but the coal train itself, which, power and payload, end to end, will be integral all the way from mine to destination, no matter who is in or around it, or whose tracks it is running on.

Paul's thumbnail sketch of Kansans was in a category with his profile of ranchers in Wyoming, another of the six states that frame Nebraska. He described a public hearing at which a Wyoming official outlined a proposed program for the sterilization of coyotes. A rancher lifted his hand, and said, "We don't want to fuck the coyotes, we want to get rid of them."

We heard the screech of wheels slipping on the morning frost. The sand light came on in front of Scott. He depressed a plunger, releasing sand. We saw an eagle where Paul had seen a bobcat in summer. We ate smoked trout, the result of a fishing trip that Paul and Scott had made together. We ate an excellent piquant meat loaf that Scott had brought from home. And we ate reconstructed turkey breast in Subway sandwiches, sheepishly contributed by me. They mentioned approaching landmarks as we entered the blocks in which the landmarks would appear: an Indian burial mound, other humps that had covered ammunition during the Second World War, an immense cottonwood at Mile 188 (a redtail was sitting in it), Rosie's Crossing (an unprotected farm crossing). "She raises hell if you block it."

All through the morning, we met loaded coal trains—on Track 2, coming the other way. Five in the first two hours. Seven miles of coal. In the loaded coal train CNAMR, we had come down the day before from North Platte to Marysville, two hundred and fifty miles. CNAMR was on its way from North Antelope Mine, in the Powder River Basin of Wyoming, to a power plant on the Meramec River, a Mississippi tributary close to St. Louis. In Union Pacific hieroglyphs, the destination always comes last. Our CTSBT would fill up at Black Thunder Mine and emerge as CBTTS.

In the cab of a coal train, imagine the difference if the coal is there behind you. Trains that carry automobiles, mixed-cargo "manifest" trains, and intermodal container trains can weigh as little as four thousand tons. CNAMR weighed nineteen thousand tons. When loaded coal trains lengthen out to a mile and three-quarters, they can weigh as much as twenty-three thousand tons. Nothing heavier rolls on rails. Diesel power on its own could scarcely budge that kind of weight. The diesel engines inside locomotives are there to generate electrical power. Separate electric motors turn each of the six axles. To move the throttle to Notch 1 and start up such a thing is to wait for perceptible motion. Soon after Notch 2, the pressure of acceleration comes into your chair and begins to run up your back. Move the throttle to Notch 3, and you may feel that you are driving the North American Plate.

Paul said, "It's a touch."

Scott said, "You feel the train in the seat of your pants."

After Notch 4, even your underwear can feel the train extend. By Notch 5, you are beginning to develop an interest in whatever might be happening a couple of miles ahead. Notch 8 and you are flat out—minding the loaded speed limit, fifty miles an hour—and thinking ahead at least one county. Below Notch 1 are two neutral stages—called Set Up and Idle—and below them are the eight notches of the dynamic brakes. Across the dynamics, you can feel the coal pressing on your back, feel the train condense. There could be an off-the-wall analogy to an eighteen-speed bicycle but it does not immediately come to mind. Beside the track from time to time, you see a small post with a black X on it—seemingly no larger than a playing card. It signifies your proximity to a grade crossing—any kind of grade crossing. A farm crossing with no signs. A signed crossing from the era of Stop Look & Listen. A crossing armed with blinking lights. A crossing armed with blinking lights and automatic gates. A whistle-guard crossing that plays a recording that sounds like a train. In the two hundred and fifty miles of the North Platte–Marysville turn, there are a hundred and forty-one Xs beside the track, a hundred and forty-one grade crossings. If you are driving a train past them, at each X you depress on the console before you a metal mushroom that would not be out of place in a pinball machine. As it sinks into the console under the butt of your hand, the locomotive produces its classic sound. Or, as the clarinettist Skip Livingston e-mailed the tubist Tom Spain, "I've been listening carefully. The trains differ—different locomotives have different pitches to their horns. But I did hear one while I was moving snow on Sunday morning, and I was able to get to the piano before I lost the notes. They were A-sharp, E, and F-sharp below middle C, which made it sound like an F-sharp-7 chord (minus the C-sharp). The instruments that would come closest to the sound would probably be trombones."

Passing an X, you first play one long chord on the mushroom. Then you repeat it. Then you tap a short toot. Then, if you are virtuoso, you play a final long chord that begins to fade exactly when you nose over the crossing. With so much to do, your hands are almost always touching something on the console. But if you let fifteen seconds go by while you do nothing at all, the alerter will let out a full-scale pentatonic scream. The alerter is the modern version of the "dead man's pedal." The old engineers had to keep down that pedal or their trains would screech to a halt. Now the alerter screeches, and goes on screeching like a smoke detector, until you come to and force it to shut up. The alerter has its own mushroom.

Paul sat on the left—conducting. He had his own speedometer, his own mushroom for the horn. He had his thick sheaf of papers full of orders and warrants. He wore a beige baseball cap with red lettering that said "CORNHUSKERS." Lanky and limber, spectacled and scholarly, he was fifty-seven, and under the cap he hadn't much hair. Scott, far right, looked down into computer screens and up at cab signals, which reproduce inside the locomotive the signals outside, along the track, and are more than helpful in mist and fog. He was fifty-four—and, as it happened, five feet four—and under his red University of Nebraska ball cap was a receding brush cut. Their two seats were like upholstered thrones, as was a third, between and behind them. They had refrigeration, bottled water, and—a few steps forward and down toward the front door—a hand-cranked toilet of the type that is found on private vessels. No toilet paper in the toilet. No sink. No mirror. This was not the yacht Britannia. Toilet paper is in individual crew kits supplied at terminals by the company.

The space that contained us was as warm as an office. For Scott and Paul, it hadn't always been so. In older locomotives on days like these—fifteen degrees below freezing—Paul had soaked paper towels in water and lined the doorjamb with them so they would stiffen up and prevent the gelid atmosphere from taking over the cab. Paul and Scott had had much to do with the conditions of the workplace, and the pay, the hours, the rotations of the pool. In this district, Paul was the chairman of the United Transportation Union and, until recently, Scott had been the chairman of the Brotherhood of Locomotive Engineers and

Trainmen. Crews are paid by the trip. After you finish a trip and "tie up" on a computer, your place in the rotation starts at the bottom and rises through the pool, the collective term for turns in the district. The smaller the pool, the readier the work, clearly—but perhaps so ready that you are not adequately rested before your next company call. So there is paradox in the pool, augmenting the heavy tensions between labor and management that date from the nineteenth century. Scott's brotherhood of engineers is the oldest union in the country. "Management's strategy is divide and conquer," Paul remarked, and changed the subject to plan their next fishing trip. Scott has a twenty-foot Crestliner 202 Tournament, with two live wells, a 175-horse Evinrude, a 15-horse Evinrude kicker, and an electric motor as well. In Kansas City two years back, Paul bought Scott a T-shirt that said "UNION FISH STRIKE MORE."

Scott took a dip of Levi Garrett.

Paul said, "I've only got one bad habit, and that's working on the U.P."

Paul's grandfathers were engineers. One went west from North Platte. The other went east from North Platte. Paul's father was a conductor. After two years in college, Paul "hired out on the railroad," but was soon drafted and sent to Vietnam. Later, he was a switchman, then a yardmaster, and then "came out on the road as a brakeman," and was promoted to conductor in 1976. Scott Davis's great-grandfather was a fireman who "got hurt and became a physician." Scott's father was a building contractor who moved where work required. As a result, Scott went to three high schools—in Ogallala, Stapleton, and Hyannis.

Paul: "He was voted the most popular sophomore three years in a row."

Scott joined the Union Pacific when he was twenty-three. He dug ditches on a signal gang, climbed poles, and "became a fireman just when the coal thing was starting." As an engineer, he took his first train by himself to Scottsbluff, on Thanksgiving, 1976. He "waited all day for Burlington Northern to bring coal." For Thanksgiving dinner, he ate day-old rolls.

The coal thing would change their lives—their workplace, their leisure time, their relative prosperity. From mines near the center of America, the coal thing would revolutionize American railroads, slow the spread of creeping desuetude, reverse—to a large extent—their antiquation. Before the end of the twentieth century, it would all but jam solid the busiest trackage. It was the direct economic result of the Clean Air Act of 1970. The immense coal reserves of northeastern Wyoming had been no secret to anybody, of course, least of all to geologists. While a good coal seam in Pennsylvania might be seven feet thick, drill cores and seismology had long shown coal beds a hundred feet thick in the Fort Union formation of Wyoming. There was a small mine from the era of steam locomotives, but on a larger scale no one was interested in this vast domain of coal, because there was comparatively little heat in it. In British thermal units, it was thirty per cent poorer than Appalachian bituminous coal. So the open range above the Powder River coal was not further opened. Ranchland ran to the horizon in an absence of artificial light. That part of Wyoming—in its vegetation, wildlife, and vacant beauty—had been well characterized in 1960 by the establishment there of a national grassland.

Beyond the detriments of Powder River Basin coal was the

signal fact that it was as much as five times lower in sulfur than Appalachian coal. With the Clean Air Act, power plants were required to scrub sulfur out or burn low-sulfur coal. The five hundred power plants that use coal to light, heat, cool, and compute fifty-two per cent of just about everything in the United States were suddenly swivelling their attention to Powder River coal. A combination of companies built the Orin Line—the longest new rail line in the United States since the nineteen-thirties. At various sites along the Orin Line, large machines removed a hundred feet of overburden to begin an invasion of the planet unprecedented in scale. Belle Ayr, Black Thunder, North Antelope, Jacobs Ranch—in fewer than twenty years, mines of the Powder River Basin were the largest coal mines in the history of the world.

Coal trains go into the Powder River Basin like tent caterpillars up a tree. The Orin Line is not much more than a hundred miles long, but sixty-five loaded coal trains—collectively, a hundred miles of rolling coal—come down it on an average day. Sixty-five empties go into the mines, and sixty-five loads emerge. They go to Texas, Arkansas, Louisiana, Mississippi, Alabama, and Georgia; they go to Michigan, Wisconsin, Minnesota, and everywhere between. They are unit trains—each a so-called set, each on its way (with few exceptions) to one specific power plant.

CTSBT, having come up through Alexandria, Belvidere, Carleton, Davenport, Edgar, Fairfield, Glenvil, and Hastings—alphabetical Nebraskan railroad towns—was now descending among the farms of Hayland Hill, nearing the Platte River. Paul said, "In Nebraska, they bury a farmer only three feet under."

I said, "O.K., why?"

With an air of stating the obvious, Paul said, "So he can still get a hand out."

Scott said, "A wealthy farmer has two mailboxes."

Beyond the broad and braided Platte was Gibbon Junction, where the two-track line from Marysville met the U.P.'s Triple-Track Main. Like the on-ramp of a freeway, the lesser tracks went through a long curve to make an acute angle with the main. Reading signals, Scott had gone down from notch to notch through the dynamics, and was now drifting, as he put it—creeping slowly around the curve until his nose was in the angle, where he stopped. Parked there was a Dodge Grand Caravan—Texas S53ZNT—with a man in it who was taking pictures. The Triple-Track Main—Gibbon Junction through North Platte to O'Fallons, Nebraska—is the most heavily used freight line in the world. Gibbon Junction joins southern traffic to central traffic running east and west. Since the blending of tracks there occurs in fewer than six acres, it is the sort of place where espionage leading to sabotage could be particularly effective. This apparently trespassing man, on a bitter-cold January morning, had left a grade crossing, driven on ballast beside the tracks, and squeezed his Grand Caravan into the narrowest part of the junction V, where his lens was on us. While we sat and waited for an eastbound coal train to go by on its way to Council Bluffs, the van backed across the double tracks and into virgin snow, where the camera returned to action.

Since September 11, 2001, scenes like that have made certain people extremely nervous, but not Paul or Scott. "These train buffs, they'll do anything," Paul said. "I've had them driving down the highway taking pictures of the train." Throwbacks to the nineteenth century, train watchers, known in England as train spotters, are people who go on planned outings to look at trains. They are sometimes described as a dying breed, but the Reaper evidently is not impatient. In the United States currently, there are well over a hundred thousand train watchers, a national subculture whose antique passion is accompanied by a knowledge of railroading that often has greater breadth and depth than the sophistication of most people who work for railroads. Where tracks are, they are; but they tend to cluster. At Tower 55, in Fort Worth, where the Union Pacific crosses the Burlington Northern Santa Fe, a guy was seen making notes. In no time, the F.B.I. showed up and confiscated his notebook. Never mind that he was only a train watcher taking time off from his job as a police dispatcher.

A Wyoming-coal train is not a common sight in New England. Run one into New Hampshire for a test burn at Bow, on the Merrimack River, and word of its coming will quickly spread. Think of it. Three B.N.S.F. diesel-electrics in distributed power coming through the mending wall. A mile and a half of Powder River coal. Train watchers will meet it in western New York and follow it all the way in like bait fish escorting a whale. My cousin John, in Siskiyou County, California, is a train watcher. He says he's "going training" and he disappears. When he gets out there, he knows what he is looking at.

Some years ago, I was at a kitchen party in the home of Willy Bemis, in Amherst, Massachusetts. The room was full of biologists, full of shoptalk, beer, wine, the shouts of children, the contributions of a barking dog. Willy is a world-renowned anatomist of living and fossil fishes, and these were his graduate students and colleagues at the University of Massachusetts, chatting fish, while off in a corner, where a source of incidental music might have been, was a TV monitor with a video in it showing nothing but slowly moving trains—whole trains, coal trains, intermodal, manifest, autorack American trains. When seven thousand feet of train had lumbered across the screen, the screen was entered by another train. I thought I was looking at a screen saver, but it was a quantum less lively. If Andy Warhol had rotated the Empire State Building ninety degrees, he could have approached the mesmerism of those endless trains. Willy, who has since taken up a distinguished professorship at Cornell, knows almost as much about trains as he does about fish.

The Andy Warhol of those trains in Willy's kitchen was Dick Eisfeller, of Greenland, New Hampshire, a train watcher who long ago turned pro and has made nearly two hundred videos, many of them longer than Hollywood feature films. Beside selected tracks, he films, without sleep, every train that moves past him for twenty-four consecutive hours. Completing his editing at home, he dims the rumbling sound track from time to time and tells you in a soft monotone what is going by, what its destination is, and how it relates to the national plexus of rail freight. He is not without competition, but while others show two locomotives, four boxcars, and six giddy gorges, Eisfeller is uninterested in scenery, and he alone consistently shows whole trains on one stretch of track across twenty-four hours and comments on every train. "Others sell thousands, I sell hundreds" is the way in which he summarizes his market niche. Willy Bemis says that among the train videomakers Dick Eisfeller is "probably the most knowledgeable, the most interested in railroad operations. He has an almost scientific approach, a mission to document things. He's interested in the business of the railroad. He knows where a train is coming from and where it is going, and whether it is daily or weekly, and whether it is on time. He knows what is in the cars. He knows the context of other trains on the same tracks."

In me, there was nothing of the train watcher, train spotter, train buff, or rail fan until there came a day when Willy Bemis (about to move, and cleaning out his house) sent me his collection of Eisfeller films. In twenty-one hours of stupefied absorption, I watched whole trains in the "Kansas funnel," whole trains on the Orin Line, whole trains in Nebraska on the Triple-Track Main. A very large percentage were coal trains, half a light-year of coal trains, bright aluminum coal trains, the coal convex in each car, like rounded tablespoons of black sugar. The title of one of Eisfeller's films was "24 Hours at Gibbon Junction."

Eisfeller is a chemist with patents on coatings that make your car look metallic where it is actually plastic. "The key ingredient is indium. If you evaporate it in a vacuum on a plastic surface, it forms little islands, so if you coat it with clear plastic it doesn't corrode." He worked for Textron until 1994, when he was downsized for being, in his word, outspoken. He had sold his first video a year earlier, and decided to go into the field full time. He had been a rail fan since childhood. In Chadwick, Illinois, Burlington Zephyrs went through his grandparents' farm. In his twenties, he "started chasing trains" and "collecting paper"—timetables, schedules, dispatcher sheets, consists. (Accented on the first syllable, "consists" is a railroad term for what a train is carrying.) Eisfeller goes into railroad yards, opens Dumpsters, and rummages through them for consists. He knows people in railroad companies who give him lineups—lists of trains expected at a given point within a specified number of hours. In his laptop, he has a topographic atlas. He has grade profiles. He has a scanner, on which he listens to engineers and conductors talking to dispatchers. He generally knows when he has time to move from one site to another. When he is beside a track and a train is coming, he often knows what train it is.

When he happened to be filming in Pennsylvania not long ago, I went out near Hershey to watch. Across twenty-four hours, he set up his tripod at ten places in seven communities, mainly in Myerstown, where, with a lumberyard's permission, he spent the night. He had awakened at 4 A.M. to drive down from New Hampshire, and now, in a typical working moment long after dark, Norfolk Southern No. 500 was approaching eastbound with "a hundred and fifteen gons of coal." A hundred yards east of Eisfeller, a horse-drawn Amish buggy clattered across the tracks on Railroad Street just before the gates went down. Like a fisherman starting his outboard motor, Eisfeller yanked a cord, turning on his generator. Suddenly, three thousand watts of halogen light sent a ball of day across the tracks. Eisfeller ran to his digital camcorder with dual mikes and nineteen-power zoom.

Consider the engineer, approaching this unexpected nova. Already, he was pushing on his horn, the grade crossing fewer than twenty seconds away. And now his locomotive was about to go up in a cloud of halogen light. Eisfeller shined a flashlight on the camcorder by way of explanation. "Let's face it," he said. "I'm doing a weird thing out here."

He never acquaints railroads with his plans or asks them for permission to do what he does, preferring not to defy their denials. He sometimes calls on local police and lets them know what he is up to. He shoots from public parking lots and state and municipal parks, as well as from private land. Engineers now and again report him to their dispatchers. On western trips, he has been confronted four times by dicks of Union Pacific.

The air was shivering cold, but he was wearing a cotton shirt and an open windbreaker, with no apparent interest in its function. Bald, bluejeaned, wearing white running shoes, he had a round face, an amiable mustache, a significant corporation. He drives everywhere, even to Wyoming. With his theatrical lights, his camcorder, and that hundred-and-thirty-pound generator, he is not rich in alternatives. His 1999 Windstar had a hundred and sixty thousand miles on it, a malfunctioning heater, and failed interior lighting. Camcording, he has stayed awake as long as three days and two nights. On interstates between filmings, he goes into rest stops and sleeps in the Windstar sitting up. "I'd be a good case study in sleep deprivation," he told me. "I've had people knock on my car thinking I'm dead. One of the times when I was most dead was on the U.P. Triple-Track. I try not to push myself."

Gibbon was another kind of junction for me. Arriving there, CTSBT crossed the Platte River just about where—years earlier—I had collected a bagful of stream-rounded pebbles whose bedrock sources turned out to be in the Rocky Mountains, as much as five hundred miles from Gibbon. The pebbles set me off on a project in forensic geology, which led to Ronald Rawalt, a mineralogist and paleontologist who was also a special agent with the F.B.I. He met with me in Omaha and described some of the cases in which his geological sense of what came from where had led him to the solution of heinous crimes, including the murder of a policeman in Pennsylvania and the murder of a D.E.A. agent in Mexico. Rawalt's home was, as it still is, in North Platte—the consummate railroad town, site of the largest railroad yard in the world—and Rawalt, unsurprisingly, knows almost as much about trains as he does about rocks. Now, long after I collected the pebbles, my base in Nebraska was in Rawalt's home.

I had tried for some time to find a way to travel in coal trains, but the quest had not gone well. After what seemed like fifty-five dozen unreturned messages, I made the breakthrough discovery that Burlington Northern Santa Fe and Union Pacific were not in competition with New Jersey Transit. I thought of Ron Rawalt, in North Platte, and sent him a note about the situation, saying, in effect, that I was in a kind of maze, walking back and forth, and getting no help from the hedge leaves. A few days later, Rawalt and I were in downtown North Platte having breakfast with Scott Davis, Paul Fitzpatrick, and John Hasenauer, the local secretary-treasurer of the United Transportation Union.

Rawalt's F.B.I. work rarely involves rail traffic, but instances have come up when he has had to stop trains. Near Scottsbluff once, he came upon a tractor-trailer stalled on a grade crossing with two coal trains approaching from opposite directions. The truck driver was desperately trying to pry open a signal box. Rawalt called Union Pacific's Harriman Dispatching Center, in Omaha, and Harriman stopped both trains. If this had occurred where cell phones were nonfunctional, Rawalt might have effected certain connections on his own that would "red-board the whole system," shutting down the Union Pacific for tens if not hundreds of miles. But a simpler way to stop a train, he said, is "to strap a torpedo to the ball of a rail." A torpedo is an explosive briquette.

Acting on a tipoff one morning, he drove down Route 30, the highway beside the Triple-Track Main, looking over a manifest train for signs of a "top-ten fugitive" who was a serial murderer known to ride freights. The engine number was the one he had been given. He saw a figure in a boxcar. He called the Harriman Dispatching Center and was advised that if he wanted the train to pull up right beside him the train would heed "emergency vehicle instructions." To wit: "Place a fireball on top of the car and stick your thumb down outside the window."

A fireball is a red dome light. Rawalt had one and he turned it on. He stuck his hand out the window, thumb down. The train sounded suddenly like an orchestra warming up. Rawalt took the fugitive off the train. "He was armed with a knife, not a gun. He was not the fugitive murderer. But we ran him, and he was wanted out of Texas. There was a felony warrant for his arrest."

Felons are few among the transients on rolling trains, who travel from freight yard to freight yard, lily pad to lily pad. "They get off as the train slows down. Then they move to the other end of the yard. These guys carry schedules. There are more of them than there were in the nineteen-thirties."

Because of transients, freight cars that carry automobiles have become even more shuttered than freight cars that carry cattle and hogs. Railroads transfer two-thirds of new automobiles, and today's autorack cars appear to be made of steel venetian blinds. Somehow hoboes squeeze into them nonetheless. They like to ride the trains inside the automobiles. Each one has a couple of gallons of gas in it, because automobiles are driven on and off trains under their own power. Transients, settling in for a trip, turn on the automobiles' air conditioners in summer, heaters in winter. When an automobile runs out of gas, the transient moves to another. If the railroad responds by removing the keys and shipping them in tamper-proof bundles, the hoboes respond by defecating and urinating in the automobiles, breaking windshields, and knifing upholstery. In winter, hoboes seeking warmth on coal trains bury themselves in coal.

Railroad police are "commissioned," and they have arrest powers. When they are not busting autorack squatters, they are sometimes in pursuit of the people they describe as graffiti vandals, and whom others regard as Renaissance artists. The billowing cumulus of graffiti color reaches only partway up the sides of boxcars, hoppers, and gondolas, because that is as far as the artists effectively can reach. They are careful to mask out or otherwise avoid the reporting marks on the sides of freight cars (letters and numbers of identification), because they know that the reporting marks will quickly be restencilled if graffiti paint obscures them, and the art will not survive. They are proud of what they do. They stand admiring it as they are arrested. While I was in a rail-yard office one day, a company bulletin scrolled across a screen announcing that railroad police in Sacramento had at last arrested a graffiti vandal named Crooks.

On CNAMR and CTSBT, when we went through speed-restricted zones—bumping and rocking if there were problems in the track—we came eventually to a green metal flag. It marked the end of the zone but not of the speed restriction. The engineer had reached the green flag, but his last car had a mile and a half to go. Scott set a counter at seventy-five hundred, to count down in feet. When it reached zero, it went off like a microwave. The counter was once a human being riding in a caboose. The human being had a walkie-talkie, and he would say to the engineer, "We've got the green flag!" Those were his last words. While graffiti bloom and hoboes persevere, the caboose has been replaced on the end of the train by a small red box full of wires and chips.

Working cabooses do exist. If you set up a tent at Gibbon Junction and spend the summer, you might see one. Typically, they had a conductor, an assistant conductor, and several brakemen in them—the conductors handling paper waybills, the brakemen now and again walking beside the train to look for hot bearings or equipment that was dragging. The older cabooses were made of wood and had coal-burning stoves, which were wonderfully warm. Advanced technology came in the form of oil stoves, which were not wonderfully warm, and crews threw baggies full of diesel fuel into the burning oil, hastening the demise of the caboose. A pair of trains would give each other "roll bys"—crewmen in each caboose inspecting the other train. If a train had a problem, it stopped. Crewmen walked forward and fixed the problem. The engineer then pulled the caboose up to the crewmen. Now, in addition to Scott, the entire crew is Paul. If there is trouble, Paul walks back to it, and then back from it, as much as three miles, maybe in deep snow, while Scott waits, while stockholders wait, while the Federal Reserve waits, and Sisyphus is working on the railroad. Yet the electronic detectors that have replaced the crews in the cabooses see, hear, and feel more than the crews could. Ten, fifteen miles apart, the detectors are everywhere along the tracks. They enter the cabs of locomotives as cavernous virtual voices reporting what they find, reporting what they do not find, and offering reassurance. They look and listen for dragging equipment, out-of-round wheels, hot journal bearings, excessively high or shifting loads. The presence of flat spots will show up quickly on the wheel-impact load detector. An electronic-evaluation car with lasers and ultrasonics can inspect the track itself at fifty miles per hour. Collectively, railroads promote these features as "health monitoring."

William C. Vantuono, the editor of *Railway Age*, says that a unit train, such as a coal train, with no local switching work, could run without a conductor. So long, Paul. Scott becomes a crew of one, and even one-man crews may soon be a fading custom. In some rail yards, you find working locomotives with no one in them. Ron Rawalt casually predicts that "trains will before long be going coast to coast under remote control with no crewmen at all on board." Needless to say, these foreshadowings have not gone unnoticed by the United Transportation Union and the Brotherhood of Locomotive Engineers. Just step into a yard office among the gathered engineers and conductors and you will soon hear something like this: "Kids barely know how to throw a switch and pull a pin and make a train up, and they're running these R.C.L.s. We lost fifty engineers' jobs when they went to remote control. A guy with two years' experience is running remote control, replacing an engineer with twenty years' experience." Scott Davis, reviewing the subject, did not show much alarm. He said, "The railroad wants to go on one-man-only. They're not going to get that."

Meanwhile, the multiplication of coal trains and the accompanying rise of the intermodal stack train have brought congestion to the rail network and slowed down traffic in ways that robots might to some extent relieve. By federal law, train crews work a maximum of twelve hours. If their time runs out, they are "dead on the law," and they must absolutely stop the train and get off, the difference notwithstanding if they are out in the middle of the Great Salt Lake Desert or two miles from home. While more and more trains compete for track space, the crews' hours are a constant in equations full of variables. When time runs out and the result is a "dead train," trains behind it are affected, and trains behind them, until—as Dick Eisfeller once found—"U.P. eastbounds trying to get into Chicago are backed up halfway across Iowa." He once referred to Nebraska as "the land of the standing coal train," and, employing a phrase of wide use in the industry, said of Union Pacific, "U.P. stands for Unlimited Parking. Parked trains are almost anywhere, waiting for new crews. The situation can go on for days or weeks." When train crews die, they are usually near a highway, and vans go out to get them. In Nebraska, they are picked up by armadillos. Armadillo Express is the name of an independent service company that has achieved prosperity picking crews off stranded trains. Nationwide, there are a dozen such companies. Not infrequently, they carry fresh crews as little as a mile from railroad yards to bring in dead trains. Those fresh crews are called dogcatchers.

The most hyperactive dogcatchers are in North Platte, because North Platte's Bailey Yard, at nearly three thousand acres, is not only the largest railroad yard in the world but also among the most crowded. Trains waiting for admission to Bailey die where they wait. When Paul and Scott pulled CTSBT into North Platte to tie up from their turn, eighteen miles of coal trains (twelve units) were already inside the yard, and half a dozen eastbounds were lined up waiting to come in. Crewless locomotives were rearranging autorack trains and varied blocks of manifest trains. The wye was busy, and the balloon track— places where cars and locomotives are turned around. Two tank cars, poised on top of the East Hump, in silhouette looked like carpenter ants. Coyotes live in Bailey Yard. Wild geese overwinter at its water-table lakes. When you get down from your train, a van picks you up and drives you, say, two miles to the yard office, where your own car is waiting, sometimes covered with snow. Annually, about three hundred million gross tons of freight pass through Bailey Yard, where public grade crossings were eliminated years ago. Five streets of North Platte are on elevated causeways over the yard. Train watchers from many parts of the world make pilgrimages to the elevated causeways. If their skin is dark, they were obviously sent by Al Qaeda. Informants call the F.B.I.

The main purpose of the yard is to classify freight cars in the way that UPS and FedEx sort packages in Louisville and Memphis. The robot locomotives shove manifest trains up small parabolic hills—the East Hump, the West Hump—where single cars or small groups of cars are set free at the summits to roll downhill into groupings of parallel tracks, which are called bowls but in plan view resemble the strings of harps. The West Bowl has fifty tracks, the East Bowl sixty-four. Each gravity-powered "cut" of cars rolls into the bowl below and stops on a track where other cars with a similar destination are assembling as a new train. This may not represent a frontier of technology, but it is a distinct advance over "flat switching," the traditional technique of pulling the pin from a coupling, then shoving the whole train until it reaches a certain speed, then slamming on the brakes so that whatever has been uncoupled leaps free, rolls on overland, and is switched onto a designated track.

The yardmasters of Bailey work in glassy polygonal structures that look like airport control towers. Scott Davis took me into the West Hump Tower, where his yardmaster brother, Marty, was nearing the end of a shift. On the top deck, Marty sat alone in a very spacious room with a panoptic view, while two others worked in a similar space one flight down. Outside on the hump, a pinner was pulling pins and simultaneously operating, from an electronic device slung on his chest, the robot locomotive that was pushing trains up the hump. Inside the tower, one of the men on the lower floor sat before a computer screen and talked to the pinner through outdoor loudspeakers. On his screen, he could read the destinies of the cars on the hump, and he was telling the pinner where to pull pins to make cuts. As cars rolled off downhill, the computer was throwing switches all over the West Bowl, but if the computer were to overlook something it could be upstaged manually by the other man on the lower floor, who sat before a desklike surface covered with levers that operate switches. Marty Davis, yardmaster, alone on the floor above, seemed watchful, like a coach observing the calls of his offensive and defensive coördinators. At the shift change, Marty was replaced by Gib Larsen, who closely resembled King Lear. His hair was a sort of robe—a floor-length white robe. As we left the tower, Scott said, "He's into mountainman stuff. He has buckskin pants, buckskin shirts. He goes to Rendezvous days in Ogallala, where he throws axes."

In the crew room in the yard office, computers were lined up as if it were a public library. Arriving for work, engineers and conductors log in for orders there; and after their turns they tie up on the computers before they go home. When Paul and Scott had picked up their printouts for CNAMR, the crew room was jammed with dogcatchers. Trains were dying left and right, in part as a result of the freezing weather. Mary Hanna and Carol Townsend were not there. They and two hundred and fifty men were the District 2 engineers. The district's conductors were all men. There were not a few speckled beards, and mustaches large enough to resemble the lower halves of crossing signs. Most of the crewmen were clean-shaven guys in ball caps. Everyone wore hard-toed six-inch boots. While the crew room was actually a management-driven processing pen, it had the hubbub of a union hall.

As Scott's and Paul's time ticked, we waited three hours before we were driven to CNAMR, which was parked in a fuelling pit. What an ambitious word—"pit"—for a place to put something seventy-five hundred feet long. There were loaded coal trains on either side of CNAMR. We climbed into the lead locomotive, and waited for the completion of air tests, fuelling, mechanical inspection. A hundred yards ahead were a blue flag and a device on the track that would derail the train if it were to move forward while the flag was present and authorization was not.

Finally, a radioed voice came into the cab: "Five-eight-six-four east to the east run. Through yardmaster. Over."

Scott said, "Five-eight-six-four east out."

He also said, "We got a lunar, Paul," referring to a signal that at last had something positive to suggest. The releasing of the air brakes began at the two ends, and moved toward the middle. The train's very long integral air tube was like the air sac of a rope fish. At 12:54 P.M., we were actually moving—five miles per hour—and Scott set the counter, saying, "So I'll know I'm off that pit and can get up to yard speed." He was up to twelve when a yellow light put him down. He set the dynamic brakes. Bumpily, the hoppers compressed. We stopped.

An hour later, we had not moved an additional inch. Beside us was a Z train—an intermodal meant for fast travel, but its status for the moment was no higher than it would have been had its name begun with C. Eventually, the towering double-stacked boxes stirred, and Paul said, "This shooter's starting to pull." In time, we followed the shooter, slowly, through the east end of the yard. Over a fence to our left was Central Nebraska Packing, where horses, until recently, were prepared for human consumption, and are now processed for zoos. Over a fence on our right, some healthy-looking palominos were grazing through snow, enchanted surely that a coal train lay between them and the house across the way. So far, it had not done us a lot of good to be drawn by thirteen thousand horses. An hour and a half after we began to move out of the fuel pit, we were still in Bailey

Yard. But now we got a flashing green. We swung right over a movable-point frog and onto the Triple-Track Main. Scott said, "Fourteen-twenty. We're out!"

Over the hundred and eight miles between Bailey Yard and Gibbon Junction, a couple of hundred miles of freight trains are in motion every day. While the advent of the Powder River coal trains has doubled the volume, it has more or less quadrupled the viscosity. The hot intermodals, the high-priority perishable services—the shooters—are not what they used to be. Commonly, they average eighteen miles an hour on the Triple-Track Main.

We met coal trains, Q trains ("westbound hot shots"), coal trains, autotrains, rock trains, grain trains, coal trains, Z trains, manifest trains. A sixty-six-hundred-foot stack train coming almost straight at you seems like a city about to collapse. At least a third of the trains were empty, not only the westbound coal trains returning to the Powder River Basin but autotrains, rock trains, grain trains, and ballast trains—all going back to somewhere for more. We went by twenty miles of motionless trains, waiting to get into North Platte, queued up on a plain so open and vast that we went over farm grade crossings that had no lights or gates, just the big wooden X of Stop Look & Listen. We passed lone grain elevators that resembled the United Nations building and were so large that they had their own switch engines.

From North Platte to Gibbon Junction, we descended seven hundred and forty feet, an average grade of .113 per cent—a slope much too subtle to be seen by the human eye. The descent continued at the same average rate all the way to Marysville, which is fifteen hundred and ninety-nine feet lower than North

Platte. The significant grades along the way—Hayland Hill, Hastings Hill, the divide between the Big Blue and Little Blue— reminded me of fish in a river. I couldn't see them. Scott could. I would not have known they were there had Scott not made remarks from time to time about "coming up into these hills" or "pulling a pretty good grade." I could feel grades, surely—feel the uphill deceleration of nineteen thousand tons, feel the release when they were over a summit and rolling free—but even on the named hills the track looked, to me, essentially level. If you ride a bicycle, you know when you are going uphill, even where the gradient is so slight that your eye doesn't pick it up. In a nineteen-thousand-ton train, your physical perception of grade is much the same as it would be if you were on a twenty-pound bicycle—especially if your name is Scott Davis.

Run a coal train out of the Powder River Basin and down to Kansas and Arkansas and across the South into Georgia. The steepest grade you encounter is 1.5 per cent, on track that to the eye seems close to level. You can discern that it is going up or down, but it will not remind you of Crested Butte. It will seem less steep than the East Pacific Rise. Yet a loaded coal train running wide open in Notch 8 can attack a 1.5-per-cent grade and soon be beaten down under ten miles an hour. The steepest mainline railroad grade in the United States is Saluda Hill, coming off the Blue Ridge of North Carolina at five per cent—a thousand vertical feet in four miles. It is not presently used. To get up it, trains were cut into thirds. To get down it, Dick Eisfeller says, "they were extremely careful, put it that way." The base of the hill is called Slaughter Pen Cut. In the Hudson Highlands, of New York, the Mt. Beacon Incline Railway, also out of service now, went up a grade of sixty-five per cent, lifting passengers fifteen hundred feet to views of the Hudson River. I rode up the Mt. Beacon Incline Railway once and was able to discern the angle. In a litany of comparative grades, Mt. Beacon doesn't really count. The locomotive was made by the Otis Elevator Company. The steepest surviving mainline grade is near four per cent—at Raton Pass, in the Sangre de Cristo Mountains, between Colorado and New Mexico. Glorieta Pass, near Santa Fe, is 3.0. In California, the steepest grades in the Sierra Nevada reach 2.4—a grade that can be expressed as a one-mile ramp to the roof of a twelve-story building, nothing more. In the so-called Punch Bowl below Cajon Pass, in the San Bernardino Mountains—entrance to the Los Angeles Basin and once the route of the Super Chief—there are three tracks, with grades, respectively, of 2.2, 2.2, and 3.0. The routes of the heavy coal trains rarely include grades much over one per cent. The roadbeds may look flat, but the difference in steepness between 1.2 and 1.5 can be prohibitive.

Whatever the route, somewhere between origin and destination there is going to be a ruling grade—the one that is more challenging than any other. Trains are made up to meet ruling grades—barely. If you need thirteen thousand horsepower to get up your ruling grade, you'll be given three AC4400 locomotives. Many summits are marked by metallic yellow flags with black triangles on them. If something slips, or you lose an engine and you don't make it past a yellow flag, call an armadillo.

Direct-current diesel-electric locomotives are fine for hauling autotrains, intermodal containers, and sugar beets, but alternating current is the better way to move the weight of coal. A.C. traction motors—the result of a newer technology—can handle more current and pull more loaded coal cars. In the D.C. days of the twentieth century, railroads ran trains with as many as five locomotives. Now, with A.C. traction motors, trains of the same gross tonnage and on the same routes can be driven by three. A coal train is so heavy that it should be limited to a hundred cars if the locomotives are only on the front end, because with greater length and added tonnage the couplers between cars will start to break; the train literally tears itself apart. In the middle nineteen-nineties, slave locomotives under computer-coördinated radio control were added in the middle or at the rear of trains, to push in synchronization with the pull from the front, taking pressure off the couplers. That is when coal trains grew in length to a mile and a half. The pull-and-push method, integrally operated by the engineer, is known as distributed power. A few exceptional coal trains are two miles long.

When something linear is draped across a great deal of landscape, it will be required to go uphill and downhill simultaneously if it tries to move at all. It crosses a summit, and its front begins descending while the rest is still climbing. If it is a coal train and there is a restricted-speed zone down ahead, many thousands of tons will strain the dynamic brakes while many thousands of other tons still need a great deal of applied power. Between North Platte, Nebraska, and Marysville, Kansas, a scene exactly fitting that description was a two-mile eastbound rise that led to an overpass where Union Pacific crossed the Burlington Northern Santa Fe in Hastings, Nebraska. The restricted-speed zone was half a mile down the far side. Scott had to deal with the antithetical stresses of the "train action" by continuing to apply positive power and simultaneously introducing what manuals call "brake propagation." This was possible only with distributed power, and he had long since "thrown the fence," de-synchronizing the locomotives at the two ends of the train. The computer screen in front of him that related to power was now split by a vertical bar between the data of the front locomotives and the data from the rear unit, which was still pushing while the lead units were down in the dynamic brakes.

This was a place where a train could "get knuckles" (break couplers), and U.P. trains, in fact, had got six knuckles on Hastings Hill since Christmas. This is Scott's description of what was happening now: "You have to be within one throttle notch up or down with head—for example, two dynamic on the head end would allow throttle 1, 2, or 3 on the DP. It is not against the rules to be in dynamic brake 8 on the DP and 2 on the head end, but common sense will tell you that there is a possibility of pulling your train in two. There's a twenty-five-mile-an-hour slow order at Kicks Road, which is only about half a mile from the top of this hill. In order to get a hundred-and-thirty-three-car loaded coal train—nineteen thousand tons, DPU—over the hill without breaking in two, what you need to do is you need to have the rear DP unit shoving in about Notch 1, and you need to control the slack with the lead two DPs in dynamic, and you'll have to hold that train back at fifty-mile-an-hour until you reach the bottom, and then you need to be shoving with the DP in the eighth run to push the slack against the head end in order to come over that hill at twenty-five-mile-an-hour and keep the slack bunched in so it doesn't break in two."

It didn't.

By 7 P.M., with our headlight drilling darkness, CNAMR was going fast enough to explode a rooster, feathers everywhere, like a shower of sparks. A "rooster" in this context was a cock pheasant, which flew nose-to-nose into a thirty-eight-million-pound coal train. Minutes later, on the microwave radio, we heard a westbound train report to the dispatcher that the train in front of us, an eastbound manifest, was throwing real sparks from its twenty-seventh car from the rear. Signals flashed yellow. The train in front of us was ten miles down the track, and to Paul and Scott its situation brought a single thought: If we get stuck behind this manifest, our time will run out and our own train will die. Scott began moving the throttle down through the notches and into the dynamics. Within twenty-five hundred yards, he had brought CNAMR to a complete stop. If he had crept along, drifting, as he could have under the flashing yellow signals, he might have crept into a block so close to the stricken train that the dispatcher would not be able to get him around it. So Scott was preserving distance. The dispatcher was in Omaha—a hundred and twelve miles away, measured with a string—but he was in charge of all signals, all switches, and all movement of trains in many tens of miles before and behind us.

The signal structures over the tracks loomed black and nearly invisible now, but their lights had taken on a planetary brilliance—green, flashing yellow, yellow, red, and lunar (the high white that tells you you can creep past red). These same colors, stretched into long horizontal lines, were lighting up a wall in Omaha as if it were the wall of a disco. Trains in Arizona, California, Missouri, and Colorado were also running in patterns expressed on this wall, and on the wall opposite—the two sides of a narrow, tunnel-like room three hundred feet long. Iowa, Nebraska, Wyoming, Utah—in all, about nineteen thousand miles of the Union Pacific were under control from within these walls, in the space known to the company as the Harriman Dispatching Center and to the people who work there as "the bunker."

It looks like one—theatrically dark, below grade, the caverned core of a two-story building, and reinforced with such redundant masonry that it is rated to withstand "the force of a telephone pole hitting it at a hundred and eighty miles per hour," an assertion that in this part of the country is not immune from testing. The bunker calls to mind Mission Control in Houston, but even louder is the echo of those old films about the Strategic Air Command zapping the hell out of the Soviet Union from a deeply inhumed command center in Omaha. Four hundred dispatchers work at Harriman, about sixty at any given time. They wear ball caps that say things like "DAD TO THE BONE." Fingers on keyboards, feet on radio pedals, earphones under the caps, they sit at consoles in partitioned cubicles looking down into as many as eight computer screens and up at the colored lines—the sometimes flashing bands—on the walls. The lines are tracks, and some of the colors are rolling trains. If a paid inmate or a college student were to be brought here to undergo clinical psychological testing, he'd be babbling in the street in thirty minutes. Dispatchers have left Harriman to go into air-traffic control, imagining a simpler life. In the words of John Reininger, a supervisor in the bunker, "Air-traffic controllers have the great luxury of another dimension. Air-traffic controllers find this more complicated. We'd *like* to have a train change its altitude to get over another train—it won't work."

A raised axial platform, supervisory in nature, is flanked on either side by a hundred yards of dispatchers, sitting in their cubicles, about five feet lower. Each is separated by clear partitions from neighbors left and right, whose territories are adjacent and average three hundred miles. Crew-change points will often coincide with the edges of dispatchers' territories. In rear projection, the polychromatic representation of the railroad on the wall directly ahead of each dispatcher depicts what is going on in the dispatcher's territory, and a glance to the left or the right shows the traffic that is approaching. If something is flashing, it needs attention; and something is generally a train, for which the dispatcher is clearing the way. In Reininger's words, "He owns the track, so to speak."

The multiple lines of color representing trains and tracks are not everywhere parallel. Where tracks converge, as at Gibbon Junction, the lines assume swastika patterns and the wall resembles a Navajo blanket. Where a stretch of track is occupied by a train, it is lighted bright red. Where a stretch of track has nothing on it and will not have for a while, it is white. A computer is thinking about it. Green track is clear for imminent use. Brown is for manual mode, computer uninvited. A computer has planned a train's experiences two or three hours ahead of the train. The dispatcher watches the plan as it unfolds, and overrides it if necessary, whereupon the relevant stretch of track on the wall turns brown. Malfunctioning switches appear as vertical blue rectangles, like small postage stamps. Specific symbols represent specific trains. Small arrows show plotted directions. Small Hs represent switch heaters. Such is the detail that on the axial platform a supervisor lifts a pair of binoculars to look over a dispatcher's shoulder and scan the rear-projection wall fifteen feet in front of her. Dispatchers at Harriman have spent entire careers on one stretch of track. If a coal train is making a very long trip from mine to plant, as many as a dozen dispatchers will see it through. Dispatchers have in their hands the safety not only of train crews but also of track workers, not to mention the surrounding public. After twelve weeks of classes, they are trained on the job for about three months. It takes them five years to become really efficient. Above each dispatcher's cubicle is a red strobe light set on a shaft like a torch. If a crisis develops in a dispatcher's territory, the red light begins to flash so that everyone in the general area will see it if the dispatcher is off peeing.

Some television directors look at fewer monitors than dispatchers do. Dispatchers' screens in the bunker can display data from trackside sensors and scanners. They chart winds and flash floods. Any emergency situation will cause a window describing it to pop up on a screen. As snow falls anywhere in Harriman's nineteen thousand miles, switch heaters are turned on from Harriman.

Under Centralized Traffic Control, you can run a train on any track in any direction. You can run three trains side by side all headed west on the Triple-Track Main. Where the trackage is wired for C.T.C., signals are all two-sided. I remember riding in a Metroliner in Maryland and standing in the front of the front car, where—through two windows—I could see the track ahead. Over the engineer's shoulder, I could see, lit up, a digital readout of the train's speed. The engineer was wearing a tie. There were four tracks. Gradually, the Metroliner had drifted to its left and now it was flying south at the left-hand extreme, on what is customarily a northbound track, at a hundred and eleven miles an hour. A pickup in front of us ran a gated crossing. We missed the pickup. On down the far-left track, we were soon looking directly into the headlight of a locomotive. We kept going. Somewhat shy of the headlight, the Metroliner slipped over to the next track, and shot past the other train. Centralized Traffic Control.

Under C.T.C., the dispatcher at his console controls all movement, and can set all signals and throw all switches. The system involves microwave towers, satellites, and fibre optics (strung along the tracks like the nineteenth century's telegraph wires). Train orders and track warrants used to be presented on actual paper given to the crew. Where they needed to, they stopped the train, walked ahead, threw switches by hand, and made signals with their arms in varied configurations, like football referees. A fist to the forehead was trainspeak for headlight. If you cupped both hands over your breasts, you were talking about a tank car. As with hand-swung red lanterns, all that was replaced by the block-signal system, which remains in operation in a lot of terrain. Blocks average two miles. If something is stalled four blocks ahead of you, you go from green to flashing yellow to yellow to red. Under block signals, a fast train coming up behind a slow train has no alternative but to slow up and follow. Under C.T.C., a fast train can go around a slow train. Trackage still exists that has neither C.T.C. nor a block-signal system. The term for it is "dark territory." In dark territory, all instructions—even train orders—are verbal via microwave radio. Coal trains on the old Rock Island branch between Fairbury and Hallam, Nebraska, are in dark territory. They must receive a track warrant by radio from the bunker, and must give the track warrant back to the dispatcher when they leave dark territory. The town of Hallam not long ago was utterly destroyed by a tornado. All that was left was the power plant, at the dead end of dark territory.

In 1969, I went to Campbell County, Wyoming, with Floyd Elgin Dominy, who—decades earlier—had started his career there as a county agent advising ranchers, who were fighting severe and sustained drought, to build small dams and impound water in stock ponds. Dominy had risen to become Commissioner of Reclamation, the agency in the Department of the Interior which impounds water for as much as two hundred miles behind such constructions as Glen Canyon Dam, Grand Coulee Dam, Flaming Gorge Dam, and Hoover Dam. Proudly, he drove the swelling grasslands of the high, dry range, while I scribbled airy notes about the "wide, expansive landscape, the beguiling patterns of perspective, the unending buttes, flat or nippled, spaced out to the horizon like stone chessmen." The grasses stirred under the wind and the range seemed uninhabited farther than the eye could see, but the ranchers in 1969 were still tucked into the draws, and their cattle were drinking from a thousand ponds. Dominy had lived in a stone dugout with his wife and infant daughter. For heat and cooking, they had a coal-burning stove. Dominy dug the coal himself out of a hillside.

The Orin Line, known locally as the Coal Line, is in Campbell and Converse counties, Wyoming. It was cut through Thunder Basin National Grassland and now includes among its branches the branch to Black Thunder Mine. Where people like Dominy dug, by hand, coal that no one else much wanted, draglines the size of naval ships are exposing it now. On CTSBT, I mentioned that I meant to revisit Campbell County someday soon, to go where CTSBT goes, and to see the Powder River Basin (of which Thunder Basin is a part) as it has come to appear in the twenty-first century. Scott, who drives more than a million tons of coal from North Platte to Marysville per year, said he had never seen the source of the coal and had long been curious to go there. What was I doing "the day after tomorrow?" We could drive up to the Coal Line in his car and maybe catch a train into a mine. The mine turns in the southern Powder River Basin begin and end at Bill, Wyoming, and that was no big deal or distance from North Platte—not much over three hundred miles.

In his Suburban, we were barely nine miles from his home

when we approached the tracks at Birdwood, the west end of Bailey Yard. Lights flashed, gates dropped in front of us, and we watched the arriving headlight of a coal train. "Son of a bitch!" Scott complained. In no great hurry, the mile and a half of train went by, then a second son of a bitch came along before the first one cleared.

We went northwest on roads that were almost always close to tracks. Scott never looked at a map or paid much attention to road signs, but—to see where he was—he looked routinely at railroad mileposts. At another grade crossing, another coal train stopped us. We entered Wyoming in a freezing rain. In the B.N.S.F. yard at Guernsey were ten parallel coal trains. Through the rain, we saw sunlight on snow of the Laramie Range. Before long, the rain against our windshield turned into snow. North of Lightning Creek, the pump jacks of oil fields dotted the range. Bill had a regional school in a double-wide trailer, four kids in the school. As if Bill were pretending that it was not the only town in four thousand square miles, the school, the post office, the general store, and Dry Creek Community Hall were closely clustered. The post office, 82631, was boarded up, the Zip Code defunct. The town's resident population was one—the store-keeper. Sitting in Bill's railroad yard as we arrived were eight miles of coal trains.

Scott arranged for us to deadhead on CCTBT, coming from St. Clair, Michigan, and going to Black Thunder Mine. The train was scheduled to leave Bill at seven-forty in the morning, with David L. Morgan, conductor, and Eric M. Renstrom, engineer. At seven-forty in the morning, we had all been waiting in the crew locker room for upward of an hour, but no call was forthcoming for CCTBT. An hour later, there had still been no call for CCTBT, or for any other train. About a dozen crewmen were waiting, gathering the minutes of their twelve hours. The dialogue might have been coming off a circular tape:

"Fucking CRZ—can't remember shit."

"Today is National Pick-on-Tom Day."

"Shit. I can take it."

"Fucking CRZ—can't remember shit."

There was writing over a urinal in the grouting of a cinder-block wall: "Republicans Like to Cornhole Each Others + Wives + Chickens." Some of the guys wore chains on their boots to deal with winter. There was a lot of Mephistophelian facial hair—the caterpillar sideburns, the full beard, the mustache as bilateral semaphore.

Dave Morgan said, "Welcome to the Coal Line. Meaning you wait, and wait. Daytime dispatchers are a pain in the ass." And he laughed. Then, referring to the day's traffic, he added, "We've got about a hundred trains in here as we speak." And he laughed. Dave was a big guy—six-three—handsome, with a cavernous voice; and the laugh was explosive, like a chain saw starting up. The saw had a problem in its fuel line, always choking out as abruptly as it started, as if he threw a switch in mid-yuk. He wore jeans, a jean jacket. His thick brown hair was parted near the middle. He said he had waited in the locker room as much as eleven hours and thirty minutes to be called to a train.

Mary Ellen Sherwin, an engineer, came into the room. She had waited from 9:50 P.M. until 1:50 A.M. the night before, and had then driven a train to and from Belle Ayr Mine. Sixty-six years old with long white hair, she wore jeans, a jean jacket, and under her jacket a V-neck cotton sweater with horizontal grays and whites like the broadened stripes of a railroad hat from the days of steam. Addressing Dave Morgan, she remarked, "You asshole."

Dave replied, "That's Mister Asshole to you."

She said, "Where are you going?"

He said, "Thunder."

She had grown up on a ranch northeast of Bill, and now lived in Douglas, thirty-five miles south. She left for home.

When she had gone, Dave said, "They don't make enough jeweller's rouge to polish off her edges."

After four hours, a crewman spoke of "waiting on the railroad, all the livelong day." At ten-fifty-seven, the address system finally mentioned Dave's and Eric's train. Three minutes later, we were in the cab. At eleven-fifteen, we moved, into a whiteout fog.

If you would like to torture someone, either drip water on him for thirty-six hours or take him up the Coal Line. Eric stopped at a red signal where the yard tracks of Bill met the main roadbed. On a turn of ninety miles, we had travelled a trainlength, a mile and a half. The dispatchers who were controlling the movements of every train on the line were in B.N.S.F.'s dispatching center in Fort Worth, Texas. Ours spoke often and even hopefully to Eric and Dave, but there was nothing she could do. The line belonged jointly to the two largest railroads in America, and so many coal trains from so many places were there to collect the coal that the congestion had gone critical and the line was arteriosclerotic. Not that we could see the other trains. For ninety minutes, we stared forward at two red dots in fog.

Dave Morgan said, "As long as we don't see something going by us going into Thunder, we're O.K." Each train is a "slot." Mine to mine on the Orin Line, railroads work out loading slots, like airlines sharing an airport. At twelve-fifty-eight, a light turned yellow and we moved. Looking up at the signal, Dave said, "You got to have faith that that son of a bitch ain't lying to you, ha-ha-ha-h . . . ," and we slid onto the main, heading north up the leftmost of the three tracks under Centralized Traffic Control. And soon we were flying, or so it seemed, crossing the Dry Fork of the Cheyenne at twenty miles an hour.

The virtual voice of a trackside scanner addressed the interior of the cab, saying, "No dee fex. Temm purr ah choor fiff teen duh grees." The fog densened. A headlight suddenly appeared in it, and we were meeting a coal train coming down from Caballo, a small mine by Powder River standards, yet larger than every mine in the East. The train had made fifty-seven miles in ten and a half hours, but it was speeding up some and went by us in nine minutes.

The roadbed was visible enough, and Scott Davis remarked that we were looking at a state-of-the-art railroad—triple track with crossovers, concrete ties, the ballast so neatly bevelled that it looked like a new driveway. Wood ties are still in use elsewhere, and are more flexible, but concrete ties are what you want if you are annually running over them four hundred million gross tons of coal trains. (Not readily visible was the great quantity of coal dust that had filled in the ballast and, in months to come, would cause a couple of derailments by impeding the drainage of unusual rains.)

At one-thirty, we were stopped again, for what turned out to be ninety minutes. We had gone seven miles. "Fluidity" is perhaps the most hallowed word in railroad operations. The Santa Monica Freeway between Sepulveda and La Cienega is more fluid than the Orin Line between Bill and Belle Ayr. Think of Bay Bridge traffic backed up to Sacramento, think bumper-to-bumper backward from the New Jersey Palisades to the Mississippi River. Dave and Eric, sitting back, had their legs draped across their consoles. I had to look over their toes to stare, and stare, and stare at the red signals, in every moment wanting and expecting them to turn. With C.T.C., the fog was only a symbolic factor. Dave said, "It feels like we're all alone out here, but we've probably got sixty to seventy trains on the tracks up ahead. This is what it's like on the Coal Line. At least they didn't fix you up with nothing bogus. Ha-ha-ha-h . . ."

Eric went out the rear door of the cab and along the catwalk to the second unit, where he picked up a TV dinner he was cooking in the heat between the turbo and the main engine block. Until recently a conductor, Eric was a new engineer. With a full helmet of light-brown hair, fine features, alert eyes, he resembled the film idol Robert Redford but was better-looking. As he ate, he said, slowly and quietly, "I still have to learn how to get a handle on the stress side of it, trying to find a happy medium between caring too much and too little."

"We're parked," Dave said, his voice less optimistic than the trackside scanner's. Turning to the economics of the situation, he added, "We're really nothing. We're pretty much the plankton of the whole picture. Ha-ha."

An empty beaner drifted by—EMHKBTM—on its way from Tennessee to Black Thunder Mine. In other words, something was going by us going into Thunder. A beaner is a B.N.S.F. train. "E" for empty, in its B.N.S.F. seven-letter name. Beaners kept appearing: CCAMSLP, on its way from Caballo Mine to Smithers Lake, in Texas; ECEBATM, returning to Antelope Mine from a plant in southern Illinois that no longer uses Illinois coal. B.N.S.F. is made up of the collective remains of the Chicago, Burlington & Quincy Railroad, the Great Northern Railway, and the Atchison, Topeka and Santa Fe. A fallen flag is a railroad that no longer exists. In the eye of the beholder is whether B.N.S.F. is a streamlined modern enterprise or a bouquet of fallen flags. Either way, it is America's second-longest railroad, and its recumbent flags also include Spokane, Portland and Seattle; Northern Pacific; and St. Louis–San Francisco, the old Frisco line.

If you develop a monopoly on the railroads in Monopoly, you are holding four fallen flags. After the breakup of Conrail, in 1999, most of the old Eastern railroads became parts of Norfolk Southern or parts of CSX. Illinois Central is a fallen flag. It is part of Canadian National. These train mergers are like bluefish wars. Southern Pacific, which nearly merged with the Santa Fe, was consumed by Union Pacific in 1996. The modern Union Pacific is actually a consolidation of eight or ten railroads—a network, and more like a communications grid than a straight-line railroad. Its antiquarium of fallen flags also includes the Missouri Pacific, the Western Pacific, the Missouri-Kansas-Texas Railroad (Katy line), and the Chicago & North Western, which was struggling to build the Orin Line when U.P. came along with its mouth wide open. As Paul Fitzpatrick had summarized all this, "The U.P. went from a family-type company to a military-type company with the mergers, but we finally got them to think a little bit like what we think they should."

Around 3 P.M., a loaded U.P. coal train, coming down from the Antelope Mine, went by us on the middle track. Of the two red dots we were staring at, one above the other, the upper one related to the track we were on. The lower one was there to indicate a diversion route. The lower one turned yellow but resembled gold. After Eric put the throttle in Notch 1, we actually moved, crossing over from Track 3 to Track 2.

Traced from a map, the Coal Line has the raceme structure of a bluebell or a lily of the valley, as dainty an image as nature can provide for a stem whose flowers are coal mines. Black Thunder Junction, 5:45 P.M., nineteen degrees, dark, snowing.

Eight miles into Black Thunder, the branch line ended in a great loop, where the long train would pass through a loading silo while swinging around to go back the other way. Going into Thunder, we approached a switch that was closed but should have been open. What to do? Leaving the cab, Dave said, "I go over and flop the switch. This is known as a one-eyed crossover."

Crossed over, we soon stopped, as ordered, near a foot-bridge, before going over a scale. The snow was heavy now, like bugs filling up our headlight beam, but through the swarm we could see the silo, as large as a twenty-five-story office building, sheathed in light. Eric took the lead locomotive over the scale at 1.5 miles per hour, then went up to 3.5 for the rest of the train. Reading the tare weights on a screen in the cab, Dave said, "This is a pretty consistent consist." While the hoppers behind us were crossing the scale, we went under a conveyor belt that was carrying coal from a remote pit into the silo complex. The belt was three miles long. From nearer pits, coal was being brought in by haul trucks too large to share the name with anything else called a truck. Their tires looked the way bagels would look to a virus. Black Thunder was working four pits, and the whole spread of it was far too extensive to be comprehended from a train, but Scott Davis and I had driven around the basin after we arrived.

The mines were mapped in blocks: "West Overburden. Middle Overburden. East Overburden. Coal." The pits were excavated canyons. They were a couple of hundred feet deep and two and three miles long. The walking draglines gnawing at the overburden needed tall rigid masts to help support their four-chord booms. They were eight stories tall and weighed four hundred tons. Their booms were hundreds of feet long. Like the locomotives that would haul the coal away, the walking draglines required electric power. Their walk was a saurian heave, an exponential lurch, friction smoke rising from the ground around them. As they walked-dug-walked-dug their way up the coal seams, their tails dragged along behind them. The tails were cables six inches thick delivering electrical power made with coal to draglines digging coal. We saw three D11 bulldozers shoving overburden to the edge of a canyon and over the side, going back for more overburden, and returning to the lip, always stopping a foot or two short of a two-hundred-foot plunge.

Scott said, "I thought railroads were dangerous, but, man, these coal mines are really dangerous." In the presence of nineteen-thousand-ton trains, three-hundred-ton haul trucks, and hundred-ton bulldozers moving on unstable ground, blasts are routine and rocks fall like bombs.

"Those big trucks could back over a pickup and not even know it," Scott said.

The pickups knew it. They carried whip antennas twenty feet high with bright-red lights at the top.

The faces of the canyon walls were for the most part jet black—beds of coal eight to ten stories thick. With distance westward toward the Bighorns, the seams go deeper under the overburden. In fifty more years of westward digging and filling, the seams may be too deep to mine, at least in the way that they are mined now. At that point, the Powder River Basin will still contain—at the rate of sixty loaded coal trains a day—enough coal for two hundred years. It began as peat in Paleocene bogs about sixty million years before the present.

We had seen old ranch buildings falling into the ground, and a few cattle standing up. A sign: "LIVESTOCK AT LARGE." Windmills were still pumping water for cattle. On the horizons, there were no trees. Deer and antelope were everywhere at play, much too young to care what had happened to the range.

About six months before the present, I read Kim Stanley Robinson's "Red Mars," a heralded work of science fiction that describes the colonization and mineral exploitation of the fourth planet. Robinson's characters excavate Mars with backhoes, front-end loaders, tractors, graders, and "one John Deere/Volvo Martian bulldozer, hydrazine-powered, thermally protected, semiautonomous, fully programmable." There are "giant dump trucks . . . full of black boulders."

" 'Monsters like this are all over the planet,' he said to Nadia. . . . 'Cutting, scraping, digging, filling . . .' "

The monsters are "equipped to be teleoperated from indoor stations, their decision algorithms handling the details," while human operators peer at screens.

" 'Watch your screens, you lazy bastards!' "

Colonials from "rich northern countries" mine the Great Escarpment and "the island mesas of Nilosyrtis." One of their pits is "a kilometer in diameter, seven kilometers deep." They use the "Allied hydraulic impact hammer," and they "drill cased holes through large boulders" with the Sandvik Tubex boring machine.

"The train to Burroughs carried mostly freight, thirty narrow cars of it . . . running over a superconducting magnetic piste." Between Earth and Mars, strings of orbiting vehicles, also called trains, come and go in "a continuous procession" run by "a large force of local traffic controllers."

And now CCTBT was about to turn into CBTCT. Its nose was close to the silo. It was moving steadily at .4 miles per hour. Scott Davis and I went out of the cab and back along the catwalk in the noise and the snow, stepping over to the second unit, and continuing along its catwalk to the far end, because the second unit was facing backward. We got into the cab there and watched. Next to us was the first of a hundred and thirty-four empty hoppers. The looming silo was something like a grain elevator, reaching out with great arms to the crushers that supplied it. Moving inside, the lead locomotives passed three control booths, whose bay windows were not entirely black with dust. As the first hopper drew abreast of a booth, a pair of steel sheets was lowered from above, coffering the interior of the car in the way that a dentist places baffles around a tooth he's about to fill. Then coal dropped, explosively, between the sheets. A hundred and fifteen measured tons fell into the coal car in one second. A six-kiloton cloud shot up into the silo's black interior. Under the crash of coal, the aluminum hopper staggered, wrenched downward, and looked as if it might flatten. From above, the baffles were lifted. The coal in the hopper was maybe five feet above the rims, a calculated fluff that would settle down. At .4 miles per hour, the second car was now in position. The baffles came down, and the coal fell. Crunch, cloud, and the next car was in position. Emerging from the silo on a slight curve, we watched twenty cars totter in the dust under the weight of falling coal before the interior of the silo passed out of sight, with more than a mile of hoppers to follow.

We were scarcely eastbound off the loop when Dave's and Eric's time, under the hours-of-service law, ran out. Eric stopped the loaded coal train. We all descended. A fresh crew got on, and the van that had brought them carried us away, past a very large sign that said:

THUNDER BASIN COAL COMPANY

WELCOME TO

BLACK THUNDER MINE

DON'T GET CAUGHT IN

THE WEB OF UNSAFE ACTS

In the Powder River Basin, a congestion of trains may be tedious while you're in it, the railroading seemingly inefficient, but that is just an illusion lit up in red signals. The place is not as organized as an anthill, no; but it is something like one. From the mines along the Orin Line, twenty-three thousand coal trains annually emerge—that is, about thirty-four thousand miles of rolling coal, going off as units to become carbon dioxide, sulfur dioxide, nitrous oxide, water, ash, and heat, and to air-condition a population so needful of comfort that the demand for the coal is greater in summer than in winter.

Here is one example chosen not at random but for its distance and size: Coming and going, loaded and empty, thirty-five sets—thirty-five dedicated unit coal trains—are in almost perpetual motion between the Powder River Basin and Georgia's Plant Scherer, twenty miles from Macon. There is a loop at each end, eighteen hundred miles in between. Owned by a consortium led by Georgia Power, Plant Scherer, in megawatts produced, is the largest coal-fired power plant in the Western Hemisphere. It pays more than anyone else for the transportation of Powder River coal, and not long ago B.N.S.F. snatched the contract from Union Pacific.

Trains with names like CBTMMHS go down to Guernsey and then cross Nebraska and drop through Missouri to the Ozarks, where they test tonnage versus horsepower on 1.5-per-cent grades. B.N.S.F. had to lengthen its sidings and fix up its track for the coal trains, as did Norfolk Southern, which absorbs the trains at Memphis. New crews take their turns from Memphis to Sheffield, and Sheffield to Chattanooga, and Chattanooga to Atlanta's Inman Yard. The run from Inman and back to Inman via Lamar County is known inside the trains as the Scherer turn.

By the grade crossing in Juliette, Georgia, a fried-green-tomato sandwich is as good as it is famous at the Whistle Stop Café. On a freezing winter day, when the temperatures in Georgia were not much milder than they were in Wyoming, I had a fried-green-tomato sandwich for lunch with my longtime friend Sam Candler, of Sharpsburg, Georgia, and Joe Fulford, a Norfolk Southern trainmaster, and Adam Crate, whose title was Road Foreman of Engines.

Close to the Ocmulgee River, Juliette is a hamlet in the pinewoods—a cluster of houses near the grade crossing by the trackside café. In the early nineteen-nineties, the town flashed with borrowed vividness after Hollywood used it as an on-location set for a memoir that included a steam locomotive coming through the pines and killing a young man whose foot had been caught and wedged in the rails near the Whistle Stop Café, which looks to this day as it did in the movie.

I was still enjoying my fried-green species of BLT when the nose of a locomotive appeared in a window and stopped. Its presence in this place was no less incongruous than the appearance of Chief Red Cloud at New York's Cooper Union to deliver an address in Sioux. Instead of a modest Norfolk Southern locomotive, there from the mountain West on this antebellum single track sat Burlington Northern Santa Fe 5639, color of reddish wheat, with seven thousand feet of coal behind it in the trees. Lee Stuckey was the engineer, Brian Nix the conductor—Inman to Inman, the Scherer turn. On a yellow slip above Lee Stuckey's head were the initials of Black Thunder Mine.

Over wooden ties, we went down through the loblollies in a narrow series of S curves, the trees so tight to the train that on this clear day visibility from the cab did not extend much farther than it had in the fog in Wyoming. More forest curves eventually led to a long left where we could look back at the beginnings of CBTMMHS's hundred and twenty-four cars. Then, to our left, we passed a long yard with five parallel tracks, where five coal trains could, if necessary, be parked, or "staged," waiting to advance and drop their coal at Plant Scherer. That should have suggested the dimensions of the scene to follow, but the significance of the yard did not really register with me, and the effect was near total when we bent around a long curve and the dense curtain of pines seemed to open theatrically from left to right, revealing a loop of track at least a mile in circumference around an infield filled with a million tons of coal (earthmovers and bulldozers crawling like insects on the coal), and, on the far side of the loop, a trestle forty feet in the air and eight hundred feet long, and behind the trestle a pair of rectangular buildings a quarter of a mile over the ground and close to three hundred feet high but dwarfed beneath the overbearing immensity of four hyperbolic cooling towers that came into view one at a time, their broad flared rims five hundred feet above the ground, and two smokestacks a thousand feet high, reaching above the scene like minarets. It was an electrical Xanadu in homage to a craven need, its battlements emitting cumuli of steam.

After being switched to the right at the top of the loop, we started around it counterclockwise. Coal trains are so heavy that they are routed through the loop in alternate directions, to distribute the assault on the track. In the infield to our left were five hundred acres of Campbell County, Wyoming, fifty feet deep—the million-ton reserve known at Plant Scherer as the "pile." CBTMMHS circumscribed the pile until—close by Plant Scherer—it stopped at the head of the unloading trestle, which extended before it between rows of bright lights. This train had left Wyoming five days ago. Plant Scherer would burn everything in it in less than eight hours.

Sam and I descended from the cab, the better to watch the unloading. Like the New Jersey Turnpike high over the Meadowlands, the trestle was supported on concrete croquet wickets that divided the space below it into twenty-one bays. Between yellow railings, the red-orange locomotive began to move onto the trestle, followed by stainless hoppers heaped with coal. Bin doors opened in the bottom of the first car, and, in three or four seconds, down through the trestle fell a hundred and fifteen tons of coal. The sound was nearly as explosive as the sound of the filling had been in Wyoming. At some plants, coal cars are rolled over—literally flipped on swivel couplings—but such rotary dumping, spectacular as it may be, is too slow for a place like Plant Scherer, which Jeremy Taylor, an authority on coal trains, has called "the most efficient unloading operation in the country," with its trestle, its electric contact points, its compressed-air opening of the hopper doors. The train was moving at three miles an hour, and the cars were unloading like sticks of bombs. The coal was mounding in the bays. As each load began to drop, a geyser of dust shot upward from the car. Down in the bays, the dust coming off the fallen coal spread out in a thick black cloud.

There were sprayers to diminish the dust but the sprayers were frozen. Sam had radically changed. His face had blackened. His beard was much younger. Now the locomotive stopped hard to shake up frozen coal. In the bays of the trestle, mountains quickly grew, and big yellow Cats did what they could to smooth them. As coal floods the bays, it can fill them high enough to derail the train. After the locomotive had gone far past the end of the trestle, the cars kept coming and the geysers kept rising. The uncontrollable dust far below had the look of an occurring disaster, the spreading clouds dark and flat as if they were derived from incendiary bombs.

Plant Scherer can unload a coal train in thirty minutes but seldom does. If Plant Scherer takes more than four hours to unload a coal train, it pays Norfolk Southern a demurrage fee. Norfolk Southern, for its part, has seventy hours to get the train from the Mississippi River to Plant Scherer and back, or Norfolk Southern pays a demurrage fee. Cars may have to be set out because of freezing—hopper doors frozen, the coal in solid blocks like frozen peas.

Coal under the trestle in forty-foot dunes soon filled all twenty-one bays. Sprinklers were finally thawed. A rainbow hung in a drifting black cloud. Like a chambered nautilus, the train had come back upon itself and was now completely annular. At the far side of the great loop, the lead locomotive was all but touching the hoppers that were still arriving.

Under the trestle, a chute was carrying the coal off to be crushed and then pulverized and then mixed with air for immediate burning, in the way that an automobile engine mixes air with gasoline and explodes the vapor. Pulverization helps make it possible to burn the coal at a temperature low enough to limit nitrous oxide, and the fireballs don't get much hotter than three thousand degrees. The heat, of course, boils water—eighty-one million gallons of Ocmulgee River water a day—in boilers twenty-five stories tall. Steam from the boiling water turns four generators lined up in a single room a quarter of a mile long.

Damon Woodson, a mechanical engineer at Plant Scherer who had worked in a nuclear power plant, said, "I never really understood nuclear until I came here." That million-ton pile on reserve in the train loop was equivalent to one truckful of mined uranium, he said. "The way to go is nuclear if you want to have power. To get a million BTUs, fuel oil costs nine dollars, natural gas six dollars, coal a dollar-eighty-five, nuclear fifty cents. We'll see how it all turns out."

Plant Scherer burns nearly thirteen hundred coal trains a year—two thousand miles of coal cars, twelve million tons of the bedrock of Wyoming. It unloads, on average, three and a half coal trains a day. On a wall inside the plant are pictures of yellow finches, turkey vultures, and other local wildlife on Plant Scherer's twelve thousand acres of land. Asked why Plant Scherer needs twelve thousand acres (six miles by three miles), Woodson answered readily, "Because we are thinking of expanding."

A Fleet of One — II

If you have crossed the American continent in the world's most beautiful truck, you prefer not to leave it forever. You think of it from time to time—stainless, flashing like a signal mirror in the Carolinas, in California, in Wisconsin, Wyoming, Oregon, and Georgia—and you want to climb back into the cab. Exactly thirty-six months after I said goodbye to Don Ainsworth and watched his chemical tanker as it slowly pulled away from the Port of Tacoma Truck Stop, I got back into his cab. While he was making a round trip between San Diego and Dudley, Massachusetts, I connected with him in Rochester for an eastbound-and-westbound seven-hundred-and-fifty-mile reunion with the truck.

The driver of an eighteen-wheel, eighty-thousand-pound chemical tanker needs to be thinking ahead at least a mile, of course, but if he happens to own the whole rig—the tractor and the trailer—he is also thinking through itineraries for long-haul routes in which the smartest distance to profit is not necessarily a straight line. And always, in various ways, he is listening to and looking for bears. When I noticed a police car deep in a median like a beetle under a leaf, I mentioned it to Don, and he said, "I saw him a long time ago. He's on the phone, talking to his mistress." Skirting and crossing the Hudson River, there were two ways past Albany on limited-access roads. The one through Selkirk had tolls; the one through Rensselaer had no tolls but was a den of New York bears. "Cops roost in rest areas on the free side," he said, as he admired Selkirk. He called the tolls there "hush money." It was just a bit of overhead, to be taken into account with other tolls, state fuel taxes, and terrain (long slow pulls on hills) in the business planning of his route.

In the Berkshires, seventeen miles from the New York state line, he pointed out a brown-and-white westbound sign that said "NEXT HIGHEST ELEVATION ON I-90 IN OACOMA, SOUTH DAKOTA." The long Berkshire grade had summited at seventeen hundred and twenty-four feet, and was not going to inconvenience Ainsworth in time or fuel economy. From eighteenth gear, he shifted to twelfth for the eastbound descent, and that was about all he needed to do to cope with the cordillera of Massachusetts. "It's not the Rockies," he agreed. "But it is steep enough to have a runaway-truck ramp." Massachusetts might prefer not to know that Oacoma is a Missouri River town accessible from the ocean in a yacht. We passed the escape ramp. It had been used so recently that its sand had not been regroomed.

Since that day in Tacoma when I had last seen him, he had driven nearly four hundred thousand miles, in forty-six states and three Canadian provinces. He had carried liquefied clay from Sandersville, Georgia, to Thunder Bay, on the Canadian shore of Lake Superior, delivering it in a blizzard. He had carried petroleum-based candle wax from Titusville, Pennsylvania, to West Jordan, Utah; fatty acid from Winter Haven, Florida, to

Roanoke, Virginia; cutting oil from Hilton, New York, to Cull-man, Alabama; tall oil (pine-tree resin) from Mobile, Alabama, to Oklahoma City; "elephant snot," trademarked ClariFloc, from Savannah, Georgia, to a wastewater-treatment plant in Fresno, California ("it's literally a turd attractor"); herbicide from St. Gabriel, Louisiana, to Saskatoon, Saskatchewan; calcium slurry from Cockeysville, Maryland, to Kimberly, Wisconsin ("a hard interior wash, an acid wash, failed the first time"); magnesium chloride from Wendover, Utah, to Little Rock, Arkansas; metam sodium ("a corrosive marine pollutant, a Class 8 haz-mat") from Cadet, Missouri, to Pedricktown, New Jersey; plasti-cizer from Kalama, Washington, to Duncanville, Texas; isopropyl alcohol from Merrimack, New Hampshire, to Louisville, Ken-tucky; and—to the Powder River Basin, in Wyoming—forty thousand pounds of flocculent to Black Thunder Mine.

On the present trip, he had come up through Gila Bend, Flagstaff, Oklahoma City, St. Louis, and Columbus to I-90 east of Cleveland; and he picked me up at the Western Truck Stop in Henrietta—lollipop 362 on the New York State Thruway. New York is anomalous in the matter of Thruway lollipops, as it is in many other respects. Eastbound, we rolled from 362 to 361, 360, 359, and so on. Nearly everywhere else, the numbers count up from west to east. And New York has no weigh stations. In New York you don't pull over to get weighed; bears pull you over and weigh you. They carry portable scales. They take them out in rest areas and put them under your wheels.

We were rolling over broad farmland almost startlingly flat, screened with hedgerows and blistered now and again with drumlins. It was the bottom of Glacial Lake Iroquois, which had shrivelled up as Lake Ontario. Ainsworth in his youth had lived on a small, remote farm there. Each day, he was the first on his school bus and the last off, commuting to his high school in Honeoye Falls, a town divided by a small stream and still centered on a preserved gristmill. Among fields of corn, wheat, and soybeans, Don's brother Lorne lives near Lima, a dozen miles south of the interstate. During Don's infrequent stopovers at Lorne's farmhouse, he sleeps in his only home other than the truck.

Was I aware that New York produces more milk than Wisconsin? (I wasn't. It doesn't.) Did I know that New York is third in wine grapes? A reefer overtook us, bearing the logo of Heluva Good cheese. Ainsworth turned on the C.B. "Hello, there! Where are you from?" "Sodus Point," came the answer from Heluva Good cheese. Ainsworth said, "My dad and I used to go iceboating there." Click. Was I an admirer of John Steinbeck? Cormac McCarthy? Larry McMurtry? Ainsworth's middle names could be "Free Association." "I just finished McMurtry's book about Annie Oakley and Buffalo Bill. It's a series of anecdotes, loosely strung together." Near Utica, the floor of Glacial Lake Iroquois ended in the rise of mountains, the somewhat cooler air, and the green sloping dairyland of the Mohawk River Valley—Little Falls, Canajoharie—as the road ran close by the Erie Canal. "I was in Needles, California, the other day and it was a hundred and twenty-one degrees."

"Hello, there!" he said to toll collectors. If amiability could kill, they'd fall over in their booths. This was a Sunday, but he had not—as he once had routinely—attended service in a truckers' chapel. He described himself as "an Adventist-in-training" now. "It's as close as a Christian can get to being a Jew." He was planning to order new mud flaps from Goldie's Kosher Truck Parts, in Kearny, New Jersey. Approaching the Connecticut River, he said, "In Chicopee, put your hand over your heart, because that is where *The Wall Street Journal* is set." Coast to coast, he still knew which truck stops carry "the Walleye." Politically, he tilts to the right, but not enough to capsize. He said, sombrely, of the President of the United States, "George is a lost soul."

Three years had not diminished his energy, his obvious zest for the road; and his vocabulary was still a mixture of truckspeak and idiosyncrasy, often less sortable than sand and salt. As we overtook a "pumpkin"—one of the all-orange eighteen-wheelers of the fleet of Schneider National, the largest truckload carrier in the United States—he said, "An orange litter bag is a Schneider embryo." A tractor-trailer with extra cargo space attached to the tractor was a dromedary. Seeing a murdercyclist with no skid lid, he called him a future organ donor.

Seeing flashing red lights far ahead on a Massachusetts shoulder, Ainsworth swung into the fast lane to give a wide berth to a cop with quarry—a four-wheeler having a bad day. Ainsworth was mindful of a new law. "You must get out of the right lane, if you can, when you see those flashing lights. They lose more bears in sideswipes than to people who put guns at their heads. They're tired of losing bears." Those flashing red lights were not on the roof but down in the grille of an unmarked Chevy Camaro. Bright-red lights in a police-car grille are known as unexposed cherries. A cop shop is a state-police station or "anywhere where guys in uniforms hang out." Ainsworth studies cop shops to see what is new in unmarked cars. He told me that bears specializing in big trucks drive Suburbans, Explorers, and passenger vans, "meaning baby trucks inspect big trucks—when you see one, you can bet that that cop is a diesel bear, dedicated to truck enforcement, but that doesn't mean if *you* go by him at one-two-zero he won't nab you." On the scanner, Ainsworth hears state police comparing the day's "trophy tickets—i.e.,

'What was the highest speed you nailed someone for today?' "
He went on to say, "They know who you are before they pull
you over. The communications equipment in their cruisers ex-
ceeds the cost of the cruiser." They read a license plate, run it
through their computer network, and rapidly find out if they are
about to meet Pretty Boy Floyd or a retired librarian. Beside the
easternmost I-90 New York toll booths, we saw a specialist bear
looking through a trucker's papers. "Predators roost near the water hole," Ainsworth remarked. "Tunnels, bridges, toll booths—
any bottleneck. Cops are so bloodthirsty in New York they'll
stand in the middle of the road studying you. They are looking
for expired license plates. They are looking at C.V.S.A. stickers."
Commercial Vehicle Safety Alliance. "C.V.S.A. stickers are
color-coded and shape-coded, so a cop knows when you were
last inspected. I believe in the C.V.S.A." The bear beside the toll
booths was dressed in black, a style increasingly in vogue. "They
wear all-black uniforms. Their boots are bloused, as they are in
the military. Their holsters are made out of ballistic nylon. Why
are they dressing that way? To frighten you. To intimidate you."

Police are also likely to ask for toll receipts, with which they
test the assertions in a trucker's logbook. Toll receipts are
stamped with date and time. Hours-of-service rules, recently re-
vised, limit the trucker to eleven driving hours after ten off, and
if the driving time is cumulative and not consecutive it cannot
go past the fourteenth hour after ten off. Ainsworth calls this
"the fourteen-hour shot clock." He said, "You've got fourteen
hours to accomplish the eleven in. If you want to do elective
maintenance, you'll never do it in the middle of the day." Long-
haul drivers are still limited to a total of seventy hours in eight
days, and when the seventy have been completed they now must
spend thirty-four hours off. "Take thirty-four hours off—you're

fresh, just like the Pony Express," Ainsworth said coöperatively. "I'm a born-again driver." Nevertheless, truckers feel "toll-ticket-tethered" when driving in the East, tolls being few and scattered in Western states.

To drop off the load from San Diego, we left the Massachusetts Turnpike at Exit 10, went south on I-395, and off into the neighborhood where Massachusetts, Connecticut, and Rhode Island make a triple junction. After the interstates' oceanic sameness, the silver tanker in those suburban streets was something like an anadromous fish coming out of the sea and going up a river, suddenly having to pick its way through narrow channels past bridge piers and over ledges up rapids past erratic boulders. Old Howarth Road, Oxford, Massachusetts. The groin vaulting of shade trees. The blind curves. The bouldery suburban houses. Dudley Road. Old Webster Road. The hunkered companies. International Photonics Group. Stop, start—stop sign to stop sign, light to light, the truck was jolting. The load—sixty-two hundred gallons of concentrated WD-40—weighed forty-five thousand pounds, and the surge slamming the front wall of the tank felt like a punch in the spine. Ainsworth said, "It's got a lot of surge to it, a lot of slosh to it, because it is thin."

More than any other product, in his agented and freelance operations, Ainsworth carries WD-40, picking it up from Ken East, the brewmaster in San Diego, and taking it to packaging plants in Ontario, Texas, Georgia, Wisconsin, or Massachusetts. As Ainsworth styles it, he is "the Johnny Appleseed of WD-40." Occasionally, returning west, he picks up a "secret ingredient" in Painesville, Ohio—a corrosion inhibitor made by Lubrizol and known, like a Swiss bank account, only by a number. Water displacement 40 was first brewed for the military, in the nineteen-fifties, and the brew came up right on the fortieth try. The load now surging was thin because his tank had kept its temperatures at and a little above a hundred and fourteen degrees for three thousand and thirty miles. That ovoid elongate stainless-steel tube was a sixty-thousand-dollar thermos. And, if necessary, it could add heat. "This is no F.P.U.," Don said. "This is a chemical tanker." An F.P.U. is a farm-pickup unit that hauls milk. Imagine what people saw, looking out from their living rooms on Old Howarth Road. In Waterloo, New York, on our way east, Don had spent seventy-five dollars for a "spot-free wash" so that people looking at his truck would think they were staring at the sun. Moreover, the tractor was only three and a half months old—a Peterbilt, replacing the earlier one almost identically, but in deep claret striped with tan. "This is one quiet machine," he said. "No wind wings. It's symphony-class." It had a chrome bumper, stainless-steel rock guards, and cylindrical stainless air cleaners with light-emitting diodes. Concealed behind a hinged license plate was a steel hook that could be used to pull him out of a ditch. There were, as before, no logos on the doors, or, needless to say, on the bright steel behind him. He still had his bug screen in the form of the American flag. A stainless-steel black-bristled boot brush was affixed to the lower stainless-steel step on the driver's side, enabling Ainsworth to degrime his custom-made boots as he climbs into the cab. To his inventory of caiman boots, mule boots, eel boots, and shark boots, he had recently added four sea-turtle boots, one pair dyed serpentine green and the other henna. He will not say who made the boots, because he prefers not to visit him in prison. He referred to the turtles as "domesticated." As he drew into the Shield Packaging Company, in Dudley, no one watching could have guessed that over the years leading to that moment he had hauled his spotless trailer 775,567 miles.

Shield was ensconced in what had been one of the first spinning mills in America, its windows now filled in with masonry but in a spruce and geometrical manner that had returned dignity to a vacant shell. The approach driveway was flanked by the plant and a retaining wall. The driveway's concrete surface was as clean as it had been the day it was laid. Beside a row of discharge tanks, the driveway was depressed, and a large drain grid was at the lowest point. Any big chemical spill would go into that drain—to end up where? In the nearby Quinebaug River? In nearby Lake Chaubunagungamaug? No. It would go into the packing plant and be disposed of from there. So why did a Ghanaian called James, newly arrived in the United States, come out of the plant laden with thick cardboard sheets, and carefully tessellate them under the entire truck? Because— Chaubunagungamaug or no Chaubunagungamaug—it mattered to the boss that not one drop of anything but rain land on his driveway. The driveway was as stainless as the truck.

On a railway siding in the Shield grounds were two coupled tank cars. Each could hold thirty thousand gallons, nearly five times as much as Ainsworth's truck. My glance moved from the tank cars to the truck driver. "So why not send the WD-40 in tank cars?" I asked him.

He said, "You can't supply heat in transit to a railway tank car; and service is piss poor."

On the Mass Pike, later, I asked him how it felt to be forty-five thousand pounds lighter, how the driving differed. He said, "You don't have to think as far ahead. That doesn't mean we're going to sleep up here." And, in miles that followed, he added, "The gap is the most important thing—keeping a good gap. A lot of times, people will steal your cushion. . . . People talk faster back here, and they also drive faster here in the clogged arteries of the Northeast. They squeeze into my lane and force me off into the shoulder—it's the new trend in four-wheeler driving."

Five thousand live chickens went past us lying on their sides on shelves within open mesh screening, the road breeze ruffling their white feathers, white feathers snowing in the air. In a six-wheel "four-wheeler that civilians would call a truck," they were on their way to Heaven to join Colonel Sanders.

Stopping off for "a dab of fuel," Ainsworth dropped $307.10, and also bought *The New York Times*, *USA Today*, and his beloved Walleye. In the seven hundred and fifty-eight miles I rode with him from western New York to Massachusetts and back to western New York, he paid $108.50 in tolls. When I rode with him from Atlanta to Tacoma, he paid zero in tolls.

"Why was Howard Hughes surrounded by Mormon advisers?"

I said it was news to me.

"They're sober," he said, and went on to praise Flying J truck stops, headquartered in Ogden, Utah, because they are clean and well managed.

The Petro network of truck stops seemed to be his favorite. We went into one in Waterloo that not only had the usual food, maps, showers, and hardware but also had a chiropractor, a hair salon, an Internet room, and a video horse-racing parlor with wall-size screens. "You can take a prom date to a Petro," Ainsworth asserted. In San Diego, though, no one dances at a Petro. San Diego, in its beautiful setting, clearly regards itself as aesthetically incompatible with big trucks—at least according to one truck driver. He said, "They don't allow ugly unwashed trucks into the county. They have only one tiny truck stop, not a real one. They have no support structure for trucks. The closest real truck stop east is at a casino sixty miles east. The closest to the north is in Los Angeles County; to the south, in Mexico. To the west, nothing, for obvious reasons." He later added, in a letter, "The beauty of the city makes it antithetical to greasy, smoke-belching behemoths of the highways. However short-sighted, their lack of care for trucks does not mean they are an evil town, merely truck-care deprived."

Eastbound, we had overnighted at a TA truck stop, which we reached in the evening, just before Ainsworth's shot clock ran out. "It's a fairly new, bummy one," he said, a description that was not altogether contradicted by the motel next door, where grass was growing through cracks in its dry swimming pool. With Flying J and Petro, TravelCenters of America is one of the national big three. The lot was all but full. Nearly two hundred and fifty trucks were there, a large number for the Northeast but below the size of big truck stops nationally—Bankhead, Georgia, five hundred trucks; Walcott, Iowa, eight hundred trucks. "In these New England and Middle Atlantic states you're scratching with the chickens just to find a place where you can turn your key off," Don said, as he swept his mirrors and wrestled the wheel, gingerly backing into a tight slot between two other trucks. Pull-through parking—in forward, out forward—is not as common as one might hope. Parking in various truck stops, he has to back in about fifty per cent of the time. As we walked through the lot, carrying our gear, the hum of the many trucks was not deafening; it was just voluminous. This was a humid, heavy night in the middle of the summer. At night, anywhere, if it is very hot or very cold, Ainsworth goes into a motel instead of sleeping in the truck, because he prefers not to run the engine just for heat or air-conditioning. This does not seem to preoccupy his colleagues. The hum of a truck stop in the dead of night is one of the sonic emblems of America, right up there with the bombs in air, the rutilant rockets, and the stern impassioned stress. You have not heard the sound of creature comfort until you have heard hundreds of huddled trucks idling through the night.

A company called IdleAire, in Knoxville, has heard the sound and seen a market. It sells cool air and warm air to trucks at truck stops. From an overhead insulated duct, the air comes down a bright-yellow accordion-pleated tube and enters the window of a parked truck. IdleAire's facilities are like black smokers with unimaginable pendant worms waving to and fro, looking to connect with trucks. From the IdleAire company, drivers buy adapters that fit into truck windows and snug the tubes. IdleAire simultaneously offers satellite television and Internet and telephone access. In California, Ainsworth had recently noticed that IdleAire was selling its coolness for $1.60 an hour, while trucks' idling diesels were each burning a gallon an hour, for—at the time—$2.60.

Most tractors and trailers are mated promiscuously, as a matter of business practice, but taking them all together there are some two million big trucks in the United States. When their drivers' shot clocks run out, they idle for ten hours. Two million trucks times ten hours times three hundred days amounts to six billion gallons of diesel fuel per annum burned basically to keep truck drivers cool, to keep truck drivers warm, and to keep happy presidents content.

Walking on through the sultry lot, Ainsworth said, "Misuse of a resource in short supply. Some folks call that fuel."